Social Work, the
Relations

Social Work, the Media and Public Relations

Edited by
Bob Franklin and Nigel Parton

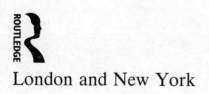

London and New York

First published in 1991
by Routledge
11 New Fetter Lane, London EC4P 4EE

Simultaneously published in the USA and Canada
by Routledge
a division of Routledge, Chapman and Hall Inc.
29 West 35th Street, New York, NY 10001

Phototypeset by Input Typesetting Ltd, London
Printed in Great Britain by
T.J. Press (Padstow) Ltd, Padstow, Cornwall

British Library Cataloguing in Publication Data
Social work, the media and public relations.
  1. Great Britain. Social problems. Reporting by mass media
  I. Franklin, Bob II. Parton, Nigel
  070.44936110941

Library of Congress Cataloging in Publication Data
Social work, the media and public relations / edited by Bob Franklin and
  Nigel Parton.
        p.   cm.
  Includes bibliographical references and index.
  1. Social service—Great Britain. 2. Mass media and social service—
Great Britain. 3. Public relations—Great Britain—Social service. I.
Franklin, Bob II. Parton, Nigel.
  HV245.S6237   1991
  361.941—dc20   90-8797
                                                            CIP

ISBN 0-415-05002-2
ISBN 0-415-05003-0 pbk

Contents

Tables and Figures

Contributors

Sally Arkley is Public Relations Officer for the British Association of Social Workers.

Louis Blom-Cooper is Chairman of the Press Council, and chaired the inquiries into the deaths of Jasmine Beckford and Kimberley Carlile.

John Callaghan is a co-founder of West Yorkshire Radio Action and its current Development Officer.

Tim Dant is a research fellow at the Open University. His recent field-work has included community care for elderly people, which he is now writing up with colleagues. He is also writing a book on 'knowledge, ideology, discourse'.

Steve Dowson is a qualified social worker who worked for nine years as a specialist in mental handicap, during which time he was closely involved with a series of innovative community-based residential projects. After a period as Senior Research Officer with Norfolk Social Services he was appointed Director of the Campaign for Mental Handicap (CMH) in 1987. CMH was founded in 1971 as an advocacy organization committed to the right of people with learning difficulties to live as full citizens in the community. It now continues this work under the name of Values Into Action (VIA).

Bob Franklin is a Lecturer in the Department of Politics at the University of Keele. Until recently he was Director of Research for the West Yorkshire Media in Politics Group at the University of Leeds. His publications include *The Rights of Children* (ed.) (1986) and *Public Relations Activities in Local Government* (1988).

Anne Fry has written for many publications including the *Observer* and *Community Care* and *Social Work Today*, where she is currently Chief Correspondent. She has written *Media Matters: Social Work, the Press and Broadcasting* (1987). She is married with a son.

Peter Golding is Professor of Sociology in the Department of Social Sciences at the University of Loughborough. He has published widely on aspects of mass communications and on social policy. His books include *The Mass Media* (1974), *Making the News* (with Philip Elliot, 1979), *Images of Welfare* (with Sue Middleton, 1982), *Excluding the Poor* (1986) and others. He is currently conducting research on the media presentation of the poll tax and on public and media perceptions of charity.

Valerie Howarth began her career in social work with the Family Welfare Association. She then worked as a senior social worker, Assistant Training Officer, Area Manager and later Assistant Director of Personal Services, for the London Borough of Lambeth. In 1982 she moved to Brent where she was Director of Social Services. In 1987 she became Director of ChildLine, Britain's first national freephone service for children.

Malcolm Johnson is Professor of Health and Social Welfare and, since 1984, Director of the Department of Health and Social Welfare at the Open University. The author of more than seventy books, monographs, articles and chapters, he has also served as Convenor of the BSA Medical Sociology Group, Secretary of the British Society of Gerontology, Scientific Advisor to the Department of Health and Social Security, Vice-Chair of the DHSS Working Party which produced the Code of Practice on Residential Care and, from 1988, Chair of the Advisory Council of the Centre for Policy on Ageing. Professor Johnson is the founding editor of the international journal *Ageing and Society*.

David Jones is General Secretary of the British Association of Social Workers.

Nigel Parton is a qualified social worker who has been teaching social workers at Huddersfield Polytechnic since the late 1970s. From 1989 to mid–1990 he was Hallsworth Fellow at the University of Manchester. His publications include *The Political Dimensions of Social Work* (edited with Bill Jordan, 1983) and *The Politics of Child Abuse* (1985).

David Perrin is currently working with BBC 2's *Taking Liberties*; he has been a journalist since 1964 and in broadcasting since 1975.

He worked on BBC Radio Four's *Checkpoint* and, at Thames Television, on *TV Eye* and the *Witness* documentary series. He was producer of the 1989 ITV drama-documentary *Danger in Mind*.

Terry Philpot is Editor of *Community Care*. He has spent his professional life in journalism, mostly in the field of local government, health and social services. He has edited a number of books including *Social Work* (1986) and *Last Things: Social Work with the Dying and Bereaved* (1989) and is currently writing a history of voluntary child care. He is a member of the social work committee of the National Children's Home. He was awarded a British Council fellowship in 1989.

Martin Ruddock has worked extensively in both the voluntary and statutory sector after qualifying in teaching, youth work and as a social worker. He is currently working at the Tamesmead Family Service Unit.

Marie Smyth is a lecturer in Applied Social Studies at the University of Ulster.

Lynne Walder has worked as a journalist on several weekly and daily regional papers in the West Midlands and Lancashire. She worked in public relations at the BBC and with a national charity before joining the Directorate of Social Services and Strategic Housing at Bradford Metropolitan District Council.

Tom White is the Chief Executive of the National Children's Home (NCH) and was previously its Director of Social Work. He was Director of Social Services for the City of Coventry from 1970 to 1985 and has worked in local authority children's departments in Lancashire, Monmouthshire and Devon. He has been past President of the Association of Directors of Social Services and past President of the Association of Child Care Officers.

Acknowledgements

Many people have contributed to this study in a variety of ways. A book which brings together the range and diversity of professional experience and expertise embraced by *Social Work, the Media and Public Relations* is necessarily a collective effort and, as editors, we would like to thank the contributors who have been supportive throughout the enterprise, who have met our various deadlines and responded to our suggestions and comments with good humour. We are especially grateful to those contributors who, in writing their chapter, have been obliged to confront again particular and unpleasant experiences of media attention.

We are also grateful to the Bradford *Telegraph & Argus* for allowing us to reproduce two stories from their newspaper in Chapter 13. Special thanks are due to Christine Bailey of the Institute of Communication Studies, University of Leeds for the substantial contribution she has made to this book.

Finally, in accordance with protocol on such occasions and, as future reviewers of the book will undoubtedly remind us, any errors, omissions, or good old-fashioned stupidities must be acknowledged as our own particular responsibility.

Bob Franklin and Nigel Parton

Introduction

Since the early 1970s it has become commonplace for social workers to accept that they receive prominent coverage in the media, that this coverage is largely negative and that it contributes to the poor public image of the profession. Social workers, their professional representatives and numerous public inquiries have been exercised by the treatment of social work in the mass media, particularly the popular press. The opening paragraph of the Barclay report commented:

> There is confusion about the direction in which they are going and unease about what they should be doing and the way in which they are organised and deployed. When things go wrong the media have tended to blame them because it is assumed that their job is to care for people so as to prevent trouble arising.
>
> (NISW 1982: VII)

In fact the growth in public concern about social work articulated by the media was seen as the major reason for establishing the working party.

The negative and occasionally hostile media reporting of social workers became even more evident in the second half of the 1980s when the Beckford, Henry, Carlile and Cleveland inquiries were reported. Social workers were centrally involved in these inquiries and subject to severe media treatment – evident from the accounts of Martin Ruddock and Valerie Howarth – while social work itself seemed to be under an unrelenting and highly critical spotlight.

If social workers claim that members of the media are unsympathetic to the profession and lack sufficient knowledge to report social service matters adequately and sensitively, journalists repond by alleging social workers' ignorance of the structure, organization and news-gathering routines of the media. Journalists often believe that social workers themselves are largely culpable for the poor press they receive because of their failure to establish working relations with journalists and their refusal to adopt proactive public relations techniques to promote a more positive public image of their work.

Social Work, the Media and Public Relations aims to examine in depth the causes and consequences of critical media reporting of social work as well as the various ways in which both social work and the media are attempting to develop a more realistic, and hence positive, image of both social work practice and the profession itself. The book brings together a variety of contributions from highly respected academics and researchers, experienced social work practitioners and managers from the statutory and voluntary sectors, as well as contributions from journalists, television producers and public relations professionals who analyse and reflect on various aspects of the relationship between media and social work. The book has been explicitly and deliberately organized to encourage chapters of variable length and style to reflect the very different but equally valuable and valid contributions deriving from and articulating different experiences, themes and approaches. Consequently, some of the chapters draw upon research and reviews of the literature, while others derive their focus from the practice of social work, journalism or public relations. A number are essentially experiential, expressing firsthand knowledge of media attentions. Throughout, we have been eager that the book should not become narrowly focused simply on 'child abuse' rather than social work, or 'the press' rather than the media. We have therefore interpreted 'social work' and 'the media' in their widest definitions, encompassing statutory and voluntary sectors with a range of client groups in different settings and a range of different media including the press, professional journals, television and radio. Much media reporting of social work, however, does relate to child abuse and many concerns within social work about the media relate to this issue. Consequently, it seems almost inevitable that a number of chapters should give significance to this particular but high-profile area of concern. To avoid this significance would be to fail to acknowledge events in the real world.

The book is in four parts. The first assumes a wide brief and attempts to provide both an introduction to the main themes and a framework for the whole book. It reviews a range of other studies and attempts to answer three questions. First, how do media report social workers and social work, including the particularly contentious issue of child abuse? Second, what are the implications of these media representations of social work within the profession and beyond? Finally, how are the persistently negative media appraisals of social work to be explained?

Part II taps the experiences of journalists and broadcasters. It reflects on their professional practices in the reporting of social work and social-service issues, as well as the ways in which their media products help to construct public perceptions of social work practice.

Part III examines particular occasions and experiences when social workers and social work have been subject to intense media and public scrutiny. These accounts reveal that the consequences of such media attentions for both individuals and social work practice can be substantial.

The final part of the book explores strategies for moving beyond the prevalent negative public images and media reporting of social work. The discussion focuses on and examines the growing public relations and campaigning activities, in both the statutory and voluntary sectors, designed to redress the balance of media reporting in favour of social workers and the people with whom they work.

Part I
Media reporting of social work

1 Media reporting of social work: a framework for analysis

Bob Franklin and Nigel Parton

Reporting of the Cleveland affair had a profound and damaging effect on the public image of social workers. The full impact of Cleveland for social work practice in the area of child protection, and its implications for subsequent child-centred legislation, are only now becoming apparent. The events in Cleveland were first brought to the attention of the public by the *Daily Mail* which broke the story with its front-page headline 'Hand Over Your Children; Council Orders Parents of 200 Youngsters' (23 June 1987). This first report presaged much in the paper's subsequent coverage; it was sensational, simplistic, highly critical of the role of social workers, too ready to accept and too willing to articulate the parents' case, but indifferent to any discussion of the rights of the children concerned. For its part, the *Daily Mail* seemed to see its coverage cast in a more benign, if not heroic, mould. The journalistic values of fearless, disinterested, investigative reporting, committed to laying the 'true facts' before the public assumed almost missionary proportions and were explicit in its headline declaration of 26 June 1987, 'The Scandal the *Daily Mail* First Brought to the Nation's Attention'. The *Mail*'s self-congratulation was subsequently endorsed by the then health minister, Tony Newton, in the House of Commons debate of the Butler-Sloss report. 'The *Daily Mail*', he claimed, 'can certainly feel it has played a very helpful and proper part in assisting in the exposure of just what happened in Cleveland' (*Daily Mail*, 7 July 1988:26).

Reporting of events in Cleveland escalated rapidly to become a media phonemenon without precedent. The first five weeks of coverage alone generated 9,000 press cuttings while 'mentions on national television news were an everyday occurrence' (Treacher 1988:15). Interest in the Cleveland affair has been sustained subsequently across all media and is evident not merely in news and current affairs output but in radio and television's more creative and artistic programming. *Testimony of a Child*, Lucy Gannon's play about a middle-class family in which the children are diagnosed as sexually abused, was broadcast by BBC 2 in July 1989 followed by a round-table discussion chaired by Esther Rantzen and including Geoffrey Wyatt and health minister David Mellor.

But media reporting of social work and social service issues is extremely selective, asymmetrical and confined within a remarkably narrow band of concerns. While cases involving the physical or sexual abuse of children – such as the Cleveland affair, the deaths of Jasmine Beckford, Tyra Henry and Kimberley Carlile – have each attracted sustained, if highly critical, media reporting, many areas of social-service provision, for example with older people and those with special needs, tend to be almost wholly neglected (Mawby, Fisher and Parkin 1979:365; Hartley 1985:29). Media coverage of elderly people in relation to welfare is confined almost exclusively to reports of deaths prompted by hypothermia and government unwillingness to offer adequate supplementary payment for heating. Occasionally other areas of social work activity seem to make fleeting but rare appearances. Again the frequent focus is work with children, although where an issue such as race (which enjoys a high news priority in its own right) touches an area of social work activity, the result is bound to be copious media coverage. Consequently, the complex issues arising from mixed-race adoption achieved a high news profile in August 1989 prompting sensational headlines such as 'White Family Must Give Up The Little Black Boy They Love, Judge Decides; BABY IN RACE HEARTBREAK', while the following day the 'Heartbroken Mother in Race Case' asked readers 'WHY DID THEY TAKE MY BABY?' (*Daily Mail*, 24/25 August 1989).

In November 1989, the tragic death of deaf and blind, 23-year-old Beverley Lewis, who suffered from cerebral palsy and lived with her mentally ill mother, was given similarly extensive media coverage. The case prompted the *Daily Mirror* to, 'call for a review of the law' and, paradoxically given the paper's stand over Cleveland, 'to give social workers greater legal powers' (*Daily Mirror*, 2 November 1989). The common element which appears to unify these otherwise disparate stories involving child abuse, older people, mixed race adoption and Beverley Lewis, is that they provide an opportunity for media to disparage social workers and aspects of their professional practice. Hardly surprising then that the *Daily Mirror* quotes approvingly Beverley's sister's challenge:

'Why didn't social workers do more when they knew she was at risk?' (*Daily Mirror*, 2 November 1989:2).

This unevenness of media reporting of social work prompts a number of interrelated questions which partly illustrate the complexity of the issues involved. What is it, for example, about social work in the area of child abuse that is so attractive to the media? What is the nature and extent of coverage given to other client groups and areas of social work practice? Are all social work agencies – statutory, voluntary, private – and all social work settings – field, residential, day care – treated in the same critical manner? Do they, for that matter all get equal attention? What sorts of images of social work are constructed in the media and how do these vary between agencies and settings? Social workers typically offer one set of answers to these enquiries. Journalists, they suggest, are unsympathetic and lack sufficient knowledge and experience of social services to report the matter adequately and sensitively (Geach 1982:15; Phillips 1979:123; Fry 1987). In response, journalists and broadcasters allege social workers seem ignorant of the structure, organization and news-gathering routines of the media and urge them to adopt more proactive public relations techniques to promote a more positive public image of their work and profession (Rote 1979:17; Fry 1987:13; Hills 1980:19).

The key to probing beyond these mutual recriminations and exploring the complexities of the relationship between media and social work, seems to lie in the suggestion that social workers, especially those operating in the statutory sector, increasingly have been presented in the media as a metaphor or symbol for the entire public sector, personifying the 'evil' which the political new right presumes to be inherent therein. Conservative antipathies towards social workers are readily understood given its suspicions about the state and its commitment to an anti-welfare spending ethic. Social workers moreover symbolize the state's altruistic concerns and by caring for the poor, disabled, elderly and sick, offer an implicit critique of the family and community which previously provided such services and which, the political right suggests, should do so again. Large sections of the media appear to have incorporated discussion of social work and social-service issues into this broader political agenda which in large part expresses the Government's sustained attack on the public sector. In this process, social workers have become vehicles for a more general discussion (typically a critique) concerning the role of the social democratic state in the post-war period as a provider of goods, especially welfare goods;

about the nature and priorities of state functionaries in the private sphere of the family; about the role, reconstruction and financing of the welfare state more generally and local government in particular; about the accountability, use of authority and hence the social auspices of welfare agencies and practitioners; about the relationship between, and the social responses to, the 'deserving' and 'undeserving poor'. In their reporting, media have increasingly tended to invest social workers with the same characteristics they judge to be pervasive in the allegedly inefficient, but overly interventionist social democratic state; ineffectiveness and authoritarianism are consequently the twin, if contradictory, themes evident in media discussions of social work.

One consequence of media reporting of social work, noted initially by Stevenson and Parsloe (1978) must be stated at the outset since its importance is fundamental and cannot easily be overstressed. Recent media interest in social work, particularly with children and families, has transformed its essential character as well as the ways in which social workers experience their practice. Social work is no longer a private activity conducted by professionals with individuals but has become subject to a number of often contradictory public concerns. Clearly, the media alone cannot account for this transformation, not least because to some extent they reflect wider social anxieties and interests. They provide, however, a crucial mediating link between social workers and the public which was previously not evident.

This chapter addresses three broad questions in order to probe and clarify some of the complexities raised above. First, how do media report social workers and social work, especially the contentious issue of child abuse? Second, what are the implications of media representations of social work both within and beyond the profession? Third, how are these persistently negative media appraisals of social work to be explained?

The term media, of course, is merely a convenient shorthand to designate a diverse range of institutions distinguished by the financial and journalistic resources they possess, the size and geographical spread of the audiences they address, their sources of funding, their news-gathering practices and routines, their judgement concerning what constitutes a good story, and the medium of communication as well as the technological delivery system which they exploit to transmit their 'messages'. Given this diversity it is both unsurprising and unexceptional that media are not uniform in their approach even to similar subject matter and that consequently variations are evident in the ways in which television, radio and the press approach social-work issues; indeed the press itself in its 'quality' and 'tabloid' variants exhibits substantial differences in its coverage of many, not least social work, issues (Sparks 1987:432; Brynin 1988:27).

MEDIA, SOCIAL WORK AND CHILD ABUSE

Media interest in social work, especially child abuse, is a fairly recent phenomenon which seems to date from the death of Maria Colwell in 1973 and the resulting public inquiry (Hartley 1985:38). Previous research reveals a mere nine articles published discussing child abuse between 1968 and 1972, with these invariably tending to reflect the views of the NSPCC Battered Child Research Unit (Parton 1985:97). Media interest in the Colwell case peaked in autumn 1974 when the report of the inquiry into the child's death was published. It was not, however, merely the scale of media reporting and interest which at the time was new and created a precedent, it was the media concern to scapegoat the social worker at the centre of the case which also marked a new departure. Media reporting was heavy with disapprobation and admonition for what they alleged amounted to professional neglect. Throughout the inquiry the media vilified the social worker concerned, who had to be protected from the public while entering and leaving the inquiry, who was questioned for twenty-five hours in evidence and who eventually had to change her name to escape public and media attention (Andrews 1974:643; Lees 1979:15; Shearer 1979a:13).

The growing awareness of media interest in social work and their impact on social-work practice can be gauged by reference to contemporary academic analysis. Satyamurti's case study of a local authority children's department in the very early 1970s, for example, analysed the way social workers' occupational identities in practice were 'shaped by features of their situation, as mediated through the main sets of relationships in which they are involved' (Satyamurti 1981:2). It also examined the strategies social workers adopted, both individually and collectively, to make their work tolerable. She argued that despite the upheaval prompted by the Seebohm reorganization – her field-work was conducted during the valedictory months of the Children's Departments – the major relationships in which social workers were involved remained largely the same 'because the major factors influencing them remained unchanged' (1981:5). Stevenson and Parsloe's study (1978) confirmed much of Satyamurti's account with the exception of a single but crucial difference. While the media receive only scant attention in Satyamurti's study they are judged to be central by Stevenson and Parsloe in structuring both social work practice and the professional climate in which it is conducted.

Stevenson and Parsloe's study of social service teams, conducted in the mid-1970s attempted to construct a picture of social workers' feelings, attitudes and priorities at that time. Interviews with 360 practitioners revealed their awareness of the growth of media interest in social work issues. 'Those of us who have been involved in social work for a substantial part of the postwar years', they observed, 'are bound to contrast the level of public interest in social services and social work with our earlier experience. One reflects upon the astonishing increase of media attention in the past decade. Scarcely a day passes without a radio or television comment about some aspect of social work or related matters' (Stevenson and Parsloe 1978:320). If development of media interest has created profound anxieties in social workers' attitudes towards their professional practice, Stevenson and Parsloe report that a

> pervasive theme running through our respondents' comments was quite simply fear. We can use the impersonal phrase 'anxiety about accountability' but it only seems to minimise the intensity of the feelings expressed to us. As was to be expected, they were most often concerned with non accidental injury to children and, in every study of area teams social workers referred not simply to the professional anxiety which such situations created, but their fear of being found wanting and called to account. This applied right across the United Kingdom and the phrase 'another Maria Colwell' was the common shorthand used by many social workers, some of whom, one suspects, had not read the report and were not using it as a symbol of the complexities of the 'tug of love' but simply of the horror of a child on their case load dying at the hands of a parent.
>
> (Stevenson and Parsloe 1978:322)

Child abuse inquiries have been the major triggers of media interest as well as their primary focus. They have also provided the key arenas for mutual recrimination between social work and the media. Following media coverage of the Colwell inquiry, it was alleged by the Beckford inquiry that social workers have become the 'butt of every unthinking journalistic pen whenever a scapegoat was needed to explain a fatality or serious injury to a child in care

or under supervision of social service departments of a local authority. It is the height of absurdity for the media or indeed the public,
to castigate social services' (Blom-Cooper 1985:5). A major reason
why the Carlile inquiry was held in private was a concern that a
number of potentially important participants, mainly social workers,
might refuse to give evidence because they feared that 'they would
be hounded by insensitive journalists, criticised prematurely and
out of context in the media long before the inquiry reported and
be unfairly prejudiced in their present employment or in obtaining
employment elsewhere in the future' (Blom-Cooper 1987:6).

The Cleveland inquiry report considered it necessary to include
nothing less than an entire section on the media which Butler-Sloss
alleged had 'played an important role in the Cleveland crisis at all
stages' (Butler-Sloss 1988:168). Media brought the issue to public
attention in late June 1987, they reported and commented exhaus-
tively on the daily proceedings of the public inquiry and publication
of the report in July 1988; subsequently they have sustained regular
coverage of the issue. While the Butler-Sloss report concludes that
media personnel generally acted responsibly, it also noted that 'such
a responsibility has not been recognised in certain quarters and in
this delicate and sensitive field where the welfare of children
requires it to be remembered it was from time to time obviously
overlooked' (171). Most critically, the report alleged that the media
had 'become a factor in the continuance of the crisis' (169).

Reporting of the Cleveland case certainly achieved a remarkable
prominence in news agendas throughout 1987 and 1988. Two other
social-work-related stories also prompted substantial media coverage at that time. The reports of the inquiry into the deaths of
Kimberley Carlile and Tyra Henry, published on 12 and 19
December 1987, like the Beckford and Colwell inquiries before
them, generated considerable public concern and debate around
the issue of the physical abuse of children. There are of course
significant differences between these cases. The Beckford, Henry
and Carlile cases illustrate media responses to instances of physical
abuse whereas the focus of the Cleveland reporting was upon
alleged sexual abuse. Second, the media concern in the former
cases was with particular instances of abuse whereas in Cleveland
media were unable to identify any specific individuals or families
and consequently were less able to personalize the issue. Finally,
the Beckford, Henry and Carlile cases were presented in media
reports as the mere tip, albeit an exceedingly unpleasant one, of a
projectedly much larger iceberg. Media, however, seemed less clear

in their assessments of the prevalence of child sexual abuse. When the Cleveland story was first reported in June 1987 it was suggested that child abuse might be quite widespread although media sources remained ambiguous on this point (Nava 1988:108). By the time Butler-Sloss reported, however, the media seemed unanimous in believing the initial number of cases at Cleveland was an over-estimate resulting from a panic or some other malfunction in the welfare system.

The media response to these cases of child abuse and the different images of social work presented in reporting, offers a potentially rewarding point of departure for the analysis of relationships between social work and the media. Media reporting of the Beck-ford, Carlile and Henry cases constructed an extremely negative stereotype of social workers which presented them as incompetent, non-judgemental, and indecisive individuals who were extremely reluctant to intervene in the private realm of family life even to protect children from a suspected abusing adult. The *Daily Mail*'s claim that social workers were 'butterflies in a situation that demanded hawks', exemplifies the stereotype (*Daily Mail*, 20 December 1987). Cleveland, however, prompted a juggling of stereotypes and a second quite contrary, but equally pejorative, image of social workers emerged. The alternative stereotype for the social worker is that of the authoritarian bureaucrat who, with little regard for the civil liberties of either the children or adults concerned, 'breaks up families' by removing (and implicit in much media reporting is the notion of unnecessarily removing) children into local authority care. The public drama of child abuse enacted on the media stage required, it seems, that social workers must be cast in the role of wimps or bullies; fools or villains (Franklin 1989:1–15).

Journalists routinely deployed key words and catch-phrases to establish the stereotypical images. Social workers were described as 'naive, bungling, easily fobbed off, easily hoodwinked' (*Daily Express*, 29 March 1985), as 'official do-gooders' with 'no experi-ence of the world' (*Sun*, 29 March 1985), as 'incompetent and insufficiently professional' (*Daily Telegraph*, 18 December 1987), as 'too trusting with too liberal a professional outlook' (*Guardian*, 19 December 1987), as 'easily manipulated, disgraced, browbeaten, conned and bearded' (*Sun*, 12 December 1987).

A different group of equally hostile and negative phrases informs the second stereotype. Social workers are 'authoritarian bureau-crats' who 'speak in a chilly jargon and take refuge in bureaucratic formulations' (*The Times*, 17 June 1987). They are, 'guided by prejudice and motivated by zealotry rather than facts' (*Daily Mail*, 6 July 1988), they 'seize sleeping children in the middle of the night' (*Sunday Telegraph*, 10 July 1988), they are 'abusers of authority, hysterical and malignant, callow, youngsters who absorb moral-free marxoid sociological theories' (*Daily Mail*, 7 July 1988). In the words of Tim Devlin MP, thé social services are merely 'another organisation with the initials SS' (*Guardian*, 30 June 1987). For local Labour MP Stuart Bell, Cleveland social services represented nothing less than 'the Salem witch hunt or the Ayatollah Khomeini come to Middlesbrough' (*Daily Telegraph*, 25 June 1987).

The diverse and contradictory character of these two stereotypes of the social worker is more apparent than real and an underlying consistency can be discerned if it is acknowledged that social workers have become a flagship or symbol for the entire public sector. The latter is commonly presented in media on the one hand as inefficient and incapable of meeting the various demands placed upon it while, on the other hand, it is allegedly repressive, interventionist and illiberal. As a symbol for the public sector social workers personify, in caricature form, all the shortcomings which the political new right assumes the public sector possesses and consequently inefficiency and bureaucratic authoritarianism become the antithetical polarities within which social work and social-work practice come to be defined. It is the underlying consistency of these two negative stereotypes of social workers which allows reporting of child abuse to set them 'cheek by jowl' on the same page or within the same programme without any perceived unease or contradiction on the part of journalists, broadcasters, readers or viewers.

At first glance it may seem as if there is a chronological progression of these social work stereotypes. In July 1987, during the early coverage of Cleveland, the social worker image was that of the authoritarian bully. By December 1987 reports of the Kimberley Carlile and Tyra Henry cases redefined the stereotype of social workers to present them as wimps, but by July 1988 when Butler-Sloss reported the bully had returned with a vengeance. This is not, however, an instance of the curious 'amnesia' which McIntosh identifies when media respond essentially to the same issue in a radically different way (McIntosh 1988:10), but a journalistic viewpoint informed by a political agenda which is increasingly Conservative and preponderantly anti public sector (Brynin 1988:32; Goldsmiths College Media Research Group 1987:19; Milne 1988:213). Social workers dressed in the (dis)guise of wimp or bully, personify the public sector and present an attractive as well as a convenient target for its critics.

SOCIAL WORKERS AS FOOLS OR WIMPS

Media reporting of the Beckford, Henry and Carlile cases followed a very similar pattern. Coverage was based around a stereotype of social workers as ineffectual, wavering individuals, lacking professional judgement and unable to recognize situations which required them to intervene to protect children at risk. In short, they were designated in media reporting as wimps or fools. On this account, professional incompetence is judged to be the social worker's trade mark and eventually when they manage to make a decision invariably it is the wrong one. The *Daily Mirror* alleged cynically that 'whenever two or more members of the caring professions are gathered together to solve a problem, a string of inept decisions will follow' (*Daily Mirror*, 6 July 1988:12). A threefold explanation is offered for this wimpish incompetence.

First, social workers are routinely presented as rather unintelligent characters lacking wit or insight of even the most elementary kind. The *Daily Express* claimed the social worker in the Beckford case was 'fobbed off time and time again with excuses which would not have deceived a child' (*Daily Express*, 29 March 1985), while the *Star*, having described Maurice Beckford as 'educationally subnormal', proceeded by quoting approvingly the judge's remark to Beckford: 'Despite your limited intelligence you seem to have had no difficulty hoodwinking social workers' (*Star*, 29 March 1985). Second, and perhaps more important than any simple lack of intelligence, is social workers' alleged naivety and lack of basic common sense. In part this naivety reflects their youthfulness and lack of experience of the world. The *Sun*'s coverage of the Beckford case, for example, included on the front page a picture of the social worker involved above the caption 'No Experience of the World' (*Sun*, 29 March 1985). Elsewhere in the paper's coverage, social workers are described as 'people who sit behind desks' and who 'tell us that a text book should govern a child's very existence' (*Sun*, 29 March 1985). But there is also a class dimension structuring social workers' naivety. The *Daily Express*, in uncharacteristic enthusiasm to don the mantle of the proletariat claimed social workers 'should be working class people like ourselves, who have lived, who know what life is about' (*Daily Express*, 29 March 1985). Finally, media allege that social workers' incompetence derives from an observable casualness in their professional attitudes and practice. The *Guardian* claims social workers possess 'too liberal a professional outlook' (*Guardian*, 19 December 1987) while the *Daily Mirror* admonished social workers for their 'laid back attitudes' (*Daily Mirror*, 19 December 1987). This professional casualness is a malaise, moreover, which infects even the most senior echelon of the social services hierarchy. A judge in one case was obliged to reprimand an assistant director of social services in the witness box and instruct him to 'take your hands out of your pockets' (*Daily Express*, 29 March 1985).

Given this style of coverage, it is hardly surprising that social workers feel that media are hostile towards them (Fry 1987:5; Geach 1982:14) or that public perceptions of social workers view them as 'gullible and too soft' (Wilton 1980:14), while clients see them as tending towards 'prevarication and procrastination' (Kitchen 1980:16).

What is quite remarkable about media reporting of these three cases of physical abuse, although the media present the matter as unexceptional and uncontentious, is their assumption that social workers should be considered as guilty for the death of the abused child as the abuser. Accordingly it is judged appropriate to label social workers as killers and media do precisely that. The *Star* cited Jasmine Beckford's foster parents' allegation that 'if her stepfather is a killer, so are Brent social services' (*Star*, 29 March 1985). The *Sun* carried a picture of the social worker alongside the heading 'They Killed The Child I Adored' (*Sun*, 29 March 1985). Social workers in the Henry and Carlile cases were similarly castigated by the press. *The Times* headlined, 'Tyra Henry Inquiry Says Social Workers to Blame Over Murder' (*The Times*, 18 December 1987), while the *Daily Mirror* alleged 'a bungling social worker was blamed yesterday for the death of four year old Kimberley Carlile' (*Daily Mirror*, 12 December 1987). The media seemed to believe that of all the professionals with whom the child may have had previous contact – police, teachers, health visitors, doctors – it is the social worker who is responsible for what has happened to the child; the criminally convicted abuser is often relegated to the position of a marginal figure in media accounts. Media criticism of the social worker in the Carlile case was so strident that *The Times* considered it prudent to remind its colleagues in Fleet Street, Wapping and Broadcasting House, that 'whatever journalists and others may insinuate, she was not killed by her social worker . . . she was killed by a brute abetted by a woman whose sense of evil had atrophied' (*The Times*, 12 December 1987). The indecisive wimp – a comic figure to be ridiculed – has a more malevolent face; incompetence can have tragic consequences and the fool is thereby transformed by the media into a villain.

The media moreover invariably present social workers as callous, indifferent and unrepentant about their responsibilities for the children concerned. There is also the suggestion that social workers cannot be held accountable, that they go unpunished for their 'crimes' and 'get off lightly'. The *Daily Mirror* combined both these themes in its search for a scapegoat. 'Social workers', it claimed, 'won't face disciplinary action over the tragic death of Tyra Henry and yesterday, no-one even said sorry' (*Daily Mirror*, 19 December 1987). A *Star* editorial announced that the social worker in the Beckford case was 'enjoying a holiday . . . 24 hours after Jasmine was brutally beaten for the last time by her evil stepfather' (*Star*, 29 March 1985). In the tabloid press, there is the thinly veiled suggestion that there may even be a premium on such professional incompetence, with social workers allowed 'to slip away to better jobs, as at least three of them have' (*Star*, 29 March 1985).

The media's habit of holding the social worker to be at least as accountable as the abuser for the death of the child is underscored by their tendency to focus reporting not on the death of the child, or the criminal trial of the abuser, but overwhelmingly on the proceedings of the committee of inquiry and the publication of the report (Hartley 1985:41). Coverage of the inquiry tends to focus almost exclusively on the role of the social worker in the affair. In 1971, 18 per cent of reports concerning child abuse in *The Times* mentioned social workers and/or social service departments, whereas figures for 1973, 1974, 1975 and 1976, had grown dramatically to 37, 34, 51 and 48 per cent respectively (Hartley 1985:41). This media emphasis has a crucial effect; child abuse becomes 'decriminalized' and becomes redefined as a social services problem. As Hartley concludes, 'Child abuse which had previously been reported as a criminal matter by the press came to be reported as a social service matter. Main news items about it began to focus on the activities of welfare workers and particularly social workers who apparently "failed" to deal with the problem effectively' (Hartley 1985:76). Shearer, goes further and suggests that from its inception, media reporting of child abuse has had the covert intention of challenging what, in 1973, were the newly established and fledgling social service departments. Media, she claimed, 'were simply waiting for the right issue by which they could "give them a kick".

. . . In this respect the case of Maria Colwell . . . provided an opportunity to criticise social service departments and the new profession of social work' (Parton 1977:113).

In summary, media reporting of the Beckford, Carlile and Henry cases was similar although it differed in important respects. Perhaps most significant here was the fact that while Jasmine Beckford and Tyra Henry were in the care of the social services department, Kimberley Carlile was not; paradoxically the media attack on the social worker in the latter case seemed greater than in the other two. Notwithstanding any formal differences, the media assumption across all three cases was that social workers were culpable for their failure to intervene to protect children in such circumstances. Social workers are judged to have it in their power to prevent child abuse, but are failing to do so. The *Daily Mail* identified clearly the reasons underlying its criticisms of the social worker in the Tyra Henry case. 'Her conviction that children should not be removed from their families', it alleged, 'pointed to a fundamental defect in her approach' (*Daily Mail*, 19 December 1987). The policy prescription seems clear. Successful preventative work in the area of child protection requires social workers to become more authoritative and interventionist on behalf of children.

THE SOCIAL WORKER AS VILLAIN AND BULLY

A second, quite contrary, stereotype of social workers emerged during 1987. Its roots lay in the Cleveland affair which large sections of the media, despite the *Daily Mail*'s advocacy of an interventionist strategy for child protection, presented as illustrative of the unaccountability of social service professionals and the potentially authoritarian consequences of the post-war welfare state. Media coverage of Cleveland was extensive and without precedent. Intensive reporting was sustained across a period of a year from the initial break of the story in June 1987, through the seventy-four days of the inquiry, until the publication of the Butler-Sloss report on 6 July 1988. The media published the report by increments. Rumours of the inquiry's findings were published in the *Guardian* on 22 June 1988. On 1 July 1988 a manuscript copy of the report was leaked to Tim Miles, the social services correspondent of the Press Association. Radio Four's early evening programme, *PM*, ran it as its lead story. The following day, every newspaper was carrying the story with the *Daily Telegraph* headline urging 'Sack Cleveland Doctors if Leak is True, says MP' (*Daily Telegraph*, 2 July 1988).

Media reporting of Cleveland was extensive but in truth it was less than it might have been. The news prominence given to the June 1987 General Election and the subsequent merger of the Alliance parties, prevented the story breaking earlier. The tragedy of the Piper Alpha oil rig the day following the publication of the inquiry report clipped coverage abruptly and served to remind how quickly even the most significant and newsworthy stories can fall from media agendas to become 'yesterday's news'. A discussion of the Butler-Sloss report scheduled for BBC breakfast time on 7 July 1988 featuring Stuart Bell, Mike Bishop (the then Director of Cleveland Social Services), and other figures prominent in the Cleveland affair, was virtually shelved in the wake of the Piper Alpha disaster and warranted a mere five minutes' broadcast time.

Media attention focused on four aspects of the Cleveland controversy; if the conclusions of the Butler-Sloss report are correct they also fuelled and exacerbated at least some of them. First, the diagnostic technique used to identify sexual abuse (reflex anal dilation or RAD) became central to much media discussion. Its accuracy was contested by parents, MPs, the media themselves and, most significantly, by paediatricians. The issue became a crucial concern for media since the absence of a reliable diagnostic test meant that the extent of any sexual abuse could not be established with any accuracy. Media 'guesstimates' of the incidence of child abuse varied massively across the period of the inquiry but by the time Butler-Sloss reported, they seemed keen to play down their own earlier high estimates with the *Daily Mirror* suggesting that the test may only indicate 'that a three year old has sat on the funnel of his toy ship at bath time' (*Daily Mirror*, 6 July 1988).

A second and related media concern was to expose and highlight disputes between the various professionals involved in the case. The disputes were both intra- and inter-professional in character. The most prominent story of the former kind was the disagreement among paediatricians concerning the occurrence of sexual abuse. Although two women police surgeons endorsed Marietta Higgs' diagnosis (*Daily Mirror*, 29 June 1987) Alastair Irvine, the Cleveland police surgeon, disagreed obliging the Northern Regional Health Authority to establish a panel of expert paediatricians to re-examine a number of the children; the composition of the panel itself became a hotly contested issue (*Daily Mail*, 27 June 1987).

Inter-professional disputes were also publicized. The most celebrated story here was Bell's allegation of a 'conspiracy' between Higgs and Richardson to 'exclude' police personnel from investigations of sexual abuse (*Daily Mail*, 30 June 1987). The story achieved a high news profile across all media. Following the publication of the Butler-Sloss report the press mounted a general attack on all the 'experts' involved. The centre-page spread in the *Daily Mail* announced 'From Social Worker to Police Chief, The Experts Let Down Those They Were Meant to Protect' (*Daily Mail*, 7 July 1988).

The third, but undoubtedly most prominent, focus for media reporting were the confrontations between parents who were often described as 'anguished' or 'innocent' and the various medical and social work professionals typically described by the words 'zealous' or 'authoritarian'. Media stories usually stressed the extent to which child care procedures can threaten parental rights and emphasized the impotence of parents compared to social workers who may have secured place of safety orders and invariably enjoy the support of the courts. The relative roles of parents and state representatives in child abuse cases undoubtedly raises enormously complex issues, but media presentations rarely explored that complexity and were typically sympathetic to the parents. The *Daily Mirror* headlined 'No End to Agony for Parents in Child Sex Story' with a story reporting parents leaving the court, 'in tight little groups, the odd tear trickling down blank bewildered faces' (*Daily Mirror*, 30 June 1987).

The final focus for press coverage was the Butler-Sloss report itself. Assessments varied concerning the report's merits. The *Independent* described it as 'strikingly child-centred and humane, constructive and full of common sense' (*Independent*, 7 July 1988), whereas Melanie Phillips in the *Guardian* claimed there was 'a vacuum' at the heart of the report which left key questions unanswered (*Guardian*, 8 July 1988). Most newspapers quoted the report selectively to endorse their previous editorial line. Consequently, the *Sunday Telegraph* review, having junked the report as 'a disappointing and inadequate piece of work', proceeded to write a eulogy of Stuart Bell and mount a forceful attack on welfare professionals (*Sunday Telegraph*, 10 July 1988). Much of the complexity which Butler-Sloss had tried to detail so thoroughly in her report was lost in newspaper reviews. With the benefit of hindsight the problems in Cleveland could be viewed with greater clarity. For the *Sunday Telegraph* they now seemed reducible to 'an outbreak of hysteria amongst doctors and social workers' and the 'prevalence of ultra feminist and of anti-family views in some medical and social work circles'. In tandem these two factors resulted in social workers wishing to 'seize sleeping children in the middle of the night' (*Sunday Telegraph*, 10 July 1988).

In addition to these themes, media reporting identified certain figures as central to the Cleveland drama and focused its reporting upon them: Stuart Bell, the local MP, Marietta Higgs, the consultant paediatrician, and Sue Richardson, the child sexual abuse consultant, were the main media targets. Their significance however, as Nava argues (Nava 1988), reflects the fact that the media presents each of them as a symbol to mobilize a distinct set of associations, values and prejudices. Bell speaks for traditional family values; Higgs and Richardson symbolize the forces which, the media presume, seek to subvert them.

The images of Marietta Higgs and Sue Richardson presented in the press have, from the earliest reportings, been negative. The captions under Higgs' photograph – describing her variously as 'accused' or 'slammed' or as a 'crusader' – betrayed press commitments. At best she was 'the doctor in the child abuse storm' (*Daily Mail*, 24 June 1987), at worst she joined Sue Richardson as one of the two 'sex row plotters' (*Daily Mirror*, 30 June 1987).

Media attitudes hardened after the publication of the Butler-Sloss report despite the fact that it vindicated Richardson and Higgs against many of the earlier media allegations of professional malpractice levelled against them. Headlining its centre page summary of the Butler-Sloss report, the *Daily Mail* announced, 'Verdict on Cleveland; Two Women Believed They Had Uncovered a Scandal . . . And For The Families a Nightmare Began' (*Daily Mail*, 7 July 1987).

Sue Richardson was persistently presented as an ideologue whose professional practice was guided by dogma rather than experience or the media's preference for 'common sense'. When her beliefs about practice in the area of child protection are cited, they were presented as extreme and bizarre. Susan Crossland in a *Sunday Times* article suggested that 'Much in her [Sue Richardson's] attitude and approach would have been better suited to an advocate in a children's rights organisation' (*Sunday Times*, 10 July 1988). Again, 'Mrs Richardson's belief that sexual abuse is, "the misuse of power by an adult against a child" is quoted as if to prove its eccentricity rather than its self-evidentness' (*Daily Mail*, 7 July 1988). Richardson's confessed scepticism about the value of working co-operatively with families in the case of child abuse was presented as advocacy of anti-family values; Richardson preferred 'to take control through a place of safety order' (*Daily Mail*, 7 July 1988).

Like all ideologues, Richardson allegedly became impatient with others involved in child protection who did not share her beliefs and readily grew 'frustrated by the police's lack of enthusiasm and seemed unable to appreciate how wary they would inevitably be about her strongly motivated commitment' (*Daily Mail*, 7 July 1988). This last phrase is particularly interesting and betrays the newspaper's partisanship since it is not clear (except presumably to *Daily Mail* readers) why anyone should be 'wary' of somebody who is 'strongly motivated' or even 'committed' to their work. On the contrary, these phrases are typically used for laudatory purpose!

By contrast, reports of Stuart Bell were extremely positive with captions under his photographs describing him as 'Stuart Bell MP' thereby investing him with authority and credibility for readers. *The Times* portrayed him as a champion of civil liberties challenged to battle by authoritarian social workers. Accordingly one picture of Bell was captioned 'Determined To Protect Children' (*The Times*, 30 June 1988). In the words of the *Sunday Telegraph*, he was 'one of the few public figures involved in the Cleveland case who has no need to reproach himself' (*Sunday Telegraph*, 10 July 1988). Butler-Sloss, however, disagreed. In her report she described his remarks as 'inflammatory' and 'intemperate'. She dismissed as unfounded his widely publicized allegations against medical and social work professionals. Butler-Sloss was also 'sad' that Bell felt 'unable in the light of the further knowledge that he clearly had, to withdraw or modify allegations which could not be substantiated' (Butler-Sloss 1988:165). But, in general, the media rarely challenged the veracity of Bell's assertions no matter how eccentric they became but presented them as 'facts'. Bell's criticisms of social work were unrelenting as he increasingly articulated views characteristic of the family and anti-public sector lobbies. Bell himself often stressed the latter commitment. His article 'Stop The Sex Abuse Industry Now' published the day Butler-Sloss reported, reviewed his major concerns throughout the Cleveland episode. Child abuse, he claimed, can be dismissed as little more than a 'fashionable obsession' imported from America. In reality, the incidence of sexual abuse is much less than social workers suggest. The 8,000 calls a day which ChildLine receives are judged to be unreliable indicators since 'free telephone lines . . . are open to abuse from hoaxers and children who just like the idea of a free phone call'. Social workers promote this 'child sexual abuse bandwagon' because it represents 'jobs, money and power'. The beneficiaries are 'an ever-increasing army of social workers . . . who are unskilled and guided by prejudice' and who 'already waste time on daily case conferences and squander money attending unnecessary seminars' (*Daily Mail*, 6 July 1988). Campbell suggested that many of Bell's arguments were inaccurate and based on mere assertions designed to achieve political ends. The media nonetheless seemed to accept them uncritically (Campbell 1988:15). His advocacy of the parents' position struck a note with large numbers of people who seemed unable or unwilling to accept that sexual abuse of children might be as widespread as the Cleveland cases suggested. By articulating their denials, Bell calmed their fears, dispelled their anxieties and restored moral equilibrium to family life.

MEDIA REPORTING OF SOCIAL WORK AND CHILD ABUSE: AN ASSESSMENT

A number of critical reviews of media reporting of Cleveland have been published. The public relations officer at Cleveland, for example, complained about bias in coverage, the publication of confidential high court evidence, misleading phone calls, editorial blackmail (give us a story or we'll print something really nasty), and the invasion of council offices (Treacher 1988:15). Butler-Sloss reported the complaints of medical staff concerning disruption in hospital wards because of media personnel trying to conduct interviews, one instance of a journalist dressing as a nurse to gain access to children in the wards and journalists blocking the entrances to wards, creating access problems for the nursing and ambulance staff (Butler-Sloss 1988:171).

The actual content of reporting can be criticized on seven counts, although these apply with varying force to different media. First, reporting was frequently sensational and trivialized the issues involved in child abuse. Sensationalism and trivia have almost come to be defining characteristics of the tabloid press and consequently many examples could be cited here. The *Sun*, for example, on the day following the publication of the Butler-Sloss report, featured the story on its front page. A picture of Marietta Higgs was headlined 'Sack Her, Child Abuse Doctor Must Go, Urge MPs'. But, despite its topicality, Cleveland was not the day's main news story. A great proportion of the front page was devoted to 'Another Sun Exclusive' and a larger headline announced 'Dad Stole My Bride'. The sub-heading explains the rather enigmatic headline 'Pat Due To Marry Next Month, But Cheryl, 23, Picks Father'. It seems nothing less than a grotesque moral perversion that such a story might be prioritized above the child abuse report (*Sun*, 7 July 1988). The important point here, however, is that no matter how serious the paper's treatment of the Cleveland issue in the article, its positioning adjacent to the other story guarantees the trivialization of its subject matter. A similar style of coverage was evident in the *Daily Mail* where Cleveland reporting carried under the headline 'We've Been to Hell and Back But Still We Can't Take Our Children Home' had to share page six with a vacuous and silly story about the owner of a pet who spent £1,000 on a funeral for his dog 'Shane the Labrador' (*Daily Mail*, 25 June 1987).

Second, media reporting tended to be biased and partisan in judgement. The often uncritical advocacy of the parents' case was apparent in headlines. 'No End to the Agony For Parents in Child Sex Storm' (*Daily Mirror*, 30 June 1987). And 'Victims of Sex Abuse "Experts"; the Continuing Nightmare of the Innocent Parents Who Stand Accused' (*Daily Mail*, 24 May 1987). In much of this coverage there is little evidence of any attempt by journalists to establish the facts, to present any statistical evidence on the incidence of child abuse, to gain expert corroboration for any allegations, or to create a dialogue between opposing groups or generate meaningful and informed debate about relevant issues. This criticism is more forceful in the case of newspapers than television. In many cases, the tabloid press simply took the parents' side, interviewed them and presented their account of events as reality. This is undoubtedly a quick, as well as a cheap way of news gathering, but the result is unbalanced headlines like 'Agony of Sex Slur Father' (*Daily Mirror*, 27 June 1987).

Third, media reporting presents an oversimplified account of events. Reports tend to concentrate on the immediate circumstances which 'triggered' a particular event – perhaps a child refusing to eat or crying – rather than the background and progression of events which led to the assault (Mawby, Fisher and Hayle 1979:15). In certain senses, simplification of issues in media reporting is inevitable given the time constraints under which reports are produced and the limited broadcast time in programme schedules. A short item on television or radio news attempts to explain, perhaps in little more than two minutes, highly complex issues which 'took an inquiry three months to investigate and fifteen months to deliberate upon' (Social Worker 2 1983:17).

Fourth, in the Cleveland case, media misrepresented important issues and routinely reported factual inaccuracies. The Butler-Sloss report for example confirmed that Higgs' diagnoses of sexual abuse were never based solely on the controversial RAD test and that the alleged 'conspiracy' between Higgs and Richardson was a fallacy (Butler-Sloss 1988:164–6). These allegations, however, persisted in media reporting after the Butler-Sloss report was published.

Fifth, coverage has too frequently been flawed by its concern to scapegoat. The need to identify individuals, usually social workers or the paediatricians in Cleveland, who could be blamed, blinded the press to the complexities of both child abuse and the interaction between welfare agencies attempting to cope with it. Scapegoating moreover misdirects attention and obscures the possibilities for analysing the root causes of abuse. Media typically present abuse as a consequence of the act of an evil, 'sick' or, in the case of social workers, incompetent and authoritarian individual, rather than understanding it as a possible outcome of a structured set of relationships and circumstances. Headlines such as 'Tyra Henry Death Inquiry Blames Social Workers' (*Daily Mail*, 19 December 1987) make less demands on readers as well as on journalistic resources.

Sixth, Tyra Henry and Jasmine Beckford were black; Kimberley Carlile was not. This difference prompted two responses from the press; both were racist. First, the racist overtones in the press treatment of Maurice Beckford were obvious. The *Star* carried an almost full, front-page picture of Beckford with the headline 'The Brute' (*Star*, 29 March 1985). An editorial in the *Sun* can hardly be deemed conciliatory in its judgement: 'Only ten years! He [Beckford] should have been put up against a wall and shot. . . . Isn't there a sound case for sterilising such brutes?' The editorial concluded with a side-swipe at the social workers concerned, 'We hope they can sleep at nights' (*Sun*, 29 March 1985).

Second, there is a clear accusation of reverse discrimination against social workers; a suggestion that they treat black people more favourably than white. The *Daily Mail*'s editorial comment on the Beckford case on 29 March 1985 asks

> To what extent were the social workers of Brent 'naive' and to what extent were they blinded by dogmas? What influence if any did colour have on the decisions they took? Was it of any significance that the foster mother was white, while the stepfather and natural mother were of West Indian origin? Is it something in their training; something in the agitprop atmosphere of the inner city; something in the unfeeling arrogance of local bureaucracy that can dull the intelligence and humanity of social workers?

The issue is addressed as a series of questions but there is an underlying accusation of differential, if not preferential, treatment of clients by social workers according to race.

Finally, reporting of Marietta Higgs, in the Cleveland case, often revealed media sexism. The *Sunday Express*, for example, reporting Higgs giving evidence to the Butler-Sloss inquiry claimed 'What disturbs me about Marietta Higgs is her calm. Her sweet smiling reason' (*Sunday Express*, 11 November 1987). It is not clear, however, why journalists should be 'disturbed' by such personal qualities which seem rather desirable in a witness and certainly preferable to others. 'Reason' is presumably preferable to 'irrationality' or 'prejudice' and 'calm' more desirable than 'hysteria' or 'histrionics'. Perhaps the nub of the *Sunday Express*' concern is that Marietta Higgs does not conform to stereotypes of female behaviour in situations of stress? Other reports contain thinly veiled disapproval of the sexual division of labour in the Higgs household. 'Mr Higgs', the *Daily Mail* reported, 'is bringing up their five children . . . while his wife pursues her medical career; he gave up his own . . . to concentrate on raising the family' (*Daily Mail*, 24 June 1987). The image presented to the reader is that of a woman who values and places her career before that of her husband and who rejects a socially allocated role as mother to protect and bring up her own children. Such an image is not guaranteed to generate warmth and sympathy towards her among most *Daily Mail* readers. Higgs is persistently presented as a person who defies many expectations of female behaviour, especially in the family context.

Our assessment so far has judged published content of reporting but, as Murphy observed, it is 'the stories that are not published and angles which are not taken which form the important subjects for analysis' (Murphy 1974:750). Three substantive issues were not addressed by media.

First, the fact that inadequate financial and human resources are allocated to deal with the problem of child abuse is rarely raised in media coverage. Acknowledging this is not to deny a related point; namely, that media reporting of child abuse, and social service concerns 'not to appear on the front page of the *Mail*' have led to severe problems of resource allocations in many social service departments as a result of the priority given to child protection work, which are discussed below. The real problem is that the overall social service 'cake' is too small. Despite such distortions, inadequate resources to support child protection work remains the 'real abuse' (Doran and Young 1987:13). A draft report from the government Social Services Inspectorate published in June 1988 disclosed 600 cases of child abuse in London alone which were not allocated to a social worker (*Independent*, 7 July 1988). Media practice here merely reflects the procedures of inquiries. The Carlile report for example stated that the 'chronic resource implications' underlying the child protection service 'go way beyond any child abuse inquiry' (Moore 1988:27). The provision of resources adequate to deal with child abuse is a central but neglected issue in media reporting.

Second, a number of gender-related omissions in media reporting have been highlighted by feminist writers. Coverage, for example, has failed to specify abusers as 'male' and those abused as 'female', preferring the non-gender specific terms 'parents' and 'children'. These terms obscure the fundamental character of sexual abuse, the reasons why it occurs, as well as policies for its prevention; they 'amount to a deceit' (MacLeod and Saraga 1988a:15). Such claims are substantiated by research studies which suggest that abusers are 'overwhelmingly male' (90 per cent), while more than 80 per cent of young people abused are female (NSPCC and Greater Manchester Authority Child Sexual Abuse Unit 1988:4–7; La Fontaine 1988:1–2).

Finally, media framed the issue of child abuse in Cleveland as a battle between the state's commitment to protect children and parents' rights to exercise an equivalent paternalism. The rights of children involved in such cases were barely heard even though a child's interests may be massively at odds with their parents', the state, or both. Butler-Sloss' observation that 'a child is a person, not an object of concern', was seized upon by media as a summary phrase embodying the major concerns of her report, but it did little to inform or structure media coverage. More than a judge's catchphrase is required, of course, to redress the vulnerability of children to physical and sexual abuse which is consequent on their powerlessness in the patriarchal family and wider society. It is unhelpful, moreover, for media to present images of children as the weak, passive victims of abuse, requiring protection by, or perhaps from, social workers. A more positive appraisal of children's competences and rights is needed which supersedes 'restrictive notions of protection' with 'liberating notions of empowerment' (Kitzinger 1988:83). In summary, media reporting of child abuse has been sensational, sometimes trivial, both pro and anti parent by disposition, simplistic, often factually inaccurate and eager to scapegoat. Occasionally it has been racist and sexist. The issue has been presented and framed within the parameters prescribed by dominant and traditional social values. Discussions of the rights of children or feminist critiques of patriarchy which seek to go beyond these narrow confines, have been largely ignored. Since 1973, however, the dominant theme has been anti social work. But what are the implications of this both within and beyond the profession?

THE IMPLICATIONS OF MEDIA REPORTING OF SOCIAL WORK

In contemporary society, the media have a crucial role in forming and shaping public opinion. Such a claim is no longer contentious although some media scholars dissented from it in the 1960s (Blumler and Wolton 1990). Media make available to people aspects of social reality which they do not experience directly and thereby make elements of social life generally 'knowable'. This is particularly significant for an activity like social work of which, unlike teaching or doctoring, most people have little direct experience. The media render otherwise remote happenings observable and meaningful and transform the private into the public realm. Consequently media discussions of social work are highly influential with significant implications in a number of arenas.

First, media reporting of social work becomes an input in the policy process. A cyclical process is set in train. Since media are influential in structuring public perceptions of social and welfare issues – often in a highly emotive and melodramatic way – they can create demands on government to legislate to placate heightened public anxieties (Golding and Middleton 1979:5), a process which has been dubbed 'legislation by tabloid' (Franklin and Lavery 1989: 26–9). The 1975 Children Act, for example, in part reflected public concerns prompted and exacerbated by coverage of the Maria Colwell case. A similar influential role in government policy is imputed to media in America (Nelson 1978:28). More recently media discussions of the Cleveland affair seem to have had important implications for the Children Bill (now the Children Act). The timing and presentation of the Act seem to reflect government concerns to calm public anxiety in the wake of Cleveland. This is not to suggest that certain types of media coverage (the persistent presentation of social workers as authoritarian and eager to intervene) bring about specific legislative proposals (the Children Act) in a crude or deterministic way. What is being proposed however is that the media play a critical role in generating a climate or culture of public opinion sympathetic and receptive to proposals for change.

There is a second area in which it can be surmised that media publicizing of child abuse has exercised influence; namely the way in which priorities are set and resources allocated, particularly in terms of social work time and expertise. Numerous research reports have commented how experienced, qualified workers in 'generic' social work posts deal almost exclusively with statutory cases involving children and their families, while other client groups, for example the elderly and disabled people, are dealt with by unqualified staff or volunteers (Stevenson and Parsloe 1978; Howe 1986). Increasingly media publicity of statutory child protection work, can be seen to undermine other efforts to develop more preventative approaches.

While central government reports (DHSS 1985) and numerous research reports (Fuller and Stevenson 1983; DHSS 1986) have stressed the importance of developing an approach to child care work which emphasizes prevention and a much more positive use of local authority care, the emphasis on child protection has made this very difficult. The increased amount of crisis and investigative work is reflected in the increased number of place of safety orders nationally and the increased number of cases on child abuse registers. The number of place of safety orders taken out trebled during the 1970s following the Colwell inquiry (Parton 1985:122–4) and subsequently increased again from a rate of 0.45 per 1,000 (0–17) to 0.73 in 1987 and 0.71 in 1988 (NALGO 1989:21). The number of children registered on the NSPCC registers more than doubled between 1983 and 1987, with a twelve-fold increase in registered cases of sexual abuse (Creighton and Noyes 1989).

Third, media play a central role in influencing public images and perceptions of social workers and what they do. Individuals' day-to-day experience of social work is minimal and consequently media fulfil an important educational function. To date, images of social work presented to the public have been largely negative but they need not be so necessarily. In 1987, of course, the stereotype of the social worker as bully gained ascendancy. The public image of social workers insensitively taking children from their families reached what seemed for some to be its logical conclusion when Thameside Social Services moved to take an unborn child into care after three previous children, in the family concerned, had died in infancy: in the upshot this child was stillborn. The press unleashed a wave of moral outrage. The *Daily Mail* ran the headline 'They

Killed Our Baby Grieving Father Accuses Social Services' (*Daily Mail*, 18 November 1987). The *Sunday Times* reminded its readership of 'public fears that helpless parents can be condemned without a hearing by an overweening and all-powerful bureaucracy' and added, 'Every year social workers remove dozens of babies within hours of their birth' (*Sunday Times*, 22 November 1987).

An alternative, more benign, public image of the profession envisages the social worker as a sort of latter-day Florence Nightingale; a middle-class do-gooder. One research study found that the 'typical social worker is tolerant, young, university educated and female. She spends her time working with children, the elderly and the poor' (Wilton 1980:14).

Many within social work, albeit largely in the voluntary rather than the statutory sector, now believe these negative images are significant and consequently have given public relations activity a much greater priority than previously.

Fourth, there is evidence that the media have an impact on day-to-day social work practice. In a general sense, their influence can be pervasive. It has already been noted that many social workers interviewed by Stevenson and Parsloe were fearful of being 'found wanting' and made to account publicly (i.e. in the media spotlight) for their actions. This fear was/is an omnipresent influence on the way social workers experience their work.

A survey of 177 social workers in six different social services departments in early 1989 were asked a series of questions about the impact a range of situations had on the respondents' recent work. Media coverage of child care tragedies was seen by two-thirds to be making their work harder. Social workers clearly experience the impact of the media on their everyday practice as very negative (NALGO 1989:43).

There can be little doubt that the media are important in influencing the professional climate and culture within which social workers operate and thereby specific aspects of practice. For example, in the area of child abuse it is not simple coincidence that the number of place-of-safety orders has increased considerably each time that a public inquiry orchestrated by the media, has castigated social workers for failing to intervene and protect the child. Social work practice has responded to accusations of being soft by using authoritative statutory interventions more and taking risks less.

Fifth, media reporting of child abuse has significant implications for broader issues concerning the civil liberties of social work staff. The latter may be denied any public platform or refused permission by politicians in their employing authority to discuss their opinions or account of events with the media. In Cleveland, for example, Councillor Bob Pitt, chair of the new social services committee, moved a policy statement restricting social service staff access to media in a clumsy and bureaucratic rhetoric which did little to conceal its censorial purpose. 'For the time being' he announced

> we shall continue the policy which has been in operation for some time of avoiding getting involved in discussions, debates and confrontations over child abuse issues which almost certainly will be counter productive and which will look back rather than forward. Neither members nor staff from the department will appear on public platforms or become involved in public debates. This is not a policy which will be in place for all time, but I do believe it is necessary at this stage.

(Pitt 1989:3)

The press release from which the above quotation was taken expresses a profound irony as well as timidity in its attitude towards media. Pitt had issued a press release to gain maximum media reporting for his announcement of the ban on discussions with the media by social service staff; a clear case of do as I say, not as I do!

In Cleveland media reporting seems to have held yet more general implications for the political life of the region. At the time of the local elections in May 1989, the Labour group were particularly concerned that the child abuse issue might be a vote loser for them and hence Pitt's 'new-speak' dictate that in future 'we will be talking about child protection not child abuse' (Pitt 1989:3). But verbal gymnastics and attempts to define issues out of existence are unlikely to resolve problems, as Stuart Bell found when he confronted difficulties in his attempts at re-selection for his Middlesbrough parliamentary seat.

Beyond these substantive impacts, there are other ways in which media reporting of child abuse bears directly or indirectly on social work practice. Social workers themselves read, view and listen to media along with other members of the general public and are not immune to the effects of their messages. Persistently negative appraisals of social work means morale within the profession suffers to the extent where some authorities are now facing critical difficulties in recruiting social work staff. Media criticism also influences attitudes towards social workers amongst related professional groups – health visitors, youth and community workers, police and medical staff – who work closely with them. How can media antipathies towards social workers and social work issues be explained?

MEDIA REPORTING OF SOCIAL WORK: AN EXPLANATION

The explanation of media reporting of social work contains at least three interrelated and mutually reinforcing elements. Each will be mentioned briefly and then explored at greater length. First, social work is an essentially ambiguous profession, riven with tensions, which render it potentially vulnerable to criticism from perspectives which view the world in far more clear-cut and absolutist terms. This vulnerability is exacerbated by the fact that political and community support for the profession, as it became increasingly incorporated under the rubric of the state, was extremely limited. A second explanation derives from political economy. It was suggested earlier that social workers have been presented in media reporting as a symbol for the public sector embodying, in almost caricature form, its alleged shortcomings. If this speculation is correct, it might be expected that the shifting economic, political and moral climate characteristic of the 1970s and 1980s, would generate a new political consensus hostile to some of the central assumptions of social work. The final component in the explanation turns to aspects of media themselves and two accounts of the mechanisms prompting journalist/ broadcaster interest in certain stories. The first borrows from Cohen's theory of 'moral panics' developed in the early 1970s to explore the nature of media reporting of mods and rockers (Cohen, 1972). A second 'media based' explanation for interest in social work, rests on what journalists call 'news values', namely the features which a story must possess to be deemed 'newsworthy'.

Social work: an ambiguous profession

Social work is concerned essentially with meeting the needs of individuals, families and communities in a personalized way. The scope and location of such activity, however, has varied over the last 150 years. Expressed broadly, the history of social work activity has seen it increasingly drawn into the auspices of the state. The reorganization of social services departments following the Seebohm report established social work as a central part of the state's activity. This change reflected the reassessment of the deficiencies of the welfare state which was taking place during the 1960s within the broader framework of Keynesian social democracy. It was judged that by and large the majority of the population had benefited from the provision of welfare goods and services but significant gaps remained; children and elderly people were particular examples of relative neglect. Two factors were seen to explain this shortcoming. First, the main state welfare services were considered overly complex, bureaucratic and impersonal and not understood sufficiently well by the less articulate and confident. Second, there were some individuals and families who generated a disproportionate number of problems in terms of delinquency, child neglect, mental illness and financial problems and consequently required specialized and in-depth intervention. These concerns were forerunners of the 'cycle of deprivation' thesis explicitly articulated by Sir Keith Joseph in the early 1970s. The central concern of the reorganized social service departments was thus to co-ordinate other welfare agencies, while trying to improve the functioning of the most deprived sections of society through individualized methods such as case-work. It would provide the personalized and humanistic dimension to the welfare state and thereby try to rehabilitate and reintegrate into the mainstream of social life those who for whatever reasons were particularly deprived or left behind. Consequently the hallmark of the new state service, and the profession which was to staff it, was to be flexible, liberal and permissive in its approach since it would be primarily concerned with those rejected or perceived as failures by the main social and economic institutions. It was symptomatic of attempts in the late 1960s and early 1970s to find technical and personalized welfare solutions to social problems. It was one of the final elements introduced within the social democratic consensus both to reform itself and to respond to more wide-ranging social, political and economic changes.

It is important to recognize, however, that modern social work's relationship to social democracy was in many ways weak and certainly ambiguous. The establishment of state social work, with its individualistic and psychologistic approach to human problems, sat uncomfortably with the predominant social reformist tendencies within the Labour Party and the Labour movement. What is particularly evident and extremely important is that the growth and legitimation of social work during the period relied little upon wider community or political support. It lacked any effective roots which might help nurture it and provide it with stability. It was established very much as a result of the efforts of the social work lobby itself which was actively seeking professional status and recognition and which was perhaps at its most confident, well-organized and optimistic during the 1960s. Important alliances were established with senior civil servants and academics as well as those within the profession, so that some of the grander claims made on its behalf were rarely seriously tested due in part to chance political processes which helped dissipate opposition. (See Hall (1976) and Cooper (1983) who provide detailed insights and assessments of the politics informing the reorganization of social services and Tom White, in this volume, who looks particularly at the role of the Seebohm Implementation Action Group.)

Thus, while social service departments embraced only a proportion of social workers and social workers only constitute a minority of social service departments' employees, it was through the establishment of social service departments that social work grew as a significant element of the welfare state. Subsequently, it is through social service departments that social work has been subject to its most vociferous public criticisms and debate. Social service departments were welcomed as the fifth social service and social work was hence no longer a minor 'handmaiden' welfare activity (Townsend 1970). It was seen to have taken over primary responsibility for areas of social life, on behalf of the revised welfare state, previously left to other agencies, including the control of juvenile crime, or the community itself. The establishment and beginnings of social service departments, however, took place essentially outside the gaze of wider public and political concerns and had little public or political understanding or support. Not only was the new service dominated by the new aspiring profession of social work, it was quickly perceived, ironically, in very similar ways to other state welfare agencies – as large, impersonal, bureaucratic and hence divorced from the communities it was intended to serve.

But in addition to these unstable circumstances of birth for the new profession there are a number of tensions at the very heart of social work, evident throughout its history, which were in effect built into the new service. In many ways social work is an 'ambiguous' profession which is attempting to fulfil a variety of different, potentially contradictory objectives (Clarke 1988). Such tensions, however, are the very stuff of social work and provide the core of what it is to do social work. Social work is essentially a messy business. These tensions, built into the fabric of social work and hence into the fabric of social service departments, have been greatly reinforced to the point where it may be experienced as not just a daunting task riven through with dilemmas, but an impossible task where the profession and its practitioners are almost set up to fail. There are a number of such tensions which can be identified.

First, the service was established to be universal – yet explicitly selective for those with exceptional needs or problems which put them beyond the normal coping mechanisms of the family, the market or the other main social services. Hence the stigma associated with the old poor law or 'the welfare' has never been fully overcome. In fact it might be argued that such stigma is reinforced in a political culture which stresses and values 'standing on your own feet' and which sees dependency on state welfare as a major malaise. To cite one of Mrs Thatcher's memorable phrases, 'There is no such thing as society, only individual men and women and their families.' Social work of course has always emphasized working with individuals and families. Increasingly, however, individual problems and family failure is seen to be caused by, as well as to reside with, those individuals and families concerned. In a culture which increasingly individualizes and privatizes family life, it becomes difficult to explain problems which manifest themselves within individuals and families as being caused by anything other than the behaviour of these individuals themselves. Simply to make a claim on a social worker, therefore, becomes a public declaration of being outside the mainstream of society and economic life. Personal troubles are castrated from their social context and structural location.

Thus, while modern social work was established to respond to the needs of a variety of different client groups, it is clear that the element the majority all have in common is that they live in poverty. They are members of the 'residual and dependent' sections of the working class (Jones 1983:12) or what we may now, more appropriately, term the 'underclass'. They are excluded from, or are on the margins of, the labour market. Becker and Macpherson have concluded from their survey of relevant research that only about 10 per cent of client referrals will be from a person in employment; approximately 20–30 per cent will be from the unemployed; 25 per cent from 'economically unactive persons'; and from between 20–35 per cent from elderly clients. Ninety per cent of clients are likely to have incomes from a source other than employment – the DHSS in almost every case (Becker and Macpherson 1986:51).

Second, social work is essentially concerned with mediating between the needs of clients and the norms and requirements of society. Expressed differently, this means negotiating care and control. Most people come into social work in order to 'help' others and improve their situations. Practitioners and the profession itself sees itself as essentially 'client-centred' so that values such as respect for others and client self-determination are professed to lie at its core. Such values subsequently inform practice principles such as 'starting where the client is' and 'moving at the client's pace' and 'being non-judgemental'. However the growth of social work has been dependent upon its *social* auspices whereby social workers are employed by and work on behalf of society. Here 'society' means the state, and the social auspices are represented primarily in the statutory functions. Social workers have a variety of statutory powers concerning their major client groups – one of which is protecting children. To fulfil these duties social workers invariably have to do things which may be experienced by the client as against their wishes but which are seen as important either to protect others or to modify behaviour so that it comes more into line with what is deemed normal.

Social workers can also be experienced as controlling in less explicit ways. They are the gatekeepers of scarce resources – financial, material, expertise, day care, residential care – both within their own departments and in others. Not only may clients not be deemed a high priority but when they are they may be asked to modify their behaviour in order to qualify.

Thus social workers have to exercise judgement, evaluate and act in ways which the client may experience as against their interests. It thus seems that social work is caught between either representing society to the client – making judgements, imposing social standards, allocating scarce social resources – or representing the wishes and needs of the client to society – advocating with other agencies and being supportive and sympathetic where everyone else may have rejected them. However this is not a circumstance in which social workers choose an 'either/or option'. This tension is at the heart of social work, continually requiring the social worker to work a fine balance to mediate between the interests of society and the needs of the client. 'In terms of the relationship which the social worker has with the individual and with the state, social work can be seen as "straddling the split" between subjective states of the individual and their objective statuses. Subjective states may be characterised for example by pain, suffering, need, love, hate; and objective statuses may be characterised by for example old age, handicap, mental illness, debts or crime' (Horne 1987:87).

Third, and perhaps more significantly for present purposes, social work has a particular responsibility for the family (Rustin 1979).

The rise of social work as a profession was very much dependent upon the increasing centrality of the family and, to a lesser extent, the community, as an object of both concern and positive support in post-war, state, social policy. While the family was seen as the best place for individuals to be reared and cared for, particularly compared to an institution, it was also seen as the source of many problems such as crime, delinquency, mental illness and, more latterly, child abuse. Primarily, however, the private family is judged the optimum locus for child rearing and in which to care for individuals. The state intervenes only on the basis of its statutory commitments when things are judged to be going wrong. Social workers have particular responsibilities for those who are powerless or dependent, particularly children, so that if the normal (adult) guardians are failing in any way, social workers should step in to protect those at risk. This need to protect children and hence to intervene in families is a very ambiguous obligation for social workers in a society which essentially upholds the value of the private family and where parents are seen as having primary responsibility for rearing children. Hence there is little social or moral legitimacy for state interventions into family life. Social workers have to rely on a variety of strategies to care for children but also to establish the circumstances which are giving rise to concerns and to establish whether those concerns are well founded.

Fourth, the knowledge available to carry out social work is a mixture of the practical, the social scientific and the personal, with many judgements being based on interpretation, drawing conclusions from very impartial and contested information. Inevitably, therefore, much of the work may be 'high risk' and progress may be difficult to measure, particularly where progress may be interpreted according to quite different evaluative criteria. Like many areas of public life success is not clear-cut. It is not analogous to winning or making a profit. As many have said, social work is often concerned with prevention or maintenance, trying to ensure that things don't get worse. It is essentially a prophylactic activity with results which are hard to measure and no guaranteed unequivocal yardstick of success.

Finally, social workers must continually assess and make judgements about whose interests they are ultimately concerned to promote. This is no easy matter. Not only does a social worker have responsibilities to the individual client, the state and society more generally, but also to different individuals who compose their client group who may have very different, even oppositional, needs and wishes. A social worker, for example, must mediate the opposing aspirations of a very elderly relative who wishes to remain at home but who is being cared for by a younger but still elderly relative who cannot cope any longer; between the very young child who is showing numerous signs of abuse but for which there is no 'hard' evidence and the parent who is under clear social stress and doesn't see that their child is any different to others in the neighbourhood. Similarly, the expectations and interpretations of other agencies and professions may be quite different. Throughout, therefore, the social worker has to negotiate, compromise and make the best of things while trying to be fair to all concerned (Jordan 1987).

In summary, social work is essentially and necessarily an ambiguous and messy occupation where the outcomes are rarely clear cut and where the methods of achieving them are variable and likely to be contested. All of this takes place where the primary clientele are the deprived and marginalized. Such an occupational structure and working environment contains a massive potential for criticism even when the social work task is being fulfilled 'as well as might be expected'. For a journalist or broadcaster seeking a sensational story, it offers a rich lode to mine.

A shifting political economy and the emergence of a new welfare consensus

The tensions within the social work task detailed above have been sharpened further in recent years. Shortly after the reorganization of social services, the political climate in which social work operated began to change and the nature of the economic base began to shift. Just at the point when social work was given a more visible and central role the foundations of the social democratic welfare state were themselves put under severe strain. The political and economic climate became increasingly hostile to some of the central assumptions of social work. The mid 1970s witnessed the onset of economic recession, the return of mass unemployment, the growth in new right ideology and ultimately the election of the Conservative administration in 1979.

Britain's worsening economy had two direct consequences for social work. First, the numbers of potential clients grew as increasing sections of the population became marginalized from the mainstream of the economy and excluded from the labour market. The numbers at or below supplementary benefit level increased from 5,140,000 in 1974 to 9,380,000 in 1985 (17 per cent of the population). By 1985 there were 15,420,000 (29 per cent of the population) at or below 140 per cent of the supplementary benefit levels (CPAG [Child Poverty Action Group] 1988). This expansion largely reflected the growth in unemployment and consequently a greater proportion of the total were children and families. There were also significant increases during the period of single parent families and elderly and very elderly people. All are traditional clientele of social services. These groups are concentrated in areas of social deprivation where the social effects of the economic recession have typically been worst – inner city areas and those reliant on heavy industry, particularly in the north.

The second consequence of the recession exacerbated the first by placing severe limits on the resources allocated to state welfare agencies to meet this expanded need. There have again been a range of consequences for social work. Because other agencies have less resources available, such as council housing, individuals will encounter new problems like homelessness or overcrowding. Similarly as these other welfare agencies are placed under increasing pressure they are likely to refer more cases to social services for help. This is particularly the case with social security and health services since they are seen to have a responsibility for family and community care. The net result is again therefore an increase in the potential clientele.

At the same time, however, social services departments will have less resources available to meet this vastly increased potential need. Spending on the personal social services, starting from a very low initial base, grew by 63.4 per cent between 1970–1 and 1974–5. As Ferlie and Judge have commented, 'The golden age for spending on the personal social services was quite clearly the first half of the 1970s' (Ferlie and Judge 1981:313–14). Growth subsequently slowed significantly following the establishment of a 2 per cent annual growth target intended to take account of demographic changes. In practice the growth in departments was quite diverse. Webb and Wistow, surveying the general pattern of spending between 1978–9 and 1983–4 noted that while some departments enjoyed enhanced budgets, 'Almost two fifths of all English social services departments received less growth over these years than was considered necessary to maintain service levels' (Webb and Wistow 1987:167). They also tried to assess whether these changes in resources were sufficient to meet the increased needs.

It is clear from the data that even in the years when the 2%

resource growth target was more than met the personal social services failed to maintain absolute, let alone per capita, service levels across the board. In other words 2% *appears* to have been an insufficiently accurate estimate, by even the most modest of standards, of growth and resources required annually to prevent a decline in the level of service provision.

(Webb and Wistow 1987:169–73)

These severe changes to the economic climate in which social work was operating from the mid-1970s onwards were accompanied by similar and significant shifts in the political and ideological climate with severe consequences for social work, both for its practitioners and its clients. Ideas which were seen as being associated with the 'radical' or 'new' right are now accepted as the new consensus or orthodoxy (Jordan 1989:ch. 2). This developed as the authority and intervention of the social democratic state was found wanting in response to problems in both the economic and social spheres. Such problems had been evident for some years but what changed was their apparent scale. Increasingly the welfare state was seen as a 'burden' upon the wealth creating and essentially private sectors of the economy. To tackle the economic problems associated with recession – both unemployment and inflation – many areas of the state's activity needed to be cut back.

The malaise was judged, however, to be even more deep-seated. The welfare state had encouraged and promoted undesirable attitudes about dependency, irresponsibility and permissiveness, all of which were undermining individual morality. Individuals were perceived to become lazier, because the state could ultimately provide, but society was also becoming more violent and more difficult to govern.

A number of legislative innovations which were regarded as shifting the legal definitions of morality in a permissive direction (viz. abortion and homosexuality), were accompanied by a steady increase in the rates of divorce, delinquency and violent crime, all of which suggested there was a reduced commitment to traditional values and ties. Institutions and values thought to be fundamental to the 'English way of life' were considered under threat, particularly from misguided liberals – especially among the new professions. Not only, therefore, was it possible to construct state social work as a direct drain on economic resources, it could also be seen as undermining very basic values, particularly those concerning the family. For the institution which was felt to be at greatest risk under this permissive and lawless morality was the family. Social workers rather than bolstering family responsibilities were seen to be directly undermining them. It is this concern for the family which helps explain the growth of a number of moral campaigns in the late 1960s and which was also at the root of a growing social anxiety amongst traditional middle- and working-class groups. The production of social anxiety amongst these groups resulted in a disposition to identify scapegoats onto whom the disturbing experiences could be focused. The scapegoats were attributed with the role of causing the various elements of organization and dislocation which produced the problem in the first place. Thus fears about the breakdown of the social order invariably began to focus on the family and those who had a responsibility for ensuring its 'proper' functioning. Such anxiety was particularly sensitive to orchestration by the media – especially concerning the ultimate fears of violence – and where the victim was innocent and defenceless, as in cases of child abuse, here the ready scapegoat became not only the perpetrator (invariably a male parent) but also the social workers involved (Parton 1981).

Increasingly such concerns became influential in changing the direction of political debate in the late 1960s and found the most cogent expression in the growth of the new right. This had a direct impact upon the Conservative Party, leading ultimately to the election of Margaret Thatcher; it also expressed many of the fears of the Labour Party and its traditional working-class supporters.

The new right stood for a new form of social organization similar to nineteenth-century liberalism which was based on a belief in the market as the most equitable and efficient means of resource allocation combined with a commitment to individual freedom of choice. It thus denied the underlying social basis to needs and problems and any responsibility for the state to ensure social justice. However, while it called for a 'minimal' state it demanded a strong state, particularly where it considered that permissiveness and violence were prevalent. By 1972–3 a number of commentators had demonstrated that Britain was dominated by concerns about the economy but also by concerns about increasing permissiveness and violence, issues orchestrated via the media of mass communications. The politics of the new right provided a framework for representing these concerns and also constructing a fundamentally different way of approaching and reordering social priorities (Gamble 1988).

In effect the public inquiry into the death of Maria Colwell provided the catalyst for ventilating these pervasive anxieties about the rationale, accountability and legitimacy of state social work. While the inquiry can be seen to crystallize the overriding social anxieties about the family and violence which were so prevalent at the time, it also provided the first opportunity to voice the concerns about this, in effect, new state activity – social work and the social service departments. A crucial element in the growing scepticism about the social democratic welfare state was a disenchantment with some of the agencies and new professions which operated it. Social work and social service departments as the most recent manifestations of this were particularly vulnerable.

As a result of more than ten years of Conservative government committed to 'rolling back the frontiers of the state', there has been a fundamental reassessment of the basic principles of welfare policy and a restructuring of the way certain services are provided. A number of elements can be identified as symbolizing the new orthodoxy. It is assumed that individuals should have freedom of choice in the way they live their lives but should be responsible for providing for themselves, their dependents and the commitment they make to others. Society should be based on a meritocracy whereby individuals should keep as much as possible of both their earnings and any property they acquire. As a consequence the market is the primary mechanism for distributing resources and satisfying want while families should provide the primary arena for meeting personal and emotional needs. The role of the state should consequently be reduced to providing only those services that cannot be met by the primary institutions of the market and the family. Specific policy initiatives have been introduced to make such principles a reality: privatization, which revives the informal and voluntary sector so that the state can take more of an enabling role; domestication, whereby the community, primarily in the guise of women, is encouraged to care for the more deprived and dependent; selectivity, so that where the state does provide this is based primarily on a test of means; and a greater reliance on explicit control and the use of legislative mechanisms for ensuring that individuals fulfil their economic and family responsibilities.

In the process certain forms of social work have been perceived as far more socially acceptable and hence constructed in a more positive light; others in a more negative light. Social work, which takes place either in proximity to, or explicitly within, the voluntary or private sectors is seen as far more legitimate, especially where such work is seen to enforce family and individual obligations. Generally, voluntary social work agencies such as the National

Society for the Prevention of Cruelty to Children (NSPCC), the National Association for the Care and Resettlement of Offenders (NACRO), and Save the Children Fund, enjoy a much more positive media representation. Such positive appraisal also reflects, of course, the much more proactive public relations strategies that such agencies have adopted.

Similarly, it seems that social work, when provided under the auspices of the state and particularly in social service departments, receives a much more critical and high-profile exposure, particularly when it is seen as not fulfilling its statutory role appropriately. These areas of social work which are far more circumscribed by tight legislative controls, even if open to different and even contradictory interpretation, potentially will be thrust into the media spotlight. This is certainly the case with children and in part explains why other areas of work, particularly with elderly and disabled people, will receive little coverage at all. In many ways, however, it becomes circular for the media, in concentrating on certain issues and hence making them visible and subject to public and political scrutiny, also make it more likely that they will be subject to more detailed legislative control.

Social work, moral panics and news values

A third component in explanations of reporting of social work focuses specifically on media, their processes of news-gathering and production, the way in which reporting of particular themes can develop under specified circumstances and the features which a story must possess before journalists consider it newsworthy.

Media reporting of child abuse has frequently been judged to conform to what has been described as a 'moral panic'. The phenomenon was identified initially by Cohen who was concerned to explain the rapidly escalating spiral of media reporting of mods and rockers and the powerful responses such coverage evoked from the public (Cohen 1972:259). A necessary requirement for such 'panics' seemed to be conditions of social crisis when traditional values and social institutions momentarily lose their credibility and waver under an attack, presumed or real, by a group which Cohen designates 'folk devils'. The media have a central role in both creating and sustaining the panic by identifying the group to serve as 'folk devils', by isolating, defining and socially censuring them as an out group, and by restating and reaffirming the traditional social values the group is judged to transgress. The latter is achieved by giving extensive and priority media access to what Hall *et al.* describe as 'the primary definers': authority figures such as judges, Members of Parliament, police officers and government spokespersons who legitimate, but at the same time help to structure, dominant cultural values (Hall *et al.* 1978:57). In summary, the media by generating moral panics, create the labels by which social problems are publicly perceived and understood. Typically such problems are cast in manichean mould as a battle between heroes and villains, insiders and outsiders, them and us. On the inside 'is the public, including the media as *vox populi*, while on the outside are the threatening deviant or suspect group' (Golding and Middleton 1979:11).

Golding and Middleton suggest three phases in the development of the 'panic'. First, there is a 'precipitating event' (for example the initial reporting of the Cleveland affair) which triggers media interest and guarantees that similar future events will be extensively publicized. Second, there is a period in which a number of 'previously latent mythologies' about the particular 'social problem' are revealed and reported, thereby exacerbating public anxieties – (media-conducted debates about the frequency of abuse, the sorts of families in which it is presumed to be prevalent). Finally, government responds to these public and press concerns – (by enacting some aspects of the Children Act) (Golding and Middleton 1979:12–14).

Moral panic theory seems at least initially to provide a pleasingly comprehensive account of media reporting of child abuse. The analysis of British political economy offered above, moreover, suggests that the circumstances of social, political and moral crisis which the theory requires as a precondition, were also prevalent during the 1970s and 1980s. Moral panic theory does not, however, transfer readily across contexts and while it enjoys some explanatory value, ultimately it remains suggestive rather than substantive. At least two aspects of media reporting of child abuse cannot be rendered comprehensible by moral panic theory.

First, and this seems quite remarkable, media reporting of child abuse identified social workers as the 'folk devils' to be castigated, vilified and designated to the out-group challenging the values of the civil community. The 'wrongdoer', the person actually responsible for the abuse of the child, was certainly the subject of media admonitions, but there was not the same degree of hue and cry in the reporting of the criminal trial of the 'abusers' that was evident in discussions of the role of social workers at the time that reports of inquiries were published; nor was reporting of 'abusers' so replete with sterotypes.

Second, Cohen claims that the second phase of panic identified by Golding and Middleton will be accompanied by 'exaggeration' in media reporting. Stories about mods and rockers, he alleged, will begin to appear routinely in media both locally and nationally and the number of reported incidents of gang violence will increase substantially. Media reporting of child abuse, however, confounded such expectations. When the Cleveland story was first reported, estimates of the prevalence of child abuse were high but a year later, when Butler-Sloss was published, media were keen to play down earlier estimates suggesting they were wildly excessive; Cleveland was already perceived and presented as a consequence of 'over-zealous', if not 'fanatic' social and welfare professionals. A related difficulty is that an over-reliance upon the concept of 'moral panics' when explaining the emergence of a new social problem may imply there is no 'real' problem. Public concern may be judged as simply the product of media 'mis-reporting'. In the case of child abuse, therefore, it is a problem with the media rather than a problem with the way we treat children that becomes the focus of attention (see Parton 1989 for a more extended discussion of this point).

A final component in the explanation of media reporting of social work attempts to understand what journalists and broadcasters themselves consider to be a 'good story' which is 'newsworthy'; the prevalence of particular stories in the media must, at least in part, express this factor. 'News', of course, in the sense of human happenings or events, is potentially infinite. But the chaos of human experience reflected in the daily catalogue of events worldwide is not, for self-evident reasons, reported comprehensively in newspapers or in radio and television news broadcasts. This complex of human experience is sifted and selected by journalists and, assuming the process is neither random nor eccentric, must be guided by certain principles. 'Principles' is perhaps a rather grandiose word for what most journalists would prefer to describe as a gut instinct or 'news sense' which develops quite unthinkingly and is honed by working experience. 'It's like riding a bike; if you stop to think about it you'll fall off', a deputy editor for BBC Television News explained to Alastair Hetherington in the latter's study of news values (Hetherington 1985:viii). Journalists' shared awareness of 'news values' informs news selection and in the process a miniscule proportion of human events becomes designated 'news' while the greater part of human experience is consigned to mere 'history'.

The presence of these 'unwritten rules' has long been acknowledged. The first Royal Commission on the Press (the Ross Commission) suggested that while 'the idea of what constitutes news varies from office to office' and that a 'paper's standard of news values is one of the most distinctive facets of its personality', there are 'certain elements common to all conceptions of news. To be news an event must first be interesting to the public.' In assessing what might be of interest to the public, the Commission listed the following pecking order headed by sport but followed by 'news about people, news of strange or amusing adventures, tragedies, accidents and crimes' (Royal Commission on the Press 1947–9:373–5). Galtung and Ruge (1981:60) list twelve factors which they suggest must be satisfied before an event is likely to be considered newsworthy, whereas Hetherington offers his own 'seismic scale' which contains the following seven categories:

> Significance: social, economic, political, human.
> Drama: the excitement, action and entertainment in the event.
> Surprise: the freshness, newness, unpredictability.
> Personalities: royal, political, 'showbiz', others.
> Sex, scandal, crime: popular ingredients.
> Numbers: the scale of the event, number of people affected.
> Proximity: on our doorsteps, or 10,000 miles away.
>
> (Hetherington 1985:8)

It is easy to see how stories focusing on child abuse and involving social workers bring together, in a quite unique amalgam, a number of features congruent with journalists' news values which they believe readers will find attractive. Some journalists are quite explicit about the value of such 'news' stories.

> Child abuse makes good copy. There is the trial which involves hundreds of column inches devoted to the details of the child's grisly end. This allows for both public conscience and appetite for horror to be satisfied at the same time. Then there is the ritual purification; the inquiry into what went wrong and the public execution of the 'guilty parties' – the social workers.
>
> (Hills 1980:19)

A predominant feature of western news values, underlining the attractiveness of child abuse stories for journalists, is the obsession with 'bad news'. In the words of *Sunday Times* journalist Ian Jacks, 'Bad news is to journalism what dung is to rhubarb' (Jacks 1986:1). So far as media reporting of social work is concerned, the emphasis on 'bad news' suggests that a tragedy such as the death of a single child in care, is more likely to receive media attention than the successful handling of 1,000 social work cases concerning children. Successful case work may be routine but the routine is not newsworthy. In the words of the old journalistic adage: 'Dog bites man is not news, but man bites dog is a scoop.' But there is a related point here. Routine successful social work conducted over a period of months or even years does not form the subject of media coverage because it does not generate an 'event' to report; successful work of this kind is ongoing and has no natural terminus when it can be judged as completed. Melanie Phillips makes a statement which to journalists has more than a slight ring of the self-evident; namely, before a story can be reported 'something has to happen' (Phillips 1979:123). Consequently, as Tindall observes, 'The death of a child at the hands of its parents is more likely to be reported than the poor care the child has been receiving for months prior to his death or the painstaking efforts of the social worker involved to prevent such a tragedy' (Tindall 1981:7). The systematic journalistic preference for stories which contain and express particular news values guarantees that certain aspects of social work practice congruent with them such as child abuse will achieve a high news profile while other areas of work will be largely ignored.

SUMMARY AND PROSPECTS

The argument outlined above suggests that social workers have become a symbol for the public sector and that media presentations of social work articulate a broader antipathy to the role of the social democratic state as a provider of goods, especially welfare goods and services. Changes in political economy, in tandem with attendant ideological shifts, during the 1970s and 1980s have created a new welfare consensus in which the 'ambiguous' profession of social work has become subject to greater public critique. Public criticism has in turn fuelled the willingness of certain aspects of the media to adopt an increasingly hostile posture towards social work and thereby complete a vicious circle.

Social work's reaction to media reporting has been as heterogeneous as the profession itself, but two broad responses can be identified. The first appears wholly negative, signals a complete rupture of discourse with media and seems to prevail in some social services departments. The strategy advocates social work's withdrawal from public discussion and is based on the philosophy of 'keeping quiet' and 'keeping your head down' in the hope that problems will 'go away'; a curious, unhappy and ineffective amalgam of ostrich and Micawber. It is the media philosophy of 'no comment'. But retreating from established relationships with media suggests that social work risks losing any opportunities which might be available, no matter how slight, to contribute to structuring the content of media reporting of its professional practice.

A second more positive response to adverse media reporting has been the development of increased public relations activities by the social work profession. These have been evident in both the statutory and voluntary sector as well as social work's professional body, the British Association of Social Workers (BASW), which made its first public relations appointment in 1989.

The last five years have witnessed a substantial growth in public relations departments in local authorities. The size of departments, measured by the human and financial resources they possess, varies considerably with the most well-resourced typically sited in the larger county, metropolitan district and Inner London authorities under Labour control (Franklin 1988a:ch. 2). Local politicians in all parties have come increasingly to understand that the 'professionalization' of relationships with the media can generate considerable public relations benefits; not least an enhanced public image for the local authority. The local government public relations officer's brief however has, to date, been to handle media relations for the entire authority in which social services is merely a single, albeit significant, department. But there are signs that public relations officers are being assigned to specific directorates to deal with sensitive and potentially 'newsworthy' matters. Bradford, for example, appointed a public relations officer for social services in 1987, with Kent making a similar appointment shortly thereafter. Notwithstanding these developments, the statutory sector has seemed more reluctant than the voluntary sector to adopt public relations to promote its social service provision. This is perhaps unsurprising given the political environment in which local government PROs must operate. Conservative politicians' allegations of propaganda on the rates and the Local Government Acts of 1986 and 1988, which placed severe restrictions on local authority publicity and public relations activities, have done little to prompt creative media relations in the statutory sector (Franklin 1988b:37).

In the voluntary sector, the development of public relations is more advanced, but has similar objectives. Major groups such as Save the Children Fund, National Children's Home, the Children's

Society, ChildLine, and many others, each have commitments to a long-term public relations strategy. Voluntary agencies such as West Yorkshire Radio Action (WYRA), moreover, have been established with a specific brief to facilitate voluntary groups' access to local media, not merely to improve their public image, but to exploit media to make contacts with potential volunteers and clients and to help groups to achieve their overall objectives.

In addition to this commitment to a sustained public relations strategy, the voluntary sector has displayed a greater willingness than the statutory sector to engage in short-term campaigns, frequently involving press and poster advertising, intended to raise public awareness of particular issues. National Children's Homes 'Children in Danger' campaign discussed by Tom White in Chapter 12 is a model example of such a campaign. This developing professionalization of social work's media relations has undoubtedly been beneficial in promoting an improvement in public, as well as media, understanding of some of the complexities of the issues involved in social work practice.

The 1990s is likely to witness a number of changes in the way social services in the local authority and voluntary sectors are organized and presented. Developments arising from the Children Act 1990 and, more particularly, the White Paper on Community Care, will require departments to be more sensitive to consumer interests and public perceptions of their service provision. Many are currently rethinking their priorities during a period which will undoubtedly throw up new challenges and tensions. Departments will no longer be able simply to let demand and service delivery be left to their own devices. The way services, policies and practices are presented and packaged will have a growing influence on the ways in which they are experienced, used and purchased. In an era of greater public and financial accountability it will be important for departments to try to secure some influence over what comes to be regarded as 'good' social work and 'quality' service. Public relations will undoubtedly have a crucial role to play in structuring such judgements.

Recent changes in media prompted by government policy, as well as initiatives stemming from within media themselves, offer a mixed bag of opportunities and constraints for social work's future media relations. The proposals in the 1988 white paper *Broadcasting in the 1990s: Competition, Choice and Quality*, embodied in the Broadcasting Act 1990, envisage television and radio operating in a deregulated, competitive market in which consumers (viewers and listeners) and not producers (broadcasters and programme makers) will make the decisive choices about the types of programmes to be broadcast. Critics argue that the commercial necessity to minimize programme production costs, while maximizing audiences (and hence advertising revenues) will lead to a reduced range and quality of programming. In a deregulated market existing broadcasting companies will need to cut programming costs quite dramatically. In anticipation of such competition Central and Scottish Television announced 150 journalistic redundancies at the end of 1989, Tyne Tees Television implemented a pay freeze, while Yorkshire Television imposed new contracts and conditions of service on staff. News and current affairs programming, which are the major outlets for the reporting of social work issues, are prime candidates for any cost-cutting exercise because production costs are high and they are labour-intensive. Reductions in journalism staffs and financial resources suggest that the current 'under reporting' of social work matters will be exacerbated by the changes envisaged in the Broadcasting Bill.

But there are more positive aspects to these probable changes deriving from the Broadcasting Act. Research, for example, reveals that it is precisely in circumstances of economic stringency and shortages of staff, that newspapers can become reliant on news sources other than their journalists and are consequently willing to publish press releases issued by 'non-news' organizations. A study of press releases issued over a two-month period by the press officer in a northern county authority revealed that 96 per cent of releases resulted in stories in the local press, with one release being published in eleven different papers. The extent to which press releases were subject to any editorial process, moreover, correlated directly with journalist staffing levels, with each of the free newspapers in the study publishing the press release verbatim (Franklin 1986:32). Reductions in journalism and broadcasting staffs therefore need not necessarily presage negative consequences for the reporting of social work issues but may create new opportunities for social workers to participate in structuring coverage of social service issues.

Changes in media practice emanating from within media themselves signal further possible improvements in the quality of press reporting of social service matters. The introduction of Private Members' Bills to secure a statutory Right of Reply and Right to Privacy were unsuccessful in 1989, but prompted a Government-sponsored review of journalistic news gathering and reporting practices. Politicians in all parties and large sections of the public had become concerned about the quality, content and journalistic practices of some tabloid newspapers. The newspaper industry, eager to offset potential legislation, introduced a number of reforms. The *Sun* and the *Daily Mirror*, for example, appointed press ombudsmen to consider complaints about any aspect of the newspapers' coverage. In November 1989 each of the national daily newspapers announced, with varying degrees of enthusiasm, their agreement and commitment to a voluntary code of editorial practice which promised to redress readers' grievances via a number of mechanisms including a right of reply. In early December 1989, the Press Council published a set of new procedures to improve standards of journalism including a telephone 'helpline' for people wishing to complain about a particular newspaper article. It remains unclear how effective such mechanisms will prove in counteracting press excesses in certain areas, though such a code is certainly to be welcomed.

In June 1990, the findings of the Government-initiated review were published in the Calcutt report. It makes a number of recommendations with potentially beneficial consequences for the reporting of social work issues, including the possibility of a body with statutory powers to regulate press coverage in agreed ways and to protect people from 'unacceptable' intrusions of privacy (Calcutt 1990).

Neither the hostile press reporting of social work practice, nor the ability of social work to influence media reporting and public perceptions of its affairs, is likely to be substantially affected if the analysis developed in the chapter above is correct. If media reporting is interpreted and understood as a reaction to the ambiguous character of social work under circumstances of political, economic and ideological change, it suggests that only structural changes in the nature of social work, or in political economy and the new welfare consensus, might radically shift media presentations of the profession. But such reasoning smacks of determinism and a recourse to a media strategy of passive fatalism. A proactive media-relations policy may be able to achieve only limited objectives, but these are extremely valuable and there appear to be few alternative positive strategies.

Part II

Journalists, broadcasters and public images of social work

2 The professional press: social work talking to itself

Terry Philpot

That neck of the newspaper world which we still quaintly refer to as Fleet Street, although Japanese banks are more common there than linotype machines, often gives the appearance of a battleground, with its abortive launches, circulation wars and dive-bombing standards. But the professional social work press can boast its own Boot Hill. In a market where the tendency is for the larger fish to eat the smaller ones, *Medical Social Work*, *Mental Welfare News*, *ASW News*, and the *Bulletin of the Association of Moral Welfare Workers* were absorbed, not by greedy capitalists, but by the fledgling *Social Work Today*, launched in 1970 as the official journal of the then newly formed British Association of Social Workers (BASW). There was good organizational logic informing what happened: social work, after the Seebohm report (1968), was going generic, with a generic professional body, and the times demanded an all-purpose journal.

It was not, however, only a concern for readers' professional interests that caused the new journal to be transmogrified a few years later into a fortnightly and then a weekly and to forego its role as an academic journal dissecting current theory and practice, so much as the new commercial forces being unleashed in professional publishing. Seebohm had also given birth to a vastly expanded, more highly professionalized social work, populated with staff who would require, in their professional lives, accessible reference points not met in the ponderous pages of existing journals. There, length had too often been equated with value and authority. But even before BASW had placed a toe tentatively into what were to prove the perilous waters of publishing, *New Society* had been launched in 1962 to cater for the burgeoning sociology and social science courses, teachers, students and their interests.

The magazine failed entirely to see what commercial prospects were offered by the Seebohm changes but, without any effort on its part, the advertising pages increased. The then *British Hospital Journal & Social Services Review* (later the *Health & Social Services Journal* and now the *Health Services Journal*) at one time entertained the idea of splitting in two to create another (social work) magazine. But it was not to be. It felt too safe in its predominantly health administration interests and failed to appreciate the significance of the new breed and extent of social work coming into being. A market was opening up with no one making any real effort to cater editorially for its readership.

Thus was *Community Care* born, if not into virgin territory, at least into a field where the plough had not furrowed too deeply. The results of the magazine's launch in April 1974 soon became evident. Some people, weaned on a diet of what had previously constituted professional journalism, were not unreasonably sceptical: contemporary copies may look dated now but at the time bold headlines, photographs, a staff of professional journalists, even the occasional burst of humour, did not appear to be what serious social work journalism was about. (One well-known contributor, a reader in social work and author of many of the standard texts but long an apostate of his former views, confesses now his anxiety that the magazine was printed on glossy paper!)

But, equally, there were many more who appreciated this journalistic liberation. Any scepticism was not shared by advertisers, who took to the magazine from the beginning and have done so ever since with increasing commitment.

If *Social Work Today* had absorbed the magazines of the organizations which were to amalgamate to create BASW, that magazine's increasing rivalry with *Community Care* tolled the knell for other magazines, which had been launched in the (mistaken) expectation of making large sums for very small investment. The two tabloids, *Social Worker* and *Social Services*, were short-lived. *British Hospital Journal & Social Services Review* attempted to make up lost ground by entering into a publishing contract with the then Residential Care Association (RCA; now the Social Care Association) by publishing *Residential Social Work*. It was unable to sustain it and the publication was absorbed into *Social Work Today*, which then became the official journal of the RCA as well as that of BASW (a fact much disguised by that magazine's predominant field-work interests, and greater involvement with, and control by BASW).

But the blessings of the market have proven to be as ambivalent here as in other parts of the economy: some magazines disappeared, two thrived. *British Hospital Journal & Social Services Review* forsook all interest in social work and consolidated its health interests and *New Society* soldiered on, oblivious to where the world of public sector publishing was going, eventually to be absorbed by the *New Statesman* in 1988, its identity now only to be found in yellowing files of back copies.

Yet other magazines have entered the field – and stayed. *Insight* was founded in January 1986 and aimed, with the Association of Directors of Social Services (ADSS),

> to be in the forefront of a clearly defined, rapidly growing move towards acknowledging that excellent management and excellence of practice far from being incompatible are in fact vital stablemates in a common enterprise: the delivery of the very best of services to those in need of them.
>
> (*Insight*, January 1986)

Alas, the combination of a publisher who knew little about social work and an association that knew about publishing but deluded itself that it knew the recipe for publishing success, meant that within two years the magazine was facing financial crisis. Late in the day it nearly ruinously attempted to become a broad-based journal, thus alienating its ADSS colleagues but failing to beat *Community Care* and *Social Work Today* at their own game. In June 1988 it was purchased by Reed Business Publishing as an independent sister paper to *Community Care*. Alas, despite changes which seemed to set the magazine on the right path, it fell foul of a slump in advertising and closed in November 1990.

Residential and Day Care Weekly appeared in October 1987, marked out in a number of ways as distinct from its competitors. It is a downmarket tabloid (that is, it is rarely given to publishing articles longer than 1,000 words and it is written in the style of popular journalism). It caters for day care and residential staff in the voluntary, public *and* private sectors. It has stayed its course and shows every sign of remaining.

If, as is claimed, the press lives by exposure, is this also true of professional journals? Professional magazines do, indeed, disclose, though close ties with associations are potentially compromising. It is undoubtedly true that in the past *Social Work Today* has failed to report fully on the negative aspects of BASW's activities (notably during its financial crisis in 1980). And though the sale of a half stake in the magazine to Macmillan Press in 1988 meant the end of direct BASW control (even if exercised only as an ultimate sanction) and a new joint management under BASW/Macmillan Ltd., it seems unlikely that the magazine would go too far in unnecessarily ruffling the feathers of one of its owners. After all, do not BASW members still regard it (as it is) as 'their journal'?

The relationship of BASW to its journal (under both former and present arrangements) indicates a frequent misunderstanding about the (supposed) pressures under which commercially owned magazines operate; namely, that editorial integrity is inevitably compromised by market pressures. Of course, such magazines have to be profitable, and not only that but they also have to meet the commercial targets set for them. That is accepted and it would be foolish to the point of extinction to believe otherwise. But *Social Work Today* cannot stand aloof in such matters. Its considerable profit contribution to BASW over the years and its more recent £2 million sale with a percentage of the profits means that from any common view it is 'a commercially motivated journal' (to use *Social Work Today*'s own former description of commercial social work journalism). The truth is that the political and bureaucratic imperatives of an organization make it more likely that an association, as owner, would take a more detailed and controlling interest in the doings of the editorial department than a commercial one. At the same time, it is also likely to have less knowledge and sympathetic understanding of, the publishing and journalistic processes and *mores*.

Community Care and *Insight* enjoy absolute editorial independence. This is not without cost: social services departments have on occasion stopped advertising with *Community Care* most often less through objection to honest criticism, than for the simple fact of the magazine reporting disquiet among employees. This is to fail utterly to understand what professional magazines are doing and to attribute to them a role which, if adopted, would ensure the rapid departure of even the most junior of their editorial staff.

The professional magazine is not there to offer a lifeline to its readers, in the sense of a weekly pat on the back, an uncritical support. Commitment to social work is, indeed, the wellspring of the professional press, but that is not the same as the reader being led to expect exculpation for every decision, or a defence of indefensible action.

A social services department's refusal to advertise with a particular magazine must be seen as merely a gesture: in the kind of publishing where the magazine must give a good service to readers through the medium of classified advertising (the lifeblood of most magazines), the one which is doing its job in that way is not one which the advertiser can afford to boycott. Put differently, my hope has always been that *Community Care* has been long enough established, respected and understood by those who read it, that it is recognized as being a fair magazine, treating its subject area (which must include the doings of departments as much as the discussions of practice and policy) dispassionately.

The primary function of a professional magazine (indeed, of the media as a whole) is to reflect the facts and changes of the world which its readers inhabit, to try to be, as the playwright Arthur Miller said of a good newspaper, 'a nation talking to itself' (*Observer*, 26 November 1961). National newspapers interested in some of the same issues as a professional magazine have the considerable advantage of daily publication: the ministerial statement or report released two hours after we close for press is, to say the least, dispiriting. But the professional magazine has column inches on its side: it must angle its news to suit its readers' interests and has the space to explain more fully. It is not appeasing them, but allowing them to read news which it uncovers itself or to read the reporting of events which those readers cannot expect to find in a national newspaper, no matter how well motivated, for that newspaper must reach the common denominator of its total readership. True, we reshape pages, change publishing schedules, cut stories and drop others but in favour of more of the same, of what is breaking in social work. The government's long-awaited response to the Griffiths report gained a reasonable amount of coverage in the quality press, including editorial comment. Coming in the middle of the dismantling of the Berlin Wall it might have been relegated further back or lost altogether. Griffiths, the Children Bill, young homeless people or the latest report from the Royal National Institute for the Deaf have to vie with hostages, elections, bicentennials, the Queen Mother's birthday, and crime, in the pages of the national press.

A professional magazine, too, has time and space to allow reflection. After the first news stories and reactions, there are the series: when the Wagner report appeared in 1987 *Community Care* devoted not only a set of articles to it but held a conference (with the National Institute for Social Work) and produced a book (Philpot 1989). The response to Sir Roy Griffiths' report merited an interview with the minister, followed by a series of nine articles, while the progress of the Children Bill was also marked, in the features pages alone, by nine articles. With the publication of the White Paper, *Caring for People*, there was, *inter alia*, a special twelve-page pullout supplement. And when the Children Act reached the statute book there was a detachable guide. When Eamonn Rafferty analysed what was actually published in the social work press and the way in which it went about its job, the analysis defied firm conclusion. He found 'a rich tableau of social work experience' (Rafferty 1989:100). Had he analysed the national press in a similar way might he have expected to find, in its reflection of the chaos, significance and trivia of daily life, anything firmer, products of a more deliberate hand? What is it, then, which prompts editorial decision-making, in style, format and content in the professional social work journal? Are the imperatives which motivate one those of social work or journalism?

The style and content of *Community Care* are dictated by its original motive to treat social work as a serious subject and to bring to that consideration the tools, skills and understanding of a professional journalistic staff. That seems to be obvious and reasonable, unless one believes (as some social work bodies still do in the conduct of their own affairs) that communication is the last place one expects to find a communicator. Thus, when in November 1988 *Community Care* caused a *frisson* among some readers by redesigning and appearing in the larger and unfamiliar format, it was done first to establish a clear design identity which others could only follow at the risk of being seen to copy too blatantly. Second, the larger format allowed greater use of white space which, in its turn, allowed a bolder use of illustrations, typeface and type-setting which we hoped (and experience and research has found) would make the magazine more accessible.

The journalist is motivated by a curiosity about other people, in the unusual, in the man who bites the dog, not the dog that bites the man; the hallowed definition of what constitutes news. In doing this journalists cannot expect that those in whom they take an interest will always respond positively, and this is true as much for the investigative journalist who uncovers scandal in the City or politics, as it is for the reporter trying to discover the truth about a shortcoming in a service or the claims made by staff against management. Journalists do not assume their informants are right: they only assume that they have been told something worthy of attention.

Seeking order in chaos is the prerogative of theologians but, at a less elevated level, it is also the role of journalists to seek not only to disclose, but also to educate and explain: to attempt to understand where paths are leading and, if possible, to see over the ridges ahead.

Community Care's role has been broad from the beginning but particularly over the past six or seven years in that it has developed different but complementary ways of trying to understand the present and mould the future. Thus, seminars, books and an annual lecture have become integral to what we try to do. I do not claim that every lead is taken from the professional press or that every good idea emanates from it alone. I would argue, though, that the now long-established social work press, in its present, weekly, highly professionalized form, makes it very difficult to distinguish, at times, which source is feeding which. But on some matters, undoubtedly, professional journals have led in the absence of social work's ability to do so. Such a failure on social work's part may be due to other and (to it) more pressing priorities. Thus, no professional association held a conference on or published a guide to social work and the press: *Community Care* did both in 1989 (Fry 1987). Or the failure may be due to the inability of social work to understand what is happening: the implications of the Single Market in Europe in 1992 are not fully understood nor much discussed. A special supplement (*Community Care* INSIDE, 28 September 1989) and a series of articles (*Community Care*, 20 September – 18 October; 9–30 November 1989) was, we hoped, both an earnest indication of our intentions and a prompt in the face of widespread professional indifference. Again, the resources a magazine can command, in its ability to reach very large numbers of people, may act as a spur. *Community Care* assisted the publication of the Barclay report (1982) with a major conference and a book (Philpot 1982) and, as I have said, acted similarly with the Wagner report (1988) and Philpot (1989). Professional associations and trades unions have spoken much about violence to staff but I would doubt that their impact has been as great as the collective forces of the journals in raising consciousness about its extent and impact.

What comes across the editorial desk is a constant supply of press releases, books, reports, stories, articles (at least fifty a month, unsolicited, in our case) from which must be sifted what needs to be published. Sometimes the requirement is no more than a straightforward news report, or that may be followed by the longer news feature, or the feature in the latter part of the magazine, or a series of articles. The judgement which one makes here must be journalistic – that is, is this what interests or should interest the reader? But that judgement must be informed by an understanding of what it is believed the readers are interested in, what their motives and aspirations are.

Rafferty makes the criticism that the social work journals 'in many cases inhabit the high ground of aspirational social work'. And he goes on to suggest: 'It may be frustrating at times to social workers in the field who are working with inadequate resources to be told about the importance of some principle or another' (Rafferty 1989:99). I plead guilty to wanting the occasions to inhabit that high ground, not least because I worry that less salubrious tenants might take up residence. In staking my claim there I do so assuming that the reader, as a social worker, *is* guided by 'some principle or another', even if, at times, in the difficulties and routines of the day, it may seem distant. The discussion of principles aside, readers have other interests: to understand what is happening in and to their profession at a practice level.

For those who think otherwise, there is no secret formula for the creation and production of a magazine. Hindsight, as elsewhere, would be helpful, but it is the ability to see ahead which one would like. And this, in the fog and uncertainty that encompasses social work, where the illusory certainties of some of the reforms of the past now make cowards of us all as soothsayers, is rarely given.

Journalists and social workers share certain material needs to go about their work: funding, training, knowledge of their respective fields. But they may have something else in common, for it is a truth not always universally acknowledged that instinct and a feel for what one is doing are just as, if not more, important. There is not a day when I'm not reminded of that.

3 Reporting social work: a view from the newsroom

Anne Fry

Much of the bad press received by Britain's social workers clearly reflects the fact that they are working in a more hostile political and cultural climate than ever before, and are viewed by some sections of the public and media as an anachronism in our 'help yourself' society. In Thatcherite Britain the prevalent view is that success and personal achievement is possible given the will. But it has also produced a feeling of hostility towards those whose limited abilities and reduced circumstances mean that, in reality, success can be little more than an elusive dream. This has undoubtedly reflected badly on social workers who are their unpopular representatives, supporters and advocates.

As a professional journalist, I have noticed how even the term 'social workers' can prompt some journalists to abandon all pretence of fairness and balance. A cursory examination of recent tabloid press coverage of social work matters reveals that most adopt a highly critical posture towards the social work profession. This is particularly so in relation to child abuse, where large sections of the media apparently start from the premise that social workers got it wrong and then seek supporting evidence. The popular press too often seems spectacularly ill-informed and makes little honest attempt to present a balanced picture. Journalists in the national, trade or local press who take a less prejudiced view are usually specialists with a particular knowledge of social work. They also have a vested interest in accurate reporting since they have to keep ringing the same contacts and can't afford a cavalier approach.

Another factor which concentrates the journalist's mind is the financial dependence of some specialist publications on public sector advertising. Trade journals and newspapers which derive a substantial income from public sector recruitment advertising are more likely to be read by social workers – and more likely to provide sympathetic and accurate coverage. They simply cannot afford to get it wrong for millions of pounds can be at stake.

EXPLAINING A BAD PRESS

Social work suffers a bad press for a complex assemblage of reasons. Part of the problem currently faced by the social work profession stems undoubtedly from journalistic ignorance and a willingness to attach the 'social worker' label to a whole range of inappropriate people, including voluntary workers and social security staff. Some journalists even seem totally unaware of the major institutional differences between key areas like social services and social security. The general public seem equally ill-informed. Consequently, social workers are an easy target for criticism because of this lack of public awareness about what they actually do, apart from allegedly removing children from the ever-loving bosoms of their families.

The social work profession must carry its own share of the blame. It is notoriously bad at explaining both its professional philosophy and its practice. There is often a lack of clarity about objectives and too great a willingness in some quarters to hide behind jargon and unfathomable initials. But, as each of the chapters in Part IV of this volume reveals, this is changing, albeit less decisively in the statutory sector. Poor public relations skills are certainly one reason why social workers and social services departments traditionally get a hostile press. Press releases from major organizations can be so badly presented and photocopied that they are destined straight for the bin. Spokespersons can appear vague and the organizations they represent woolly. But there really is no excuse for such an amateurish approach in these high-profile days for social services.

However, even when social services and social workers do get their public relations strategy right, they must still confront the undisguised political partisanship and prejudice of broad sections of the British press. The politically right-wing tabloid and quality newspapers, by far the most numerous in terms of numbers of published titles, circulation and readership, seem more likely to take a hostile view towards social workers and their supposed shortcomings, while the numerically fewer politically left publications, with more modest circulations, may take a more supportive approach.[1]

Another factor which may contribute to press antipathies is that British newspapers remain largely dominated by white middle-class men, some of whom may have little sympathy for what they consider to be 'do-gooding' professional women whom they perceive to be making a living out of supporting the needy in 'prosperous' Britain.

Public and press images of the social work profession have been diminished yet further by recent industrial action in social services, coupled with the impact of the social work strike a decade ago. The sight of professionals on a picket line who are presented in the media as having reneged on their responsibilities towards those at the bottom of society's pile is bound to attract criticism, no matter how just their cause.

Certainly, the adverse publicity generated by the national social work strike was a blow from which the profession has never fully recovered. A more generalized but highly significant factor in explaining media attitudes to social work has been the change in the political climate since social services departments were established in 1971. They were then operating in a mood of expansion and optimism for the future; such a mood has long since dissipated.

Perhaps the most crucial factor underlying the current journalistic hostility towards social workers is their handling – or as many would see it post Cleveland – their mishandling of child sexual abuse. In Cleveland, social workers and doctors were castigated by journalists for removing children from their homes. Paradoxically, in the Beckford case they were roundly condemned for leaving the child in the parental home. Faced with such contradictory advice, it is hardly surprising that the social work profession is sceptical about large sections of the media. Indeed, a number of social work journalists are equally sceptical about large sections of the media!

Part of the problem in relation to child sexual abuse is the incredulity it sparks off. For a long time this meant that the issue was substantially under-reported. Some years ago, I mentioned to a national newspaper news editor a magazine survey which showed that sexual abuse of children was a growing problem in Britain. He was genuinely shocked and responded by saying that his newspaper could not possibly run such a story. His paper was, he explained carefully, a family newspaper. In my view, that was precisely the reason why the article should have been published. Predictably, no story appeared. No such resistance exists now when newspapers are increasingly willing to write about formerly taboo subjects. However, at a time when it is almost impossible to open a newspaper without reading about some aspect of this worrying problem, it is tempting to speculate whether the current preoccupation with the topic might be attributed to the titillating sexual element. For, as every newspaper proprietor knows, sex sells newspapers.

Writing about a controversial social work topic, such as child sexual abuse, requires tact, but there must also be determination to get at the facts. At times, the social work profession hides behind the curtain of confidentiality when difficult stories hit the headlines. Although this is understandable, it is not always commendable and can be counter-productive. Of course, the opposite strategy of being frank with hostile journalists can also backfire. I have lost count of the number of despairing social work managers I have known who have spent ages briefing this breed and then sadly discover that their views do not appear in print. This may be because there wasn't enough space on the day of publication, or, more usually, it may be that the newspaper simply was not interested in publicizing the social work viewpoint.

Many directors of social services are apprehensive concerning the press – no doubt understandably in view of the adverse publicity they attract. But this healthy scepticism can on occasion lead them to assume that any note of criticism is necessarily hostile and unhelpful. This, of course, is not the case. A journalist who is exposing failures in the state safety net is performing a useful public service. In my own experience, even when 700 words in an 800-word profile about a leading social services figure are complimentary, the subject invariably beefs about any criticism the article contained. This obsessive craving for the laudatory is unrealistic and indicates that the profession has not quite come of age in public relations terms.

GETTING THE STORY OUT

Despite the reservations noted above, there are encouraging signs that progress is being made with the leaders of the social work profession being increasingly frank with trusted journalists when difficult stories are about to break. This is certainly one of the most encouraging developments in the fifteen years I have worked as a social work journalist and, in my view, represents the way ahead.

For their part, journalists in recent years have come to recognize, increasingly, that social work offers an untapped source of good stories. Social work is controversial and is often about failure. It contains many of the ingredients which form the basis of a good story – human interest, life and death, sex and conflict. A good story – contrary to popular social work belief – is not about some worthy policy development, practice initiative or social services personality. It is about raw emotion, disagreement between professionals and, best of all, culpability.

Given these ingredients, newspaper stories about social work focus on fairly predictable if unimaginative and misleading concerns. Four particular examples spring to mind.

First, news editors are always on the look out for stories involving sexual misconduct. Such a story might be about a social worker raping a girl in his charge. This is a particularly newsworthy topic from a journalistic point of view, since it involves a sexual element, the betrayal of trust and confirms the prejudice that the wrong type of person often goes into social work. As noted above, many journalists regard social workers and other 'do-gooders' as a soft target for criticism. They often perceive them as rather woolly, out of touch with reality; dreamers rather than doers. Newspaper executives, who are in business both to form and reflect what they regard as public opinion, are quick to home in on any failure, whether real or perceived.

Such a story will be particularly widely publicized if, as is occasionally the case, the worker was sent by a staff agency which did not vet him properly. And the story has even greater potential if the social services department, which spends large sums on recruiting such 'miscreants', can be shown not to have checked his references thoroughly.

Second, and a variation on the above theme, are the residential workers who exploit the residents in their charge, whether they are children or old people in council care. Public indignation is rightly fuelled by such tales of breach of duty towards the vulnerable. There are, however, many other aspects of residential care which might reflect more accurately social workers' concerns in this context, but they attract little press coverage.

Third, social services stories involving lack of control over children in care also enjoy wide publicity via the press. Again, these appeal to as well as reflect the journalistic and public perception of social workers as people who condone bad behaviour and are unable to exercise proper control. The journalist from the popular press may not understand that the children may be sexually precocious and damaged emotionally by the breakdown of family life which precipitated the admission into care. Thus anti-social behaviour involving drugs, drink and sex, which might be concealed from the press if they involved middle-class white children in the community, become the subject of lurid headlines.

Finally, any misdemeanour by a senior social services manager is sure to hit the headlines if the person is dismissed or ends up in court. Many of these headline stories, appearing in the tabloids, originate from stories in the local press reflecting local journalists' well-honed contacts in the town hall, including social services directors (SSDs). The stories are then transported in an upwards news spiral into the larger regional or national newspapers and become 'big news'.

However, sometimes newsworthy stories are hushed up or simply missed by the media. Whether or not something is widely covered by the press is in part luck and reflects how crowded media news agendas are on a particular day. If, for example, there is a tragedy or even a story involving the Royal family, a social services scandal may get fairly small billing in the press. Bob Franklin and Nigel Parton comment in Chapter 1 how the Piper Alpha tragedy curtailed media coverage of the publication of the Butler-Sloss report. Conversely, on quiet days in August splash headlines can usually be predicted for any story about the failure of social services.

But so-called 'silly season' or not, journalists from the popular press are always on the look out for stories about the social services, especially where they might involve local councils dubbed by the tabloids as 'loony left'.[2] Such stories typically focus on the council's advocacy of equal opportunities policy. Thus Southwark, Brent and Islington are among the soft targets when it comes to strange, not to say mythical, tales about gays and lesbians being given large sums of public money for what appear to be rather curious projects. Efforts to promote racial equality may be sneered at, particularly if services for the white community are in any way lacking.

Stories about white people fostering black children are news, particularly if the children are removed by the local social services department for any reason. Certain elements of the press revel in such stories which appeal to regrettable but sometimes barely concealed racial prejudices and can be used for moralizing leading articles.

Local newspapers also capitalize on prejudice by splashing stories about mentally handicapped and mentally ill people being rehoused in the community in the face of neighbourhood protests.

The interesting thing about major social work stories is that one seems to spark off another, prompting a giddy escalation. Thus, a rape case may encourage a local journalist to look for similar tales to be equally highly publicized in the local paper. A story about abuse in an old people's home might also prompt similar journalistic interest and larger headlines than the story might normally warrant. Journalists working on a trade publication or a local newspaper may be interested in a human interest story about an old people's home but it would not usually hit the national headlines. The focus is too narrow for such a wide readership, unless scandal is involved. There is, however, often interest in the dangers of hypothermia. And the death of an independent old person living alone in the community can be used as an excuse to attack the local social services department, even if any offer of help was spurned. Again journalistic prejudice can overwhelm factual veracity.

The national press is especially keen to cover a running story, preferably involving a tragic set of circumstances. This is why child abuse, particularly child sexual abuse, is judged to be such a winner. These stories are 'good' from a journalistic viewpoint because they shock readers and sell newspapers. They are, moreover, usually running stories where developments can be catalogued from crisis to unsatisfactory outcome; from official inquiry to condemnation of the key social services personnel involved. A child abuse case like the one involving Jasmine Beckford is a perfect example of how the media operate. Following the child's tragic death, the court case involving Maurice Beckford received ample coverage while the circumstances of the tragedy provided scope for editorials condemning Brent Social Services Department. When the report was published, and professionals were found lacking, much of the adverse publicity again centred on social services. The need for journalists to file their reports to meet their papers' deadlines was important here. The timing of the report's publication time did not allow journalists to read the report sufficiently thoroughly and consequently they immediately and, in the circumstances perhaps understandably, focused on social workers' mistakes.

Regrettably, this scapegoating has become an almost inevitable part of reporting such matters. Although reports typically allocate blame to the social worker and social services department involved, newspaper stories can be unbalanced by their failure to reveal the substantial part played in the case by other professionals.

It is regrettable, too, that sometimes key figures are pursued so remorselessly by the media they have to go into hiding. On occasion however, journalists don't recognize a good story when it is, quite literally, under their noses. On the day the Jasmine Beckford inquiry report was published, Brent Town Hall was virtually under seige by the media. Journalists would have dearly liked an interview with the then director of social services, Valerie Howarth. She and

I calmly walked through the throng – no doubt dismissed by most as a couple of secretaries – and quite a lot of journalists and photographers missed their opportunity.

Certainly, in that case and in others like the Cleveland child sex abuse scandal, key professionals seem to have been harassed in a way which steps beyond legitimate journalistic practice. It is one thing for journalists to make positive and necessary attempts to contact them but it is quite another to invade their privacy in an unrelenting way. Door-stepping by the rat pack is totally unacceptable and reflects badly on journalists themselves.

A journalist's view of social work and social workers will depend on the publication for whom he or she works and the requirements of the job. Journalists working for the popular press might be totally unsympathetic to the profession and be in business to gather unsavoury titbits from contacts with a view to setting social workers up. The aim might be to present information showing them in the worst possible light. Other professionals, like nurses and doctors, get a better press because they are more sympathetically regarded and have a better image. But social workers and their leaders are, at best, seen as fairly incompetent and, at worst, as positively unnecessary. This is unfortunate, not least because they are needed as never before and referrals are on the increase even though resources are not. Ironically, a journalist from the tabloid press may grasp the need for professional intervention when it comes to child abuse but, because the voluntary sector has a better image, they think intervention is acceptable when provided by the NSPCC but less so when given by the local social services department.

Journalists on a quality newspaper are more likely to report scandals in a restrained and responsible way, and to be interested in social policy issues. They will probably have good contacts among senior social workers, particularly if they are specialist writers, and may get leaks from well-placed government contacts. They gather news by ringing round contacts who give them tip-offs, often on an unattributable basis.

The same will apply to a specialist writer and particularly a news editor working on a trade publication. The various professional and local government associations and key local government trade unions, are all good sources of news.

A reporter on a local paper will also usually have a good network of local contacts. As such newspapers rely on council advertising revenue, its journalists may be interested in writing positive stories – perhaps about fostering – as well as homing in on any catastrophes on its patch. At best, the relationship between a local paper and its social services department may be positive and marked by trust. At worst, it is marred by mistrust and mutual sniping.

THE SPECIALIST REPORTER'S VIEWPOINT

Specialist writers who are trusted by the social work profession enjoy a definite advantage over their journalistic colleagues. They are tipped off in advance about major stories, given privileged information and sometimes get useful background briefings denied to the rest of the media. They get more exclusive stories and contacts may leak confidential reports because (as Lynne Walder comments in Chapter 14) trust will never be betrayed and names never revealed. There is, therefore, an obligation to report matters accurately, particularly when there is so much distortion elsewhere. And this is quite a difficult but satisfying task. But sometimes contacts do not realize that the journalist's job is to criticize when criticism is required. People are upset when they come under fire from a trusted journalist and either send him/her to Coventry for a while or threaten to withdraw advertising. Usually, however, common sense eventually prevails and they accept that the writer is only doing a job. However, this type of misunderstanding is one of the drawbacks of working in this particular field.

More worryingly, some key professionals confuse the role of the professional journalist with that of the council public relations officer. They do not appear to recognize that the former exists to expose shortcomings as well as to promote achievement. The latter must on most occasions conceal failures, if and when this is possible.

At best, professional journalists find public relations officers helpful for providing facts and figures or access to embargoed reports, but, at worst, they are paid to be obstructive and to stop reporters quizzing key people. It always strikes me as the height of idiocy to ring a contact who outlines the situation and then tells you to ring the Public Relations Officer (PRO) for an on-the-record briefing for publication. Correct procedures are observed but it is a time-consuming way of operating.

Another problem facing the journalist following up a good story is that social services contacts sometimes have a vested interest in concealing ineptitude and scandal.

It is undeniable that at their best journalists fulfill an invaluable watchdog function in highlighting the unacceptable face of welfare. In this category I would place stories about widespread child sexual abuse against children in care at Kincora in Northern Ireland, which the authorities wished to conceal. Interestingly, it was social workers who first took the story to the press. But the sustained interest of reporters led to the appalling scandal being revealed and to compensation eventually being paid to some of the victims. It is incumbent on journalists to keep on pestering until such matters are formally investigated and some redress is made. Otherwise, scandals are merely swept under the carpet.

Journalists should try to reflect all shades of opinion, but they have a particular responsibility to protect the underdog. This point is difficult to overstress. It must be accepted by those we write about that while administrators have thick skins and PROs to protect them, the vulnerable people they are in business to protect lack such elaborate defence systems. Getting this message across is not always easy.

There are both difficulties and rewards in working in this area. I can certainly recall stories I have written about the scandalous conditions in some mental handicap hospitals, including Smith Hospital, Henley, and Queen Mary's Hospital, Carshalton. Publication in a national newspaper or professional magazine may have angered, indeed, even inconvenienced, some well-paid bureaucrats. However, the information was accurate and supplied by honourable and well-motivated people intent on improving the lot of some of the least powerful in society. I was impressed by the risks they took in exposing such unacceptable conditions and delighted that their actions resulted in hospital conditions being dramatically improved. Sometimes the interfering journalist and nosy photographer can achieve remarkable progress in the face of bureaucracy. At such times, journalism is indeed a rewarding career!

Experienced journalists have a nose for a good story and an instinct about when to pursue it. In such circumstances, it is important to ask the same question in several different ways and to expose inconsistencies in the response. There is nothing a trained journalist sniffs out more quickly than a cover-up. Reporters working in this field risk upsetting contacts when the stories they write create adverse publicity for them. They can also be miffed when a PR trip is arranged, ostensibly to cover some remarkable new development, and no publicity is given because it is, in fact, an old story. This causes disappointment but the problem is that social services managers do not always appreciate the ingredients of a good story.

Another area of difficulty the professional journalist faces when dealing with social workers and their bosses is their failure to understand that key viewpoints must be reflected in a story. This is particularly important when reporting bitter industrial disputes. Directors of social services sometimes get displeased with the union's comments and the union can be equally upset. There is an all-round, naive and rather annoying failure to appreciate that a journalist must quote relevant people. Reporting a set of controversial opinions does not necessarily mean the writer agrees with all – or indeed anything – which has been said. Indeed, journalists by professional experience and training, become adept at examining two sets of quotes and spotting where the discrepancies lie!

Particular frustrations for the specialist journalist are prompted by the social work profession's reluctance to be proactive when it comes to public relations. If publicity is sought, it is often about the wrong stories which are not in themselves newsworthy. People in social services – as elsewhere – can want publicity for purposes of self-aggrandizement rather than because there is a real story. The reluctance to be proactive is a major difficulty. All too often in the past, social work's leaders have waited for a problem to occur and then responded to it, sometimes in a fairly amateurish and uncoordinated way. Increasingly, though, the profession seems to plan its approach when a scandal looms and ensures that key professionals get adequate TV training. This was the strategy in Cleveland and the approach paid off. In general, however, a positive publicity strategy appears to be lacking and Arkley and Jones in Chapter 15 signal some of the reasons militating against a unified public relations strategy for the social work profession. But, at a time when social work increasingly occupies the centre of the media stage, devoting time and energies to developing an approach to public relations would seem a very worthwhile investment. People need to decide what message they want to put over, who their audience is and how best to reach them.

Working in this field can be a salutory lesson for a journalist because people can appeal to your better judgement. On one occasion, after leaking a major government commissioned report, a committee member lectured me on the error of my ways. This homily fell on deaf ears because a useful purpose was served by the leak and no individual was harmed.

But, at times, it is difficult not to be moved when people you know or like are clearly distressed at being given a rough ride in the national press. They have tried to do the best they can when confronted by appalling problems with no perfect solutions. As a journalist, you can only help by putting their side of the story in a factual and accurate way. This helps restore their faith and has the added bonus of giving you an exclusive story.

I remember one leading director of social services whose department had been called to account and found wanting over a battered child's death looking very reproachful when I mentioned the child's name a decade later. 'You people never leave these kids in peace do you?' he said quietly. It was undeniably and regrettably true. It is easy to forget that for social workers the sad names in the inquiry reports are real people, whom they tried but ultimately failed to help. It is also easy for a journalist to forget that directors of social services and their staff suffer personally when a tragedy occurs and an investigation finds them culpable. A journalist on the inside cannot fail to be surprised by the havoc wreaked by such events and at the subsequent demoralization of entire departments, for the ripples from such tragic events spread wide. It is entirely right that such matters are aired fully but I do sometimes wonder if the way investigations are conducted serves the best possible purpose. Large, costly public inquiries where inexperienced witnesses are virtually cross-examined in public by as many as a dozen barristers hardly seems the best way of reaching the truth. Press coverage is, inevitably, selective and does not always accurately summarize the situation.

Another danger of the present approach to inquiries is that journalists can become insensitive and blasé on reading their twentieth child-abuse inquiry report, but this is unlikely given the tragic subject matter.

AN EVALUATION

Overall, I find social work is a particularly interesting and rewarding area in which to work as a journalist. This is partly because of the wide range of subject matter it covers and because it is possible to build up specialist knowledge in a very newsy area. Another plus is that writing about social work seems a worthwhile pursuit, particularly if you are given access to confidential information which might not otherwise see the light of day. Above all, you can restore social workers' rather jaded view of journalism by reporting accurately and ensuring that what you write appears in print. Working for the trade press is satisfying because articles are not hacked to pieces by sub-editors who do not understand the subject; something which can happen on other publications.

Although writing about social work has many positives, social workers can be an infuriating group about which to write. At worst, they are characterized by a certain wordiness, compounded by an inability to get to the nub of issues and to communicate in a forthright way. Most don't make the bold statements beloved by journalists in search of eye-catching introductions for their stories. Most could be more outspoken but, given that they are so used to being slated by the media, it is hardly surprising that their motto is caution.

The only real consolation for the social work profession dogged by a bad press is that the media does occasionally change its negative attitude. For example, former Brent director of social services, Valerie Howarth, who was villified by journalists because of the Beckford case, went on to become the respected and widely quoted director of ChildLine. But the best-known metamorphosis involved the Princess Royal, stereotyped in the past as the 'Naff off' princess. Her indefatigable charity work persuaded the hacks to see the error of their ways, or at least to see the best-known 'do-gooder' in a better light. Dispirited social workers should see hope for the future in that.

NOTES

1 See, for example, the article by Colin Sparks (1987) 'Readership of the British quality press', *Media, Culture and Society*, vol. 9, pp. 427–55 and for a discussion of the political commitments of the tabloids see Malcolm Brynin 'The unchanging British press', *Media Information Australia*, 1988, no. 47, pp. 23–37.
2 See the study by James Curran and the Goldsmiths College Media Studies Group Interim Report, Goldsmiths College, London. The Association of London Authorities felt obliged to respond to tabloid allegations. See 'Its the way they tell 'em: distortion, disinformation and downright lies', ALA, April 1987.

4 Social work: 'image' and images on television

David Perrin

INTRODUCTION: THE LONGEVITY EFFECT

Television is constituted by images or pictures, but it also helps create 'images' in the sense beloved of PR, advertising and political pundits in their talk of the 'images' of people, products or parties. 'Images', in this sense, are concise reflections of prevailing public perceptions. On occasion they achieve remarkable longevity through a type of self-perpetuation and become their own touch-stone of truth, used to dismiss conflicting (possibly true) views. When false, 'images' have a built-in truth resistance rather as certain fabrics are shrink- or wrinkle-resistant. (Indeed, journalistic cuttings libraries are a physical embodiment of the process: past accounts, consulted by reporters, help define current accounts.) The whole process attains a specious, though persuasive, validity through its close resemblance to the legitimate way in which public, or inter-subjective, agreement has a role along with other factors as an arbiter in matters of truth and meaning. To overthrow a pervasive 'image' requires a concerted challenge.

Self-perpetuation can operate on 'images' which are either favour-able or foul (as on those either true or false). Social work claims that its 'image' is foul and false, with a resultant lack in public understanding. This chapter does not dispute the main thrust of that claim, which has been amply substantiated elsewhere (Wroe 1988 and Part I in this volume). It takes some issue with it, how-ever, in the light of sixteen months' working on *Witness*, a 1988 ITV series of three documentaries about social work. Before descri-bing the series and its approach, it offers some general analytical points, in the belief that, compared to other countries, the British media, whose practice is so much an *ad hoc* and unarticulated affair, examines itself all too rarely in a theoretical manner (see, for example, Klaidman and Beauchamp 1987). It should be noted that much said here about media coverage relates particularly to 1987 when *Witness* was started and to the following year in which it was made. Further, the focus on child care should not be taken as implying a view that it constitutes all there is to social work.

WITNESS AND THE 'IMAGE'

The foul 'image' is that social workers are a profession of blunderers. *Witness* arose in response to it and an earlier insight that it had to be untenable. Making a point long familiar within the profession, *Private Eye* lampooned the widespread media approach in a cartoon depicting two typical headlines, one to the effect that social workers had once again intruded and removed children and the other to the effect that they had once again *not* intruded and children had been left to suffer. Clearly, it cannot be consistently maintained that social workers are in all cases both insensitive breakers-up of families and ineffectual bystanders. Yet these are key aspects of the 'image', like *gestalts* between which the 'image' switches according to whether the latest scandal concerns intervention or its lack. While still possible, it is unsupported by evidence to hold that social workers always or even mostly get it wrong one way or the other in their total case-load of thousands.

It was quickly evident that behind the 'image' was a failure to understand the nature of social work decision-making, especially in child care, the focus of most media attention. The vital child protection decision – in response, say, to suspected sexual abuse – does concern intervention, and if protection is to protect it must often be pre-emptive and proceed on less than certain grounds; it fails, for example, if it awaits injury to confirm fear of injury. This opens up distinct possibilities for mistakes; but though decisions may appear obviously mistaken in the hindsight enjoyed both by public inquiries into child care tragedies and the prominent media reporting of the inquiries, social workers are not blunderers for having to act at the crucial stage on less than certainty. As has been demonstrated in Part I by Bob Franklin and Nigel Parton, social work is essentially an ambiguous and high-risk activity. Legislation may change procedure or, say, the balance of children's and parents' rights but, unless the goal of protection is abandoned, this just changes the type of likelier mistake.

During the months of preparation for *Witness*, scores of social workers protested to us at the wide discrepancy between coverage and actuality, and our observations confirmed this. In particular, social workers pointed to the invariable focus of coverage and its preconceptions. They asked, for example, why, when social workers were singled out for missing signs of danger to a child, other professionals such as health visitors who overlooked them were not mentioned, and why the failings of a few doctors did not earn the whole of medicine a bad name. In all, we met staff in more than a score of local authority area and neighbourhood social work offices around the country, as well as professional bodies, unions, training and social services directors' organizations, academics and teachers, the social services inspectorate and client groups. (We also attended conferences and read histories, practice guides, and policy guidelines. An eighty-page historical chronology was compiled.) Unless social workers are discounted as witnesses to their own work, their testimony showed that mainstream media coverage ignored most of social work's wide range, highlighted the comparatively few tragedies, rarely if ever responded to achievements, had scarce direct contact with social workers, was ignorant of actual procedure, and reacted negatively to social work as if by habit.

However, the discrepancy needs closer examination. If the foul 'image' is false, it is mistaken to assume that the contrary is true, namely that all is *well* with social work. Criticism remains possible even if the 'image' is overthrown. We encountered no attempts to deny deficiencies and tragic errors but, rather, an active and widespread, though little reported, debate at all levels about ways to improve practice, training, staff, resources, and so on. Indeed, while rejection of the critical 'image' was reaching a height, so too was self-criticism. Some points of internal and external criticism overlapped, such as on training, showing that the discrepancy between the 'image' and actuality is not the simple product of particular falsehoods but is due to a complex failure of perspective, balance and completeness.

THE 'IMAGE' AND ITS CAUSES

The discrepancy has many causes. Several have been widely discussed elsewhere in this volume – social work as the welfare state's most intrusive arm, its need to do unpopular deeds, its brushes with society's most dearly held values, its association with local authorities to which certain newspapers and the Government have been hostile. The key causes relevant here concern media practice, at a level common to press and broadcast journalism.

As often described, so-called 'news values' (not easily specifiable and always shifting) help determine selection of subjects, or 'stories', and their content. They make child care tragedies obvious dramatic 'stories', ripe for prominence. ('Story' is insensitive jargon for the often tragic events in the news.) Yet they rarely yield 'stories' favourable to social workers, whereas they do constantly about policemen. The resultant mass coverage of social work is a catalogue of failures, which seem more common than they are because they alone seem to be reported. Condemnatory findings by public inquiries on which reporting is based act as powerful, official back-up for a general critical stance. The effect is abetted both by the scarce access, for reasons of law and professional confidentiality, to the day-to-day load of thousands of unproblematic, untragic cases and by limits on public comments by social workers. Whether in themselves or as reflections of the evaluations of readers and viewers, 'news-values' clearly carry values about what events and emphases matter. At the same time, journalists profess (presumably 'value-neutral') impartiality. If impartiality is to be maintained, 'news values' must be constantly monitored to ensure that certain values do not predominate.

Besides 'news values', rules of thumb for proper practice operate in the media for many subjects. For example, court and parliamentary reporters are expected to acquire certain knowledge and follow certain rules. Past mass social work coverage – apart from certain specialist correspondents – has barely evolved such background knowledge and imperatives. Hence the instances of downright ignorance. Few reports are done from a wide acquaintance with social work and a sense of context, and there has been scant effort to develop these. The power of the 'image' may make it seem to some that there has been no need.

Some journalists may contend that the 'bad press' is social work's own fault, due to their ineptitude or unfamiliarity with the media. Even if social work has handled the media badly, the contention fails as an explanation. It depends on the assumption that the means – and the will – for better coverage have hitherto existed, but our earlier arguments cast doubt on this. More contacts, more adroitly handled, between social work and media might well in the past have wrought improvements, but this would have been through the development of greater understanding among journalists, and that would have been a change in the means. It is worth noting, too, the contention's odd view that social workers and not journalists are responsible for the accuracy of coverage.

A PLEA FOR TELEVISION

If television has largely been under the spell of the 'image', credit is due – as to the quality press – for several past efforts to widen understanding of social work. The 1979 London Weekend Television series *The Do-Gooders* (its professionally unpopular title notwithstanding) and the BBC's later *All Those Hard Luck Stories* – both done in co-operation with local authorities – are two examples before *Witness*. Television's recent lead in raising awareness of child sexual abuse has been acknowledgement of social workers' sensitive and difficult task. Furthermore, though television has not challenged the 'image' as it might, a charge of deliberate hostility cannot, I believe, be sustained against television exactly as against the popular press.

Nevertheless, news, current affairs and documentaries have shared in the concentration on child care tragedies and such apparent failings as in Cleveland, doubtlessly on the ground that these are held to have been the most important 'stories'. That ground, of course, is precisely what is open to debate. No doubt 'news-values' make them the most exciting 'stories', but are the few individual tragedies so clearly more important than the recent on-going social services staff and resource shortages so threatening to thousands of endangered children? Particular broadcast reports on the tragedies have been questionable, too. Social workers seem singled out as much as the perpetrators of the child killings. The events come over as *confirmations* of general incompetence ('Another social worker has been criticised . . .'). Reports in the past have not always been done from a perspective-providing background knowledge or balanced in overall coverage by reports on social work matters or issues which do not focus on incompetence.

In television drama, too, the 'image' and its unfounded generalizations have been at work, and negative stereotypes have shaped much characterization of social workers, as is clear to anyone who has observed the wide array or personalities, beliefs, competence, and dress in social work. There were complaints, for instance, about the portrayal of a 'trendy', cantankerous woman social worker rowing with police at a case conference in a 1987 episode of Thames Television's *The Bill*. Plots have usually concerned social work at its most intrusive, for example, when social workers descend on a desperate Yosser Hughes to remove his children in 'Yosser's Story' in the BBC's *Boys from the Blackstuff* in 1982.

IN SEARCH OF THE 'SEXY'

During the making of *Witness* social workers offered reasons for television's failings. One was that programme-makers took too little time to understand the subject. Journalists can accurately work faster than is thought, but speed of work tends to heighten the effect of preconceptions and habits of approach. If journalistic understanding of a subject is slight, speed will rightly appear to people involved in the subject to compound the problem.

Another reason given was that television distorts because it picks out the untypically sensational or dramatic in a subject. A programme, it was said, would always give more air-time to a rare episode in which social workers, say, took a screaming baby from parents than to the deliberations preceding the action or to another mundane but more representative episode. This is not always so but is a tendency, and one defended by many television hands on the ground that the rare episode happened and so is not a distortion and the ground that programmes must be entertaining if they are to be watched and learned from at all. Does the defence work?

In production jargon, gripping scenes such as the removal of the baby are known as 'sexy' sequences. ('Worthy' is the dismissive term for the unexcitingly informative.) The 'sexy' is greatly prized by producers. Now, even arch-advocates of entertainment in factual programmes agree that they should be accurate and that accuracy comes first. Programmes should entertain and be accurate. The two factors need not conflict; some sequences are both 'sexy' and revealingly accurate. However, if accuracy takes precedence, it imposes limits. Overall coverage of a subject is distorting if it includes only purely 'sexy' sequences, because it omits much that makes up the subject. Further, particular programmes or other samples of coverage will be distorting if they contain only 'sexy' sequences or show only the 'sexy' elements of sequences, because they will not show the episodes in the sequences for what they are. For example, key *constituents* of the action of removing the baby are the intentions and deliberations behind it, and without some inclusion of these the action is not shown for what it is. Turn up the 'turn-on' factor and, by a sort of inverse proportion, accuracy tends to diminish. That is because accuracy requires completeness and is not just a matter of avoiding untruths. For this reason it is not necessarily a valid defence of programmes to assert that nothing in them is false. Nor would it be valid if the relation between accuracy and completeness were manipulated and a highly 'sexy' account were justified by adopting a narrow perspective from which the account seems complete. (In this way, for example, an agreed-to innoculation could be absurdly presented as *really* an assault with a deadly needle.) As for the limits which accuracy imposes on the 'sexy', these are not clear-cut and fixed. What is 'sexy' and what properly needs to be said in explanation frequently compete for programmes' time in makers' minds. Judgements in any case will vary as to the proper final balance.

Many social workers also endorsed accusations that television has 'hidden agendas', either as unavowed intentions behind requests for filming access or as pre-determined approaches to a subject. The frequency of such agendas, in either sense, is hard to determine. They are far from universal, and most programme-makers by far agree, I think, that, with regard to requests for access, exceptions should be genuine and rare (exposing secret atrocities, say) to the principle that the 'truth business' should be truthful in all its workings.

Pre-determined approaches to subjects can be more insidious, in spite of good intentions. Programmes are frequently proposed within television in terms of what may be called a 'thesis' – a new 'angle' or disclosure, exclusive interviews or access. The danger comes from pressures felt by programme-makers to preserve a 'thesis'; if it breaks down, the distinctiveness of the intended programme is lost. Evidence can end up being marshalled in service of a 'thesis' rather than a programme's response to evidence. Certain facts or interview answers may be uncomfortable for a 'thesis', and rationalizations for excluding them become attractive. A programme 'thesis' proposed in terms of a presentational technique comes under strain if the facts do not quite fit the 'symmetry' of the technique, and temptation arises to 're-interpret' the facts. Programmes are artifacts. The artifact and its preservation in a desired form often become more important to programme-makers than their subject.

CAN YOU GET IT RIGHT?

Some may say that television cannot help but get social work (or any subject) wrong because programme-makers must be in the grip of *some* bias, in that any account of a subject is necessarily from a point of view (with its particular values, prejudices and so on) or necessarily composed from only a *selection* from all the possible aspects of the subject. This view challenges the possibility of impartiality. It raises questions too deep to consider at length now.

Our points of view are not invisible to us, as this view assumes, but can be identified, appraised and taken into account in the descriptions we make. We are not like the horse which cannot change its blinkers. So the presence of points of view does not rule out impartiality. Indeed, committed attention, rather than cold detachment, is arguably required by it (Deutscher 1983). The bases of selection of material are also open to appraisal and are not inescapably given. The view in question may go on to exclude the possibility of accounts being true or false by taking the further step of asserting that all description is 'subjective'. This assertion is clearly at odds with what we take ourselves to be constantly doing, namely accepting and rejecting accounts in response to what is agreed to be true and false. It also makes social work's account of itself as 'subjective' as any others, so that social workers would no longer be able to say that any accounts are wrong (or right). In rejecting the subjectivist assertion, we are not driven to say that there is one definitive account ('the truth') about each subject. Paradoxical though it seems, a variety of true accounts of a subject is possible. This does not make the various true accounts different 'truths' in some grand sense, or mean that inconsistent claims can all be true. The various true accounts are simply different selections of true statements drawn up for different purposes or from different 'angles'. The possible variety does not render them 'subjective'. The seductive subjectivist view is not only false but dangerous, in that it can be used to justify deliberate prejudice.

WITNESS: SUBJECT, ACCESS AND CO-OPERATION

The first of the *Witness* series of three programmes was a 'fly on the wall' portrayal, filmed in Bradford, of a local authority area social work team.[1] The second, traditional in style, looked at the history of social work and social policy and, with Huddersfield Polytechnic, at training. The third (done with a children and families team, a paediatrician, police and other professionals in Hillingdon, West London) used a novel drama-documentary technique of mixing real-life professionals and improvising actors to show normally inaccessible practice and procedure in a single case of suspected child sexual abuse.[2] The different styles were adopted to add insight. Access was sought with full explanation of the series' objectives, developed over four months of general research. All the social services directors approached were keen to consider access; some individual teams were wary, worried about client confidentiality and disruption of their work. Once locations were agreed, there followed between one and two months' research or liaison with participants and, for each of the first two programmes, further research between filming periods spread over two months. At moments of filming, crew presence was minimized. As well as resistance to the 'image', the approach had certain keynotes.

1 *Social workers' accounts of their work should have special authority.* This was not to put their 'side' but because they have most knowledge about social work and because the reasons and intentions behind their actions are constituents in what we were portraying.

2 *Participation in the programmes should always be voluntary.* It should also follow full advance consultation. At the chosen locations, many individuals were initially suspicious, demanding many assurances; some refused to be filmed. Most were willing to help and to appear on screen. Mutual trust was vital. Social work clients were filmed only after advance, informed consent and the social worker's judgement that publicity would not harm them. In the problematic case of a mentally ill client we took his social worker's assurance that he wanted to take part. In the Bradford area office, notices in different languages alerted casual callers to filming.

3 *Programmes would not emphasize unrepresentative episodes.* The programmes would not, as intended, be accurate portrayals of the hitherto little seen actuality of social work if they concentrated merely on 'sexy' sequences. The team in Bradford was itself chosen as representative of local authority teams on the basis of a profile built up in research. The profile, briefly, was of a team mixed in age, gender and personality, in a multi-racial urban area, with rising case-loads, static resources, and client aggression.

4 *The series would be a co-operative undertaking.* Participants helped fix agendas. An advisor from Hillingdon helped devise the plot for the third film and was a guide to procedure. In Bradford, a regular liaison committee of social workers and the production team set guidelines for a balanced content, ensuring inclusion, for example, of client groups other than children, staff supervision and of 'successful' cases.[3] We particularly wanted an elderly client's case which mirrored the dilemmas more usually

identified with child care. Social workers themselves pressed for the programme to include criticism by clients. Participants viewed the programmes at the editing stage. Such viewings were not held to be incompatible with broadcasters' editorial control but an extension of checking and consultation.

Feedback to the series was not extensive. Some social workers remarked that it was 'real'. Participants, I think, were by and large satisfied. A social work professor said it was excellent. A couple in dispute with social workers over their children wrote to say that we had been taken in.

CONFIDENTIALITY

Confidentiality, a proper key principle of social work, need not be the obstacle that it has been to media access and understanding, as analysis shows. It depends on the notion of a duty to keep confidences, which are information told one person by another under a promise not to pass it on. The principle has a possible absolute form, by which it is wrong to pass on anything at all, even where the subject of a confidence is unidentified. Social workers seem, on the whole, to follow a weaker form, by which it is not wrong to pass on information about unidentified persons. This, for example, makes the NSPCC's published 'children at risk' statistics permissible. They also extend the circle of confidentiality to colleagues, case conferences, courts, and so on. Their practice, then, is not inflexible. The essence of confidentiality is mutual *consent* to a promise. Mutual consent, in turn, may suspend confidentiality without breach of duty.

On *Witness* the procedure in Bradford for seeking clients' consent to be filmed was that social workers told the production team about suitable cases and then forwarded requests to still unidentified clients for us to meet them. Consent to be filmed was sought later, usually after more than one meeting and after full explanation of the programme. Both social workers and the team were surprised at how many clients gave consent.

Social workers should more often consider asking clients to consent to meet the media. Clients' trust need not be lost if they keep control through consent. When clients identify themselves in publicly criticizing their treatment, social workers might think, at least sometimes, of requesting consent to reply to the criticism. (Is such self-identifying airing of grievances implicit consent?) Confidentiality may, in the past, have been too handy a shield against the media. It must also be reconciled with another cherished principle, accountability, and its presupposition of openness.

SIGNS OF CHANGE

The media's high degree of attention to social work in recent years, and journalists' consequently extended exposure to the subject, particularly during the Cleveland affair, has had benefits for the standard of coverage. Emerging rules of thumb and more background knowledge are detectable in, say, television news. Reports of bereavement counselling, after the Hungerford, Zeebrugge and Hillsborough tragedies, have introduced at least one 'story' type favourable to social workers. Reporting of the case of twenty-four-year-old Beverley Lewis has confronted journalists with the fact that dilemmas about intervention are not exclusive to child care. New social affairs programmes on television may become centres from which understanding can pass to non-specialist broadcasting colleagues. The journalistic reflex of seeing the social worker as a ready target is breaking down. There are signs, too, as in the 1989 BBC drama *Testimony of a Child*, of more rounded dramatic portrayals. At the same time, BASW and the social services directors' organizations have addressed the issue of coverage and sought proactive ways to improve it. Social services departments seem readier to consider media access (see Sally Arkley and David Jones and Lynne Walder in this volume). More social workers are realizing that commitment to freedom of the media does not dictate supine submission to whatever the media ask or do.

During more than a year spent alongside social workers at the time the Cleveland affair unfolded, one could share in their dejection at the coverage (at how, for example, the RAD test was at once taken by so much of the media to be a sole, universal test of sexual abuse). Perhaps we are now leaving behind an era in which social work's failings, and these alone, were public and its achievements private.

NOTES

1 In the *Witness* team, under editor Jonathan Dimbleby, were producers Martin Smith and Ian Stuttard and researchers Alita Naughton and David Perrin.
2 This same technique and general preparatory approach was used for *Danger in Mind*, a 1989 Thames Television documentary about the pro-

bation and psychiatric supervision of conditionally discharged restricted patients from special hospitals.
3 The project in Bradford was greatly assisted by the presence *within* the social services department of a press officer.

5 Do-gooders on display: social work, public attitudes, and the mass media

Peter Golding

It came as something of a shock to pick up the newspapers in November 1989 and read a headline 'Social Workers "not to blame for death" '. True, this unusual declamation was in the liberal professions' favourite rag, the *Guardian*. Nonetheless it represented an unexpected and unlikely departure from the now familiar tone of hostile, and not infrequently virulent news coverage of social work.

The case in question involved a three-year-old boy who had been beaten to death by his drug addict father. The inquiry panel absolved the Islington social service department of responsibility, and even chastised the junior health minister for prematurely, and on little evidence, suggesting that they had been at fault. Curiously, and begging a range of questions about the relative impact of conspiracy and prejudice on the one hand as compared to sod's law on the other, another case hit the headlines the same day.

Sukina Hammond, a 5-year-old girl murdered by her father, had been taken off the at-risk register by Avon social services four months before her death. Coverage of her case dwarfed the Islington case by some margin. The *Star* offered a front-page splash, 'A Life For a Life', demanding the execution of her killer, and on page 5 ran a story which reported the 'welfare chief's confession' under the headline 'We Sent Sukina Back to Die'. The *Daily Express* front-page headline was 'How They Let Little Sukina Die Alone', and began: 'A team of social workers stood condemned last night as an investigation started into how they failed to prevent the brutal death of little Sukina Hammond.' Neither paper reported the Islington inquiry. Papers that reported both cases invariably gave greater prominence to the Hammond tragedy.

We were back on familiar territory. When the *Daily Mirror* had headlined the 'Outcry Over Death of Tragic Beverley' earlier in the same month, with the usual quoted queries like 'Why didn't social workers do more when they knew she was at risk?', it had seemed just another routine child-death/social work failure story. Indeed the torrent of such cases in the last ten years has left a tragic litany of names etched on the heart of any social worker. Maria Colwell, Karen Spencer, Lucie Gates, Malcolm Page, Tina Beechook, Maria Mehmedagi, Carly Taylor, Jasmine Beckford: the sad roll call is not only of children tragically dead as a result of adult neglect or abuse, but of the regular collective character assassination of social workers.

This evolving demonology has created a number of themes, well delineated in other chapters in this book. As the NALGO national social services officer has despairingly complained: 'Banner headlines tell us almost daily that, in dealing with social workers, the public is dealing with an incompetent – but just maybe necessary – breed of middle-class left wingers bent only on self-preservation and theorising about the world's ills' (Reed 1986:17). His caricature draws directly on press comment. The *Daily Mail* (7 July 1988) suggested social workers are 'abusers of authority, hysterical and malignant callow youngsters who absorb moral-free marxoid socio-logical theory'. Their incompetence and immaturity feature regularly. The *Daily Star* opinion (6 February 1984) is that social workers 'have such a dreadful reputation as muddle-headed do-gooders whose grip on reality is at best tenuous, and at worst non-existent'. These are the 'social shirkers' of whom the *Daily Mail* wrote (21 February 1989): 'What is so awful is the frequency with which these so-called experts make errors of judgement which to the most ordinary folk would be unthinkable.'

If they are so inadequate then clearly they are an expensive luxury, providing services which are not merely incompetent, but completely redundant. As the *Daily Telegraph* remarked after the Tower Hamlets social work strike in 1979: 'Many of the tasks they perform ought to be done by the individual concerned, or by his neighbours and relatives, or by voluntary agencies – or sometimes, by no one at all' (7 June 1979). Not the least of the ways in which this judgement is confirmed is by the regular moral obloquy heaped on the heads of those occasional errant individuals who leap to fifteen minutes of notoriety. Criminals such as the 'Social Worker Who Threw Petrol Bombs', a man whose deviant talents had been nurtured in 'the predominantly leftish egalitarian establishment of social workers' (*Daily Mail*, 2 April 1982) loom large in this pandemonium. So too do a noticeably large number of sexual adventurers in the profession. Such stories as the front page 'Video Shame of Girl Social Worker' (*Sun*, 12 February 1986), 'Scandal of the Social Worker Sex Beast' (*Daily Star*, 2 October 1980), 'Social Worker Goes on Game for £500 a Week' (*Sun*, 25 March 1986) or 'Welfare Man in Sex Scandal' (*Sunday People*, 15 November 1981) form a higher proportion of stories about social workers than visitors to their quieter Christmas parties might expect.

Unnecessary, incompetent, immoral, and inadequate; it is an unflattering portrait. Not the least of the props which has sustained this attack is the critique mounted by more professional commentators over the past decade. Writers such as headmaster Ray Honeyford writing in the *Salisbury Review* (and reprinted in *The Times*, 21 May 1984) have concluded that 'The social worker is a professional provider of excuses. He dispenses alibis to the lazy, the loutish and the confused. He consistently mistakes sentimentality for sentiment, indulgence for concern.' Academics uneasy at the growing popularity of 'radical social work' theorists have been equally forthright. Brewer and Lait, for example, argue that 'it is partly the absence of any real competence which diverts social workers into political activities as a substitute for work, and we think it is high time this subsidised fun-revolution was reconsidered' (Brewer and Lait 1980:111).

Not surprisingly, this remorseless and many-pronged attack has had a demoralizing effect on the social work labour force. Already constrained by tightening purse-strings social workers find themselves in a very different climate to the heady days of growth in the 1960s and early 1970s. A survey by the magazine *Community Care* suggested 93 per cent of social workers blamed the media for their declining public stock, and 58 per cent thought public opinion of them had worsened (King 1989:18; see also NALGO 1989).

This is a sorry tale, and it is the purpose of this chapter to enquire into the validity of this gloomy reading of the public mood, and also to offer some speculation as to the reasons for it. I do so in two stages. First the chapter reviews the evidence about the shifts in and substance of public attitudes to social work in the recent past. Second, I explore tentatively the underlying causes of the public vision of social work.

SAINTS, SIMPLETONS, SCAPEGOATS AND SCOUNDRELS: THE PUBLIC IMAGE OF SOCIAL WORK

The very regularity with which social work has taken the temperature of public opinion in the last couple of decades is itself a measure of the continuous uncertainty within the profession about its public standing. As Craig discovered in collating such work for the Barclay Committee in the early 1980s, 'More research has been directed towards assessing the public's view of social work than has been devoted to any user-groups' (Craig 1981:1). Nor is this unique to Britain. As Brawley remarks in reviewing similar work in the United States: 'For at least twenty years social workers have agonized over their poor public image and decried the lack of clarity in the public's mind about what social workers do and the low prestige of the social work profession' (Brawley 1983:25). This immediately begins to raise doubts about the roots and sources of the public image of social work. Is this image contingent on the political climate or the mendacity of the national media, or more fundamentally derived from the intrinsic nature of social work and its broader societal functions? This question will be addressed later in the chapter.

Surveys in this country have focused on a few insistent themes, themselves telling us as much about the concerns of the occupation as about the mood of the public. Loudest among these themes have been the ignorance of the public about the role and function of social workers, the problematic status of social workers compared with other professional groups, and the relative utility of social services compared with other 'caring' professions or public services. Timms' seminal work in 1962 was mainly concerned with the apparent invisibility of the nascent profession. While probation officers had recently been generously exposed in a television drama series only 7 per cent of Timms' sample had heard of a 'social caseworker' and a third had no idea what social workers did. This unfortunate comparison with probation officers persuaded Timms that 'social workers might usefully consider the ways in which the medium of television can be used to portray an accurate and helpful image of social work' (Timms 1962:3). Most of his respondents associated social work with charities and voluntary organizations, and accorded the work a lower status than doctors, teachers, the police or nurses. The predominant stereotype was of a middle-aged spinster, presumably of the rolling-bandages-for-the-troops/feeding-hot-soup-to-the-homeless variety.

In 1968 came the Seebohm report, followed in 1970 by the reorganization and integration of services prompted by the Local Authority Social Services Act. It is with the growth of social work in the late 1960s and into the 1970s that the number of such studies begins to proliferate. In 1969 a survey in South Wales repeated

Timms' unfortunate accident of timing, being hot on the heels of another television programme about probation. Social workers were now paradoxically becoming better known while their work became more obscure. The dominant theme in this study

> is related to a number of interconnecting ideas – that social workers are government employees, that a lot of the work they do is unpublicised, and seemingly shrouded in obscurity, that they have their own specialist jargon, and that they ask a lot of questions which have, to the client, no obvious relevance to the specific problems.

Somewhat melodramatically, the authors conclude, 'An imaginative mind could see something almost sinister in this' (Glastonbury *et al*. 1973:202).

Inevitably, in the wake of the Seebohm reorganization, the renaming of departments and occupations and the structural relocation of functions generated much public confusion, especially when closely followed by the 1972 Local Government Act and the subsequent reorganization of local authorities in 1974. The number of social workers doubled between 1971 and 1976. As a study in Hampshire, carried out in the midst of this period of change, concluded, 'Effective channels of communication which can provide reliable information about where the consumer or potential customer can make his own views and opinions of the services known are as yet undeveloped' (Glampson *et al*. 1977:16). But, hearteningly for the new organization, nearly half the respondents in this survey would have turned to social services if concerned about a local case of child neglect, a much higher proportion than suggested either the police or the NSPCC as their first port of call. The concern, both stimulating and detected by surveys at this time, is simple public ignorance of what social workers do, however, and where to find them.

Perhaps ignorance is bliss, for as social work, in its new integrated and professionalized form, begins to settle in to the public landscape, so do more negative and repellent images begin to emerge from the mists of public uncertainty. Surveys now begin to appear commissioned from within the profession, or from the increasing apparatus of comment and discussion it had generated. A survey conducted for London Weekend Television in 1979 found continuing confusion about who social workers were – 24 per cent thought they were the people who allocated council houses. But the relative esteem of social workers now becomes a major concern of both social workers and the surveys. In the survey by London Weekend Television it was found that 'Both those who had contact with social services departments and those who had not, rated social workers' usefulness below that of the life-saving professions: doctors, police, nurses, the fire brigade, and the ambulance service' (*New Society* 1979:248). They did, however, rank above lawyers and clergymen.

Subsequent research began to home in on this problematic image. A survey in the Midlands, shortly after the Clare Haddon battering case, began what has become a major feature of subsequent comparable work, the task of professional reassurance. As Wilton reports of this survey, 'A typical social worker is tolerant, young, university educated and female. She spends her time working with children, the elderly, and the poor' (Wilton 1980:14). Nearly two-thirds thought that social workers were 'really necessary', and, despite recent unfavourable press coverage, and the predominant image of social workers as young and inexperienced, they were seen as not guilty in baby-battering cases. The typical social worker was seen as probably a bit naive and trendy, but well-meaning. Much research that was to follow was prompted by the same concerns: 'What do they think of us?' And it was scoured for the same conclusions: 'a little sceptical perhaps but by and large, and despite the media, they still respect us even if they don't love us'. A follow-up to the Wilton study by Gardner found the same generally positive image (Gardner 1982).

It was inevitable that the Barclay inquiry into social work set up in 1980 by Patrick Jenkin, the then Secretary of State for Social Services, should be, in part, both a response to, and very much concerned with, media and public attitudes to social work. In the lengthening wake of the Maria Colwell case MORI carried out what was described as the first ever national survey of public opinion of social work, in April 1981. The results were reassuring: 'at a time when they are under pressure, both in their work and politically, social workers have a sound image to build on' was the summary deduced by one commentator (Weir 1981:218). Doctors, the police, and even Citizens Advice Bureaux workers were seen as of greater value to the community. A significant minority shared the view of one east London caretaker interviewed that 'they're mainly young university graduates without much knowledge of working people, and they don't know what they're talking about'. But while only 3 per cent offered 'interfering busybodies' as a response to a general enquiry about 'what social work means to you', 43 per cent suggested some version of 'they help anyone who needs it'. Despite the considerable coverage given to the Malcolm Page case, whose inquiry report appeared just two weeks before the survey, two-thirds said they had read nothing that affected their attitudes to social workers. Social work, a little uncertainly perhaps, and with just a touch of selective perception, seemed to have entered the new age of Thatcherism with some semblance of public sympathy, even if not as well supported empirically, perhaps, as supporters of social work may have wished or imagined.

Subsequent research has continued to resound with these same themes. Surveys respond to hostile press coverage and government pressure with reassuring rediscoveries of public support, tempered only by popular uncertainty about what social workers do and whether their inexperience and youth render them adequate to the task. In examining more recent work it is worth considering how far this reading of the research is valid.

One careful and interesting piece of research has focused on adolescents, and begins to unpick the important distinction between public evaluation of the work done by social workers and of their personal and professional competence to do it. The author's interviews with adolescents in residential homes found that they 'saw the social worker as slower, weaker, and more feminine than the teacher or policeman, as safer than the teacher, and as softer, less clever, and happier than the policeman' (Jones 1987:99). Adolescents not in direct contact with social workers were still primarily positive in their views, though some curious misapprehensions came to light. One 12-year-old thought the social worker's job is 'to keep the roads and parks clean', while a 13-year-old mustered the minimal capture of their role in suggesting that 'social workers do not . . . sabotage drains, potholes, water mains and electrical wires or cables', which is probably fair comment though less convincing as evidence of a thoroughgoing understanding of even unradical social work (ibid. 213). Local surveys tend to uncover the same very patchy awareness of what social workers do and where they do it (e.g. Hicks 1988).

The most recent substantial study of public attitudes to social work was conducted by National Opinion Polls (NOP) in late 1989. The magazine *Social Work Today*, who commissioned the research, declared simply 'Satisfied Customers' as their headline summary of the findings (Owen 1989:14). An overwhelming majority of those polled (83 per cent) said social services should be provided by local councils not by private companies. Nearly half thought social workers should be paid more (only 16 per cent disagreed). Eighty-five per cent thought social workers deserved a good public image. They clearly knew who to blame if this was not the case too: two-thirds agreed that the media tend to present a negative image of social work, though interestingly the unpublished figures show that a high proportion disagreed with this view in Scotland, suggesting something to be investigated either in the Scottish media or in Scottish social work (NOP 1989).

Once again the question of relative status was explored. While 93 per cent said social workers do a useful job, a majority, often a large majority, saw them as lower in status than doctors, lawyers, the police, nurses and teachers (in that order). In contrast to Timms' survey in perhaps more innocent times, if people suspected a child in their neighbourhood was a victim of abuse (admittedly not just neglect as in earlier surveys) people would approach the police more readily than the social services. *Social Work Today* was in no doubt that 'social services and the social work profession have received a timely vote of confidence which can only help to lift the sagging morale of a beleagured but clearly valued group of professionals' (Owen 1989:15).

That same cry of relief would no doubt be the response to much of the research that has been done on this issue. How well does it accord with a second look at the findings? Four points should be made. First, even the most generous assessment cannot but be struck by the eternally low esteem in which the public holds social workers compared to other public sector occupations or professions, including those which have had their fair share of public criticism. This relates to the second point. The image of social work is indeed largely positive, a majority continuing to believe that social work performs a useful function. However, a distinction must be made between the work and the worker. This is a separation apparent in work assessing client views where the social worker as a helpful person is distinguished from a less enthusiastic view of the outcomes he or she is able to achieve (e.g. Rees and Wallace 1982).

Against this should be set the more disenchanted reading of similar research offered by Beresford, who suggests 'All have encountered a strong sense from most people of having little say in the services affecting them . . . associated with widespread complaints and reservations about the appropriateness and quality of services' (Beresford 1988:43). Recall research like that of Wilton (1980) on the perceived callowness of social workers, despite Barclay's statistics suggesting that at the time over a third of social workers were over 35, less than a third were under 30, and 40 per cent had been in post for over five years (NISW 1982:25). The stresses and strains of recent years have actually taken the profile more towards the public image. The recent NALGO survey of social workers suggested nearly half had been in post less than two years (NALGO 1989).

Third, the research continues to suggest that the public has a less than complete understanding of what social workers do, often demonstrating a rather diffuse public image and perception of social services, itself perhaps an irretrievably vague label for any occupation desiring more public affection and comprehension. Often within both the design and analysis of the research there is a lingering implication that the public is to blame for this ignorance – 'What do they know of our problems?'

Finally, it must be noted that much of this research is limited in scope and ambition, designed to investigate the current obsessions and anxieties of social workers rather than the deeper levels of public thought and feeling. As Wroe, in a recent overview remarks, 'No research has been done to show the relative effect of the media on public images of social work. Moreover surveys have yielded confusing or contradictory results over what the public's image and knowledge of what social work is' (Wroe 1988:3). Seeking to tap the affection of the public for care and caring, surveys have not, for example, baldly addressed the public's willingness to meet the cost of statutory welfare in any sufficient depth.

This suggests that to discover the true nature of public attitudes to social work we need to look beyond these specific surveys to a wider context. There is not space in this chapter to attempt this task in any detail, but a few points must be made. The root weakness of the research I have been reviewing is its failure to explore the distinction deeply embedded in public consciousness between a lingering regard and welcome for caring and welfare, on the one hand, but a firm suspicion of statutory intervention and unjustified levels of demand on the other. In short there is strong evidence to suggest that the public likes what social work does, just not who does it and who gets it!

The clue to this lies in more broadly conceived work. For example in earlier work on attitudes to welfare I have suggested that support for the welfare system is highly conditional and thus fairly easily dislodged in periods of economic stress or change (Golding and Middleton 1982:ch. 8). In a review of election studies through the 1960s and 1970s Taylor-Gooby shows the secular decline in support for state spending on welfare in this period of rapid increase

(Taylor-Gooby 1985:26–7), though this varies with the area of welfare being considered.

More recent evidence comes from the British Social Attitudes annual surveys (Jowell and Airey 1984; Jowell and Witherspoon 1985; Jowell, Witherspoon and Brook 1986, 1987). Certainly, against the temper of Thatcherism, these suggest a growing public anxiety about declining public expenditure, and support for higher spending on public services, even if that would mean foregoing tax cuts. However conclusions drawn from such evidence are often prematurely optimistic. The same research shows continuing scepticism about the diligence and merit of the unemployed, broadened into a deep and unchanging concern to retain a distinction between the deserving and undeserving among the needy. The proportion of respondents who feel the welfare state encourages people to stop helping each other has been consistently well above a third in these surveys. Asked about their preferred priorities in public expenditure, health education and industry consistently run far ahead of welfare, though the terminology used leaves some doubts over the precise findings. But in general 'If moralistic contempt predominantly excluded the poor from welfare citizenship in the 1970s, the experience of recession appears to have engendered a fatalistic indifference rather than an active moral commitment to alleviate their plight' (Taylor-Gooby in Jowell, Witherspoon and Brook 1987:11).

What can we deduce from all this? There does seem to be a consistent affirmation of the value of social work, but it is substantially blunted by fierce suspicion of unwarranted and excessive claims for help, and consequently of the costs of an extensive apparatus of statutory caring. The image of social work must itself be distinguished from that of social workers, whose value and good intentions are not much in doubt among a public which nonetheless affords them relatively little esteem. The reassuring and morale-boosting inferences regularly derived from public attitude surveys should be treated, at the very least, with some caution, particularly in the light of the limitations of this research and the more cautionary implications of research exploring a wider array of public beliefs and opinions.

INVISIBLE DECENCY OR ILLICIT EXPERTISE: THE PUBLIC RELATIONS DILEMMA

There is, then, a problem to solve. How has this well-liked and largely accepted social role become the focus of so much public misunderstanding? This problem has much exercised those in the profession who feel frustrated and victimized by its effects. Media invective and public ambivalence have provoked frequent articles in the trade press and, as I have suggested, have been the major stimulus for the surveys described in this chapter. Representatives of social work have been clear that 'something must be done'. As the BASW submission to the Barclay inquiry suggested:

> On the assumption that clarity about the social worker's task is essential to ensure continuing public support for social work services, and investment in them, and at the individual level the removal, where possible, of negative perceptions of social workers, issues of task specification and clarification of job titles take on an importance which necessarily goes beyond professional concern into the area of public debate.
>
> (BASW 1981:57)

This task has taken on, as befits the times, an increasingly glossy sheen as hard-nosed public relations realism has been promoted by the profession's damage-limitation experts. The message now was for a more positive evangelical style: 'Only when social workers and Social Services departments see the press as a medium they can utilise will the image of the press as a threatening and dangerous critic be dispelled' (Mawby *et al*. 1979:374) was the kind of advice now advanced by friendly and concerned witnesses of the mauling social work was receiving. The Association of Directors of Social Services set up a study group on public relations to challenge the poor national image and recommended the appointment of 'a small permanent group to determine policy and prepare a programme for a long-term public relations exercise' (ADSS 1986:6). Handbooks on how to do it have begun to flow (e.g. Fry 1987), and new and inventive methods applied to the task of winning hearts and minds (Clare 1988).

Yet what lay behind the problem? The emphasis in the diagnosis has been on lack of public knowledge and the malign news coverage and commentary in the national press. The temptation is to explain this virulence simply in terms of the familiar limitations of news values and the journalistic process (see Golding and Elliott 1979). But social work forms part of a broader culture, and it may be necessary to stray a little beyond journalism to explore the issue. I can only offer two brief speculative thoughts in the confines of this chapter, one addressing the narrow range of media forms in which social work appears, the other concerned with the essential nature of the social work task.

Compared with many other superficially similar occupations social work is surprisingly rarely the focus of fiction, notably in television, but also in film and the novel. This is, on the surface, extremely odd. Drama, particularly as it has evolved in television, makes great use of those occupations licensed to intrude. Their varied and legitimate opportunities for interference in the lives of others offers occupations like policing, teaching, medicine and the law the chance to become the perfect backdrop to a rich and endless staging of human drama and heroism.

Teachers, for example, have prospered as a dramatic type, from Mr Gradgrind to the teachers in *Grange Hill*, from Thomas Hughes to Muriel Spark's Jean Brodie. In Dickens alone the full range of inhumanity is conjured into his teaching characters, 'a savage tally of brutality, ignorance, and hypocrisy, of mental, physical, and emotional bludgeoning' (Coveney 1957:85). Against such negative anti-heroics can be set the later complexities of *Cider with Rosie*, Lindsay Anderson's *If . . .* and, of course, the recurrent figure of the teacher as novelist, D. H. Lawrence and onwards.

Medicine has, of course, no less a prominent place in the realm of fiction. In television alone the range of presentation has been enormous, whether as mad scientist or silver-haired sage, community confessor or high-tech young Turk, Drs Kildare, Casey, Welby, Finlay, Cameron and their peers have offered a constant stream of complex and changing imagery about the medical profession and its mythologies (cf. Karpf 1988; Turow 1989). Alongside them nurses have angelically held hands, mopped brows, swooned in the embrace of handsome interns, and gossiped intriguingly by bedsides, from *Emergency Ward Ten* through to *Angels* or *Carry On Nurse*.

Most obvious is the pride of place occupied, especially in film and television, by the police. From the arrival of *Dragnet* in 1952 through *Highway Patrol*, *Naked City*, *Perry Mason* and on to *Starsky and Hutch*, *Kojack*, and *Hill Street Blues*, American police television has been a veritable living-room theatre exposure of that society's neuroses, ideologies and myths, just as the changing vision of British society has been reflected in the long journey from *Dixon of Dock Green* through *Z Cars* to *The Bill*. For viewers this has been a rich opportunity: 'A little like voyeurs, the audience gets to ride in the back seat of the squad car and experience first hand the seamy side of life' (Robards 1985:12).

The odd absence of social work from the list of public or liberal caring professions which populate our fiction is on the surface difficult to explain. Taking just one week's television in late 1989 there were no fewer than eighteen programmes which, as fiction, exploited the role of such occupations in some way. This included not just the steady diet of detectives, police and medics, but even vets and fire-fighters (in London Weekend Television's *London's Burning*). Of course there are not that many field social workers, some 27,000 compared to Britain's 125,000 police or 530,000 teachers. But there are nearly a quarter of a million workers in social services departments, dwarfing the 27,000 GPs, 39,000 doctors and dentists, or 37,000 fire brigade workers. Even our 6,500 probation officers have on occasion found themselves the pivot of a fiction series on television.

Arithmetic alone is not the answer, clearly. Social work has, it is true, featured on occasion in documentary series designed to expose and explore the difficulties and human drama of welfare services. Nottinghamshire SSD attracted over seven million people to their activities in a 1981 BBC series *All Those Hard Luck Stories* (Whitehouse 1982; Reynolds 1981). ITV's *The Do-Gooders* two years previously had been equally well-intentioned, as was the more recent ITV series *Witness* (see Chapter 4 in this book). But for each such example it would be possible to note a dozen comparable exercises displaying the day-to-day realities and dramas of hospital, school or police station. There is, too, the very occasional appearance of the social worker in television's feature drama. Indeed, some of the most memorable moments of television drama have revolved around such climaxes as 'the final terrible denoument at the railway station, when the children were forcibly taken from the young mother' (Sutton 1982:18) as the BBC's then head of drama recalls Jeremy Sandford's epoch-making *Cathy Come Home*. The golden age of British television drama in the 1960s and 1970s has been decorated by social realism in which the gauche ineptitude or sullen iniquities of the social worker as intruder and controller have not infrequently been featured, as most generously in Jim Allen's *Sponger's* and perhaps most memorably in 'Yosser's Tale' in Alan Bleasdale's moving capture of early Thatcherite Britain *Boys From the Blackstuff* (Millington and Nelson 1986).

Nicholas suggests that in American material the fictional image of the social worker portrays them as 'busybodies, self-serving types, or social isolates' (Nicholas 1979:419). The suggestion here is slightly different. Social work and social workers rarely appear, by comparison with other professional groups, in popular culture. Lacking any broad-based representation in culture, especially in screen fiction, social work is necessarily dependent on the one form of display in which it has been consistently and systematically derided, the news stereotype. The omnipotence of the news stereotype is a function of its lack of challenge from a wider array of more complex and variegated imagery. The reasons for this require more extended consideration. Most obvious is the dour and unattractive material of day-to-day social work. More significant may be that despite the superficial appropriateness of social work to fiction – it would seem to involve the very stuff of drama in the human condition – it lacks one vital ingredient, the possibility of frequent and successful resolution. Policemen prevent crime and capture criminals, doctors save lives, fire-fighters put out fires. The social worker's dramas are chronic not acute, and rarely arrive at a satisfactory, swift and tidy conclusion. Social workers do not have a success rate, and thus they are penalized in the realist drama stakes.

The contrast with policing is stark. As Hurd suggests:

> the television police series must reproduce in the structure of its fictional world a coherent account of the patterning of tensions and conflicts within a contemporary society . . . while at the same time displacing and referencing-out those more fundamental tensions which are essential to any basic understanding of the role and function of policing.
>
> (Hurd 1981:65)

Social work is not even given this opportunity, and thus its place in the public arena of images, motifs and caricatures has been unusually and distinctly restricted.

Such a line of thought still leaves us focused on the media as the source and site of the problem. The solution would thus lie in changes in the behaviour of the media themselves (for example, supplying more specialized social services correspondents) or in better public relations awareness among social workers, both solutions indeed advocated by sympathetic journalists (e.g. Walker 1976). A second line of thought, however, takes us back to the very nature of social work. All occupations have to explain themselves, both for internal consumption, to sustain morale and professional self-belief, and externally to maintain boundaries, esteem and confidence. Social work is no different, and as a semi-profession has to work harder than most. In staking its claim to a place in the professional apparatus of the welfare state social work has to lay claim to special expertise. The problem is that there is a peculiar dilemma set up for social work in deciding what kind of expertise to deliver.

Much of the ideological vandalism accomplished by the media has effected a decoupling of the composite notion of the welfare state. Welfare (caring, collective altruism, concern for the disadvantaged) becomes severed from and contrasted with the notion of the (bureaucratic, paternalistic, intrusive) state. A whole series of binary oppositions is brought into play here which are each straddled uncomfortably by social work.

This dilemma is intrinsic to the social work task. As Rojek *et al.* note, 'social workers resist the suggestion that occupational practice is associated with disciplinarianism. The professional self-image is . . . of a helper, a carer, and an enabler' (Rojek *et al.* 1988:133). But social workers are required to implement our demand for social order, to be a means for the containment of moral or civic disorder and troublesome incivilities. Drawing on Donzelot and on Foucault's concept of the 'disciplinary society' Rojek *et al.* argue that social workers, as agents of 'the social', are needed to 'prevent the irruption of "abnormal" or "unhealthy" acts. It follows that the social reaction against social workers is most intense when such acts occur' (149).

But if social work is given this impossible task it also has to lay claim to an unattainable legitimacy. The application of welfare principles is caught on the horns of a dilemma in that 'the main paradox of humanist welfare management is that determining the needs and rights of citizens necessarily restricts the freedom of the individual' (157). Thus the social workers' claims to expertise are bound to fall on stony ground as we set them irreconcilable objectives. To control or care, contain or empower? What do we wish the social work task to accomplish? The claim to expertise at the welfare end of the couplet is particularly bound to be problematic. As Billig *et al.* suggest:

> If the expertise is perceived as being too ordinary, then the claim can be made that anyone can be an expert in human relations . . . there is a tension between egalitarian and inegalitarian, liberal and authoritarian forces in the practice of expertise. This tension ensures that it is too simple to hope that contradictions will vanish magically with the application of well-intentioned liberalism.

> (Billig *et al.* 1988:77–9)

Yet at the state end of the welfare state couplet we constantly question the merits and capacity of the social worker, rather than other state agencies, as the best vehicle for sustaining acceptable and decent social order.

The social workers' expertise has to be applied to incompatible ends – control and order (state), and care and support (welfare). It is likely that 'the very subjects of social work – particularly child care – stand at points of ideological tension between what are, finally, differing conceptions of the good society' (Wroe 1988:30). It is a role set up for failure, and we are only too ready to punish this failure publicly at every opportunity as a means to preserve a more comfortable illusion. No wonder, then, that

> When the tabloids bay for the blood of doctors and social work-
> ers who have discovered child abuse – they too are conjuring a
> preserve of innocence – the family – where such things must
> never happen, and they are repudiating the part they play in the
> making of the world that has forfeited the innocence they claim
> to cherish.
>
> (Warner 1989:38)

This can be but speculation. However, it takes us beyond the despairing paranoia or over-optimistic technicism which can flow from a too narrow interest in the misapprehensions and malice of the mass media. If we wish to address the problematic image of social work we cannot evade a fundamental grappling with the nature and social role of social work itself.

CONCLUSION

In this chapter I have examined evidence about public perceptions of and attitudes towards social work. Much of this research is severely limited and more indicative of the immediate and prag-matic concerns of the profession than of wider and more systematic inquiry. On the surface, and despite press malevolence, social work seems to retain a broadly positive image, but situating this evidence in a wider context raises doubts about the true purchase on public affections really acquired by social work and related welfare ser-vices.

In attempting to explain this I have offered two speculative thoughts. First, social work's curious absence from a wider range of cultural fare has left it unusually vulnerable to the one locale in which it has been consistently derided, the national press. Beyond some thoughts as to why this might be, it is suggested, secondly, that the intrinsic nature of social work and its unresolved and paradoxical relationship to conflicting public demands in a welfare state are the roots of what is bound to be an enduring problem of image. Social work reflects many of the contradictions and uncertainties which permeate corrosively throughout the shaky ideological edifice of the modern welfare state.

Part III
Social work under scrutiny

6 A receptacle for public anger

Martin Ruddock

Kimberley Carlile died, aged four and-a-half, at 49 Cambert Way, Ferrier Estate, Kidbrooke, London, S.E.3 in the Borough of Greenwich, where she had lived since October 4th 1985 with her step-father, Mr. Nigel Hall, her mother, Mrs. Pauline Carlile, and three siblings. Her death was due to a traumatic subdural haemorrhage caused by an injury to the left temple, consistent with having been caused by a blow, such as a kick. At a post mortem it was discovered that she had multiple bruising and scarring on various parts of her body, some of them obvious to the family whenever she was bathing or undressed. These wounds were consistent with repeated episodes of physical abuse. At death she was dehydrated and severely under-nourished. Between the age of two years and her death she had gained only 2.5 lbs (1.26 kg).

From *A Child in Mind: The Report of the Commission of Inquiry into the circumstances surrounding the death of Kimberley Carlile*

Writing about my part in Kimberley Carlile's death is extremely unpleasant and completing this chapter has forced me to remember once again my period of work in Greenwich Social Services which started on 2 October 1985. Kimberley died on 8 June 1986 and it has been only recently, in 1989, that I have felt able to live almost completely in the here and now.

INTRODUCTION

Before Kimberley was brutally murdered, my imagined social work terror was to be involved in a case where a child's death occurred and I could be held to be partially responsible. In part that terror related to a fear of being pursued by, and then pilloried by the press. In practice the experience of being involved with Kimberley was very true to the nightmare, except in one very clear and painful way. I had been involved in a child's death and, although frightened by the enormity of the potential public outcry, I was also faced with a personal crisis relating to my part in that child's death.

I state this at the beginning, because in part this chapter is about my experiences of the press during the Kimberley affair. It is also about how it affected me in dealing with my need to mourn for both Kimberley and myself, and in preparing for an inquiry that arose from concerns about the handling of the case. Throughout the whole period I perceived the press coverage continually to control the boundaries for the players in the inquiry.

Kimberley died on the evening of Sunday, 8 June 1986. I was informed of her death the following morning and realized immediately that the assessment I had made on Kimberley was incorrect. Over the next few months, I was involved with internal inquiries, giving statements to the police, and attempting to hold down a job that had been a nightmare even before Kimberley died. I regularly heard of press activity on the Ferrier Estate, where the family had lived, and wondered whether it was going to be a front-page terror, or slightly less. Whilst waiting for the court case to begin I wondered whether the resulting press coverage would reach the level to enforce a public inquiry and whether I could emotionally or physically survive the pressure that previous social workers involved with child deaths had endured.

Eventually, and probably with an element of denial, I waited the eleven months for the trial to begin. This was a period of waiting and fearing as I considered my position and watched those around me, from management to team members, consider theirs.

THE TRIAL

On 5 May 1987, after what appeared a very long bank holiday weekend, I arrived at the Central Criminal Court and began a two-day wait to give evidence. It immediately struck me that the press interest in the case was high, with press personnel clambering to get into the press seating, and between court sittings, watching those of us waiting nervously to give evidence.

On the lunchtime before I was called to give evidence, I left the court building and was followed up the street by numerous press photographers and television cameramen. The experience was not helpful in preparing to give evidence. The treatment I received had not happened to my colleagues, and any lingering doubts I had about the size of the story were over. It was going to be big and I was to be the prime focus. The feeling of powerlessness reminded me of being a small child in school and being backed into a corner by numerous bigger children. The desire to hit out in self-defence, wink arrogantly in unrealistic defiance, or swear, were fortunately resisted. They would have made great headlines and provided the press with unneeded material!

A day later I finished giving evidence and with a feeling of relief, left the witness box. The reporters now had me at their mercy and as I walked out through the courts of justice I was pursued by questions:

'Had you made any mistakes?'
'How do you feel about Kimberley's death?'
'Do you have any regrets?'

The walk through the building seemed to take an age and I was relieved to be met by the Director of Social Services in Greenwich, Martin Manby, at the entrance. We then left the building together and were confronted by row upon row of cameramen. The experience reminded me of old war films where the front row of infantry fires, kneels and allows the second and third rows to fire. We tried to walk down the road but were confronted by too many whirring machines to break through their ranks and escape. Finally, we stopped, and allowed the clicking and flashing to take its course. My respect for the Director for standing by me, and facing this ordeal remains immense.

As the court case progressed, the coverage increased. Immediately I returned home on the No 8 bus the phone calls started. As we became more skilful at hanging up the phone the visits started and took place between 6 a.m. and 2 a.m. By the end of the first week my young children were unable to leave for school or nursery without being asked where I was and given the view of another telephoto lens. By this time I felt penned in and frightened and was fearing I was endangering my family. I had also received the first unpleasant phone call and heard locally that people wanted to do to me what Kimberley had had done to her.

On the Sunday afternoon, between the two weeks of the trial, I left home alone for the safe asylum of relatives and to walk quietly on the North York moors in Cleveland. The weather, sadly, seemed hostile and unfriendly and I felt vulnerable and alone walking the Moors, listening to the coverage of the case on a small radio.

The trial drew to a close on the second Friday. I am told Louis Blom-Cooper arrived to watch the closing stages.

That night, from another address, I watched the BBC 9 o'clock news. I was outraged when they reported, as fact, that Kimberley had a badly bruised face when the family came to see me at the office in March 1986.

This was not true but had been claimed during the trial by Nigel Hall or Pauline Carlile. Much later the BBC apologized to me in writing for their mistake, and kindly gave me permission to publicize their apology. To me, public attitudes were already affected and enormous damage had been done.

On the following morning, Saturday, 16 May, the *Sun* and the *Daily Mail* were surpassed by the headlines of the *Star* which produced a seven-page shock issue, headed 'Kim: It was Murder'. Underneath this headline were three pictures: Nigel Hall's with the words: 'he killed her'; my picture with the words: 'he let her die' and finally Pauline Carlile's with: 'she betrayed her baby'.

The vitriol and anger in the *Star* and other papers was some of the nastiest reporting imaginable and it hurt to read it. What in part hurt most was that it fed my own self-punishing feelings and made me begin to accept I was the guilty party deserving of punishment. Fortunately, friends supported me to evaluate realistically my part and reject the role of becoming another victim.

The press coverage also left me feeling that the inquiry panel would need to be amazingly singular if they were to resist the public clamour to serve me up as a scapegoat.

THE INQUIRY AND THE MEDIA

Continuing to remain away from home, but now with the supportive company of my family, I heard from neighbours that my home was still under seige with men hugging cameras closely and watching the house. I also heard with pleasure of friends who had rejected the offer to gossip. However, the local pub, which I never use, did a thriving business as individuals shared fictional tales about me.

During 1985, Wendy Savage, a consultant obstetrician at the London Hospital, was involved in a legal battle for her reputation regarding employment and the rights of women in pregnancy and childbirth. Living in Tower Hamlets, many of my friends were involved in her support campaign and knew and valued the support of her solicitor, Brian Raymond. Through them, on Sunday 17 May 1987 I 'phoned Brian Raymond and arranged to see him the next morning. Thankfully, he became both my solicitor and valued advisor.

The following morning, I climbed over the back garden fence, walked over a disused railway line, clambered down onto a canal bank and walked to pick up my car which had been left away from my home. I then drove past my front door and watched a reporter, bottom in the air, peering through my letter-box. Finally, after a tube journey in which my photograph leapt out at me from various newspapers, I arrived and met Brian Raymond and began a process that has enabled me to remain in social work.

During our first meeting he gave me some advice that he also gave Wendy Savage in their first meeting. 'Your power in the court is directly proportional to your power outside.' This comment, after a weekend of public battering which had left me feeling the most hated individual in Britain, made me realize the vulnerability of my position. The following day I visited a senior barrister to consider whether legal action could be taken against some of the papers whose coverage had been so unpleasant. His advice was that litigation was expensive, with no guarantee of success because the papers were written from the perspective of 'fair comment' and 'opinion' rather than fact.

After this, now suffering from shingles, I spent hours with Brian considering in microscopic detail my part in the case. We also considered how I could achieve reasonable coverage in either the social work press or responsible papers. From my perspective, attending the inquiry could only give me a chance to put my story. For this reason we released a press statement to the effect that I would attend the inquiry whether in public or private. Privately Brian had strong views that I had more chance in a public inquiry because his experience led him to believe that justice needed a great deal of air to survive. My own view was less confident and I was struggling just going over the case with Brian, let alone in a public, or private, inquiry.

After the press release, however, I noticed an improvement in the attitude of the press, even though they continued to phone and visit my home. Whether they respected the press release or my having the back-up power of a respected solicitor is hard to know. From this point to the start of the inquiry Brian and I continued to work preparing a statement and considering a strategy for that unpleasant process.

During the inquiry the press coverage was reasonably quiet, though on the first day a television camera crew filmed me going into the building only to realize they had not loaded the camera. They had the temerity to request me to do it again.

Between the inquiry and the publication of the report, Brian and I continued to meet to consider how we could deal with the press after the report was published.

As I had decided to resign from Greenwich Social Services and, together with the authority, had agreed the resignation should take effect from the day the report was due, I was not constricted by the demands of the employer and was responsible for myself.

My statement to the inquiry had been an honest and critical analysis of my handling of the case and we expected the panel would accept that analysis. We also hoped they would make strong comments about the working conditions, understaffing and resources in the area that led to me trying to cover an impossible workload.

To ensure the debate did not centre solely on the individuals involved, we both wrote articles which were published in *Social Work Today* on 7 December 1987, just before the inquiry report was published. Furthermore, Brian talked to journalists and shared with them the issues that we believed needed to be addressed. We also met the independent television director who made the *Dispatches* programme, transmitted on 11 December 1987 and again shared our position. Our view in all of these contacts was that programmes and articles would be written and our choice was only about whether we could affect their content. We also prepared for me to give interviews and face the media.

Our first view of the report left us astounded by its recommendations which gave the press the ammunition for a further personal assault and left me clearly the scapegoat. Also, the report hardly addressed the essentially important issues that were evidenced in numerous of the submissions to the inquiry – for example, overwork, understaffing and lack of resources. My immediate feeling was to regret the honest stance I had taken in the inquiry and to wish we had adopted a more defensive position.

It is impossible to state categorically as fact, but it is my opinion that the press and public demand for a figure to blame, make it hard for those involved in tragedies to engage fully in ensuring lessons are learnt. I also believe the personal focus of numerous inquiries, not only in the arena of social work, provide our society with an option to avoid addressing the content of the tragedy. If the event was the responsibility of Martin Ruddock, then we need not look further at the issues.

The damning nature of the report summarized in the recommendation 'that he should not in the future perform any of the statutory functions in relation to child abuse' sent me scurrying back into hiding, where I started writing again and the results appeared in *Social Work Today* on 21 January 1988. No one in previous inquiries had been sentenced in this way, no indication had been made in the inquiry that disciplinary conclusions would be made, and the sentence could not be appealed against and was permanent.

The press had a field-day and our effort to ensure the context was a primary focus of the report had failed.

Fortunately, Brian Raymond performed valiantly on television to defend my position, and other representatives of the profession also fought back. The independent television production *Dispatches* gave a balanced insight into the process and issues that came to the attention of the inquiry. It also portrayed my own evidence sympathetically.

The following day I was again shredded in much of the press, though the responsible papers included balanced comment which I believe related to the lobbying that had taken place by Brian Raymond and many others. I was also thrilled that the *Guardian* (12 December 1987:17) published a series of extracts from my submission which evidently struck a chord with many people, both in the profession and outside it, and brought an immediate sack of supportive letters. These letters are in part a testament to much that is positive in the profession. They started a personally healing process that has assisted me to rise again from what I had experienced as a mental beating. I also believe that before they arrived I was unable to allow myself to give up the feeling of guilt without being given external permission, and these letters gave that permission. Ironically, it feels as if the press both pilloried me and also gave me the means of survival.

The power of the article in the *Guardian* is summed up in one of many letters which reads:

I have just read the report (in the *Guardian*) of your evidence in the Kimberley inquiry with tears and a deep sadness for her and for you.

You did not kill Kimberley, her stepfather did. I think your evidence shows an immensely caring and honest attitude which I admire more than I can say.

Social Workers, it seems to me, stand on the frontiers of our society, asked to do an impossible job with totally inadequate resources – but worse, with no moral support from the rest of us. And when a mistake is made we cry for their blood.

I am sure many of us today feel a sense of shame and a need to assure you that we understand your dilemma.

Please enjoy the childhood of your own 4-year-old and perhaps he/she will grow up to make the world a more loving and tolerant place.

It was my own 18-year-old's idea that I should put my thoughts on paper instead of weeping uselessly at the kitchen table.

Yours

Over the next month I was pleased to give an interview on Thames Television's *London Programme*. Sadly a long interview was cut down merely to me communicating personal sadness at my part in Kimberley's death. My immediate reaction to this was to feel I would never ever be allowed to do more than to say I was sorry. However, I was later given feedback that many individuals were moved to hear this apology and as a result felt willing to consider the predicaments of social workers more sympathetically.

In mid-January an article I wrote immediately after the publication of the report appeared in *Social Work Today*. It was my last action before *returning to* employment with Family Service Units who had employed me previously.

Before the court case started I could not envisage getting the press I received on 16 May 1987 at the conclusion of the trial. On 11 December 1987 I did not dream I would work in social work again. By February 1988 I was preparing to return to work for an agency in the London Borough of Greenwich where I had worked and where Kimberley died. In part, battling back and refusing to be destroyed by the press helped other writers and commentators to look beyond my involvement.

CONCLUSIONS

Looking back at the role of the press during the whole affair the following points seem to be important:

1 The press crucified me but also gave me the means to communicate the reason why I believed the crisis had occurred.
2 The effect of the press coverage was potentially devastating in personal terms. I became a receptacle for society's anger at Kimberley's death and was in danger of believing it was fully justified.

Social Services departments should consider carefully the personal needs of those caught up in similar such tragedies.

3 Until Brian Raymond enabled me to adopt a *pro*active stance, my passivity was making me a powerless victim. I believe this is also true for the profession which continues to find it hard to be *pro*active in shaping the public image of social work. We are too frightened of making mistakes to use the media to our advantage.

4 I believe that society and the media needed me to make an honest acceptance of my responsibility before they were able to address the wider issues within the Kimberley Carlile debate.

5 I believe that I was only able effectively to fight back because I had resigned from my employer and was able to act independently and primarily in my own interest.

7 Social work and the media: pitfalls and possibilities

Bob Franklin and Nigel Parton interview
Valerie Howarth

When you were Director of Social Services at Brent, how would you characterize your relationships with the media prior to the Jasmine Beckford case?
I can probably best answer that by recounting my experiences with media in my previous job at Lambeth, where I worked for eight years as Assistant Director of Social Services during the regime of Ted Knight: 'Red Ted' as the media dubbed him. That experience was not without its ups and downs and I was certainly used to working in a very heavy political climate. But I was also practised in dealing with the media, discussing child abuse and issues about homelessness. National political issues, often related to left-wing politics, were dealt with by the press and public relations machine at the town hall, which seemed appropriate. But in relation to practice matters I was involved with the media and this prompted no difficulties from members.

Were relations with media very different at Brent?
Very much so. The first thing that struck me was that members guarded their media contacts very jealously and viewed them as opportunities to promote their own image. Lambeth members had not been politically soft, but they seemed to have an interest in serving the community, whereas these members in Brent appeared to be very concerned with personal projection, their political careers and agendas other than those relating to social services. Brent, of course, was a very bitter, hung, council. Eventually I found myself very much excluded from what I'd been used to at Lambeth, which was being able to talk to the press and television directly.

Was Brent prepared for the media interest which the Beckford case generated?
Certainly not. I think it was a miracle that they hadn't had disasters previously. The Beckford case was badly handled in a number of

ways. First, there was the complex political climate involving disputes and rivalries between members concerning who should speak to the press and, consequently, very confused messages were given to the media. Second, when I arrived at Brent, there were no clear procedures in terms of child abuse, so the atmosphere in the department was not helpful.

Were you surprised by the press response to Beckford?

I knew that there would be a press reaction but I didn't know that it would be quite so mammoth. I had been involved in other similar cases but they never hit the headlines to the same extent.

When did the story break in the press? Was that during Maurice Beckford's trial?

No, surprisingly it was when the trial had finished. We did a good deal of work with the media during the initial stages of press coverage and were quite successful in explaining, to journalists and hopefully the general public, the considerable difficulties social workers face in handling child abuse cases and the complexity of the issues involved. One set of problems arises from the issue of *sub judice*. In this particular case, for example, we didn't have the medical information, which said that the child was damaged on the day the social worker visited, or any of the other details that came out during the inquiry. But the real difficulty in dealing with press enquiries about the Beckford case was that I knew that mistakes had been made. Consequently, I found it difficult to stand up and speak whole heartedly in support of the staff in a climate which became so politically destructive. Within days of the story breaking I was instructed by the members not to speak to the media at all and this became a major problem, both from the point of view of helping the general public understand the wider social work issues and in simply answering allegations made against me personally. In effect the press were just ignored.

Was Brent's official policy to say nothing and hope the problem would go away?

I think that's giving too much credence to policy. Certainly the policy was that the director should not speak. But the members couldn't speak with one voice because there were splits not only between the political groups but within them. So there was a series of messages going out, some of them agreed by the press officer, some offered *ad hoc* when members just happened to turn up in front of a camera. Nobody was giving a coherent view. But what is required in these circumstances is for everyone to pull together, agreeing what's to be said, who's going to say it and what the message is. If you haven't got a message, which Brent hadn't at that stage, you're in real difficulty.

Were press stories merely reflecting the chaos inherent in Brent's statements, or do you consider there was press malpractice?

I think there was also press malpractice. The media were undoubtedly left to pick up bits here and there which was unfortunate. But they also made things up as they went along. There was definite malpractice.

Can you recall any examples?

Oh yes, absolutely. First, many of the press stories were wholly inaccurate. The *Guardian*, for example, printed a story which said that I resigned from Brent in the course of police enquiries. It was a total fabrication and prompted a question in the House of Commons. It was also libellous of course but my solicitor felt I had enough to cope with at the time without following this through. Second, the inaccuracies in press stories were on occasion complemented by highly sensational reporting. Several tabloids ran a story, one as a centre-page spread which ran, 'Director of Social Services Receives £70,000 from Cambridgeshire', which was a reference to compensation I had allegedly received for an appointment which ultimately I did not take up. I never had a penny from Cambridgeshire. Not only was the story totally untrue, it was juxtaposed to a headline, 'Child Has No Gravestone', which reported the fact that Jasmine's grave was without a headstone and, by implication, alleged this was my responsibility. This is nothing but sensationalism and personally very painful. But you have very little comeback against such malpractice. It was quite appalling when I think back to what it was like opening a newspaper every day and finding myself on the pages. But it's very difficult to avoid it and this brings up a third element in press malpractice which hinges on the various techniques which journalists adopt to gather news stories. Reporters were actually sitting outside my office and refused to go away. This became a daily harassment from press and television which we had to endure for a number of weeks throughout the inquiry period. On one occasion, I literally had to go and reason with them to allow the social worker to come from the inquiry room to use the loo. The team leader, in particular, suffered a good deal of harassment, including the press literally sitting in the bushes outside her house. Now I think that is unethical behaviour. I believe the press have every right to tell the story even in a way that is uncomfortable to those involved, but I don't think they have the right to invade people's privacy to a degree which makes life impossible. Fortunately they never found me in the telephone directory, but the police advised me never to drive directly home. I had to drive past my house and go round the block to make sure I was not being followed by journalists.

Did you develop strategies to cope with this invasion?

Yes. It was essential. It became quite bizarre at one stage when I was receiving both death threats and proposals of marriage through the post. How do you cope with all that? I personally feel that the people I share my life with suffered extraordinarily more than I did because I developed a defence system that allowed me to compartmentalize it. When finally I was told not to talk to the press, it was partly a relief but, thinking back on it, I was happier dealing with the press, fraught as it was, than simply reading this untruthful and sensational material which I had no way of answering except through my solicitor.

Do the press not have a right, even a duty, to report these issues, no matter how tragic the circumstances of the particular case or how uncomfortable such discussions may prove to those who were involved?

Yes. The problem, however, is that the press are not always ethical in their behaviour. I feel strongly that there are limits beyond which people's privacy should not be intruded upon. And I think that sitting in the bushes outside someone's house is inappropriately intrusive. This isn't getting a story, it's sensationalizing a story. It's not giving news to the community, it's pandering to their wish for sensationalism.

But it sells newspapers and presumably expresses something about the public's interest or concern in these matters?

I'd like to see some of the newspapers with the largest circulations off the streets. I feel they pander to banal instincts in people and I've seen people destroyed by publicity. It is really a question of striking a balance between press freedom and the protection of individual rights. At the present time I don't think that the Press Council is strong enough to sustain that balance. But I agree that the press have every right to report matters like the Beckford case. I don't think I had any right to be protected from their fair enquiries and I've never said that.

You mentioned that you had been involved in cases, very similar to the Beckford case, which had not been the subject of press interest. Why was that? Was Beckford simply a good excuse for the press to attack a left-wing council?

I think there are a number of reasons why the press took up the

Beckford case. First, the timing was fortuitous. The miners' strike which had dominated news reporting for the previous year, had ended and left a news gap. Second, it was undoubtedly part of the Brent phenomenon. The press was just beginning to focus on left-wing councils. Brent was the first but was quickly followed by Southwark and Lambeth. But I don't think it was simply that. The final reason for press interest in the case was that it was a chance to have a go at social workers. If you read the press cuttings of the case, social workers were presented as these terrible people who interfere in others' lives but don't do the right things. Social workers were presented as muddled do-gooders who didn't really understand what they were doing even though they were simply dealing with things that everyone knows are simple and common sense! The truth, of course, is that these issues are highly complex.

Why should the press want to have a go at social workers? What have they got against them? Is it symptomatic of a deeper motive?
I think it's the scapegoating element in social work that creates this feeling. The difference between social work and the health service is that potentially everyone needs the health service but it's the poor, the depressed, the deprived and depraved who are the clients of social work. If you examine the process of scapegoating it involves the vilification of people who align themselves with the underdog and who are prepared to accept the projections of blame for the negative aspects of what's happening around them. Social workers are very much involved with poor people and have come to be a socially defined focus for the guilt, the blame and the responsibility for the conditions of poor people. I believe it's a phenomenon which is easy to identify but we don't seem to have learnt to talk about it or think it through.

What was the impact of the media attention, of this process of scapegoating, on morale within the department? Did it result in changing priorities, or any new procedural guidelines?
There is little doubt that media reporting of the Beckford case severely undermined morale within the department and was very corrosive of relationships between social workers and the community. Most social workers found that being subject to this sort of media response was absolutely devastating. Social workers in Brent had to continue with their day-to-day work but were constantly jibed with questions like 'Do you come from the council that kills babies?' It created an extraordinary atmosphere. In the Beckford case the social worker had not used the authority she possessed but, subsequently, anyone who had an axe to grind with

social workers used press coverage as a weapon to erode their authority. The case became a sort of stick with which to beat social workers. Media coverage also had a major impact on the decisions concerning the staff involved and whether they should be sacked immediately or whether they should go to another inquiry. The reason underlying the decision that they should be sacked and then be able to appeal, was that if a clean cut hadn't been made, the media would have pursued the situation indefinitely. The impact of media on social workers' lives and careers, and on Brent, would have simply continued in a downward spiral.

So there was a decisive media influence in the judgement that was made at that time?

Absolutely, and it's a very important issue. I remember the chief executive being jubilant the day after the staff were sacked when one of the tabloid newspapers claimed it was the most courageous decision he'd made. Now in my view it was neither courageous nor in accordance with the principles of natural justice and I said so at the time. But I agreed to go along with the decision because I felt that it was the only way to stop the media persecution of the department. And it had become persecution at that point. For my part I couldn't do anything else about the matter given my position. The staff never knew the reasons behind the decision and they've never spoken to me from that day to this.

The impact of media on procedures was more apparent than real. We had been working hard and just produced new procedural guidelines. The Jasmine Beckford case was in a sense superimposed on changes that had been taking place through the area review committee. But it was quite distinct from it. The press distortedly presented events as though some of those changes had come about because of Jasmine's death. Now some matters were clearly speeded up as a result of the inquiry, but the department's active engagement in certain issue areas preceded the inquiry and was not a consequence of it.

Can we move to a discussion of ChildLine which seems to signal a very different media involvement. Instead of media standing on the outside, observing and reporting the events, they are now directly involved as participants in the arena of child protection. Do you think this is a useful development?

Yes I think it's tremendously helpful. When the media take some responsibility in matters of child protection you find a quite different approach to the presentation of the relevant issues. When *That's Life!* conducted a survey and Esther Rantzen discussed on television people being abused, they received the most horrendous letters, many of them from children who were still being abused in the here and now, whereas the programme had been trying to identify adults who had been abused who would be willing to talk about it. That's what led to the BBC survey and then the *Childwatch* programme. So there is a sort of ownership or involvement with the problem which creates a different stage in its comprehension. I also think that Cleveland was helpful in certain ways. A number of people got hammered in the media for Cleveland but it's my impression that some journalists were beginning to appreciate that such matters were more complicated than they had at first imagined. Beckford, Tyra Henry, Kimberley Carlile and then Cleveland. Superficially there may appear to be little connection, but if you talk to journalists there is a definite change in their perspectives in terms of understanding.

Can you tell us about the origins of ChildLine?

I arrived six months in. ChildLine was a combination of Esther Rantzen and Sarah Caplin, who produced *Childwatch*, becoming very personally and powerfully absorbed by the problem of child abuse and the vast number of cases revealed by the BBC's survey. I think they began to realize that the issue had never been adequately discussed in the media. The *Childwatch* programme was a watershed in terms of the way people were able to talk about child abuse. But I think it also represented something of a lost opportunity for social work. It was an occasion when I think social workers should have started saying: 'This is what we're dealing with every day, this is what the community expects us to deal with on its behalf.'

Has ChildLine enjoyed a good deal of media interest from the outset and is this perhaps because they consider the organization to be their own progeny?

Yes I think there has been considerable media interest in ChildLine and this seems to reflect a number of factors. First, there is the 'Esther factor' which is perhaps not so critical as it was at one stage of ChildLine's development. She has the ability to convey messages in a way that's helpful and easily understood by the general public. One important lesson I have learned is that you must try to use the media, but not get used by them. Second, the topic of child sexual abuse is of real interest to the public. Reactions to the topic are often confused and express a denial that it exists combined with a genuine interest about it. So the question we always get asked is, how many hoax calls do we have? Third, ChildLine is a private and charitable organization and, I think as far as the press are concerned, there is a sense of initiative, adventure and striking out to tackle problems in a new way. But, finally, I think press interest in ChildLine reflects the simplicity of our message. We have tried hard to tackle the way we give information to the press about our work. We translate real cases into stories which, while we take great care to ensure anonymity and confidentiality, essentially reflect the circumstances of the case. I think social services could develop this style of press work to great advantage but seem to have failed where we have succeeded. We have the advantage of a simple message: listening to children. But when you get past that simple message, matters are quite complicated in terms of services and what children are telling us. So we're trying to learn how to get messages across.

You seem to have brought us directly to the question of media policy. Does ChildLine have a policy about media relations?

Only one rule is written down and it is extremely important. Nobody talks to the press unless they speak to the press officer first. The purpose of that rule is not to control staff but to advise and protect them. The press officer never says to people 'don't do that' unless she feels it's potentially dangerous. She's much more likely to advise staff by saying, 'If you do it in this way you'll get maximum coverage.' The rule is meant to be enabling rather than restrictive.

But does the press officer have the power to stop you talking to media?

Yes she does. It's very important that we respond coherently to the media. Knowing how to handle the media effectively can be critical at certain times. For example, one of the difficulties I faced in moving to the post of director of ChildLine was that I was 'the Beckford director'. We anticipated that the press response to my appointment might be, 'How could the Beckford director lead a child protection agency?'

Esther, who is the press officer for *That's Life!*, and myself, gave considerable thought to how we would handle this at the outset. We decided to confront the issue head on and Esther and Bryer Scudamore tackled the *Star*, one of the papers who had been highly critical of Brent's handling of the Beckford case. To my surprise they published a wonderful centre-page spread with a photograph of me and a headline 'The Caring Social Worker They Called a Monster'. I couldn't believe it. The *Telegraph*, which had always been very fair, carried a similar story about my background. I'm convinced it was because we tackled the issue in a professional way. It was really just a matter of thinking through who had connections and how we could get the story across. By now of course, Louis Blom-Cooper had described me as an 'excellent director of social services' and he took the trouble to write to the newspapers saying that my leaving Brent should not be considered a consequence of the Beckford case.

So what is the philosophy of media relations at ChildLine?

To do a good job for children, to tell people about it and to be as open as possible, even when things are difficult.

Presumably the press officer is a central figure in conveying messages about the job you're doing at ChildLine?

Absolutely. Our press officer is vital to this organization in my view. It's essential that someone has a quality control on our responses.

What is her brief?

In the most general sense her job is to point us in the right direction so far as the press is concerned, to tell us about local press reporters, about the sorts of stories in which a particular paper might be especially interested, about how to get a particular message across, as well as to offer general advice, reassurance and help. We get an enormous amount of press enquiries, but I've turned down half a dozen television appearances very recently. There was a time when it was very important to get out there but now there are a number of people who can perform well on media and who can perhaps speak more relevantly to particular issues. We kept specifically out of Cleveland, for a number of reasons, but it didn't keep us out of clashes with Stuart Bell, in which I was quite happy to get involved. So the press officer's job is to make sure that media opportunities get correctly channelled, that we pick up the appropriate ones and that we achieve exposure in the right places – for two reasons. One is to get across the message about what we're doing but the second is that we are a charity so we actually raise our money.

Why are you turning down media opportunities now?

I think we've become more sophisticated in our thinking about the message we want to get across and the level of exposure. We are also targeting our media audiences more precisely. When we opened our Midlands office, for example, we did an enormous number of local radio and television interviews. We channelled our energies closely so that people came to know about us. It was a level of media activity appropriate for launching a new office. Again, if we're doing a local awareness or fund-raising campaign, we get a good deal of local press coverage that our press officer co-ordinates.

But our major concern at the moment is to get information to children by using poster publicity in schools. Finally, we may discriminate between invitations to appear on the media on the basis of whether or not they present opportunities to discuss questions of interest to us; for example, concerning aspects of the Children Bill or issues concerning listening to children.

Can you tell us something about the range of work which ChildLine undertakes?

When I first arrived we answered 400 telephone calls a day from children; the figure currently is in excess of 1,000 calls each day. There are somewhere in the region of 10,000 attempted calls measured by BT and we've counselled some 77,000 children and 14,000 adults since we began. A large proportion of the calls are silent. The Samaritans advised us this would happen and it's typical of every helpline. What we're beginning to understand, therefore, is what that silence is about. I think we're learning many new facets of telephone counselling which haven't been tackled elsewhere. We went to Holland to visit Kindertelefon which has been operating for ten years but, because they're not freefone and the children pay for the calls, the organization is unable to discuss problems at length with children working towards resolving or disclosing their problem. I think our work at ChildLine is new, fascinating, and we are learning all the time. But it does mean that we deal with every child problem imaginable: bullying, divorce, sibling problems, school-related problems generally, exams – we get a lot of calls around exam time – suicide, problems with social workers. You name it, it's here, from problems with pets to horrendous physical and sexual abuse. So it's essential people are trained to understand the spectrum and give a child the appropriate response.

And what is the appropriate response? How might a typical encounter with a child develop?

It depends entirely on the child's needs and that's the value of the service. The child has total power because if, as a counsellor, you get it wrong, they put the phone down. They don't have to tell us who they are or where they are and our policy is not to trace calls. It's the children's *own* service. We get a lot of children ringing who want advice and bits of information on a 'one-off' basis, but there are a number of longer-term callers. ChildLine is not passive or non-directive; we're not here, as we always say, 'to help children suffer in comfort'. We are here to try and convince them that they can change the quality of their lives. But the choice must remain theirs. The major problem is that the system we might move them into is so negative in terms of attitudes towards children. They say to us for example, 'I won't have to go into care, will I?' 'I won't have to have a medical, will I?' There are procedures that we know must take place, but if only we could be more reassuring to children it would be helpful. The medical examination is a good example. We try and persuade children of its value by saying, 'You want to be sure you're not hurt, you want to be sure you're all right.' But we can't guarantee that a child won't be very insensitively examined in the police station and endure double rape, which is how we, and the child, see it. We can't guarantee that when a child gets to court they won't be cross-examined in a way that makes them feel that what happened was actually their fault. ChildLine tries to help the child. So we try to get them to begin by finding allies in their community. Having talked through their experiences with one of our counsellors we ask them, 'Who do you have whom you can trust?' 'Who else would be supportive around you?' We have a number of quite successful cases, as far as we're concerned, where children have told their mothers about abuse by father or stepfather and the situation has been tackled entirely in the home with the mother throwing the perpetrator out. We're criticized for that but what's the alternative?

What is ChildLine's relationship with the statutory sector?

Ultimately, in many cases, the social service departments are the backstop of our service for children. Often children take weeks making the decision to move from ChildLine to social services and then it's a very careful handover. We have established good relationships with SSDs throughout the country. I could cite some horror stories, but on the whole I have nothing but praise for social services and the police. The problem with social services is that they don't have the follow-through capacity. For example, a girl discloses at 13 that she's been abused by her father from the age of 9. Her mother knew nothing about it. Dad admits the offence and goes to prison for 4 years. End of problem. But as far as ChildLine is concerned, here is a child who's been abused with all the attendant difficulties and need for help. There is a mother who can't touch her daughter because she has combined anxieties about her failure to protect her child but, on the other hand, she views her partly as a rival. She also needs help and support. The bread-winner is gone from the family and the local community has its suspicions about events. Now this is when the family needs support but it is precisely the moment that the local social services, for all the good reasons we all know about, don't have the resources to deal with the problem because they are too busy coping with the next case of child protection. At ChildLine, we're saying some resources must go into that sort of back-up. I'd say there are significant gaps. But, so far as the actual crisis is concerned, we've had nothing but really good support from social service departments.

What about the future for ChildLine?

Well there are perennial difficulties: shortage of money, counsellors, volunteers and the need for other offices. We've recently opened an office in Nottingham which covers the Midlands and we're planning to open a third, in Scotland, early in 1990. The reasons for not siting everything here in London are manifold. One of the major difficulties is in fact a communication problem: how do you store in one place so much information about all the voluntary groups and people you might use, or refer to, in terms of helping people, and how do you build up relationships at great distances? So when we decided we had to expand, regional centres came to mind. Relationships, information, cash-raising are all easier to do when you're local. The other benefit of course is stronger links with local media.

Our discussion has returned again and again to the subject of media involvement in child protection, so it seems appropriate, given your experience in both the voluntary and statutory sectors, to conclude by asking about your reflective wisdoms of the role of media in this area of work.

There is absolutely no doubt in my mind that the press has a clear responsibility to report events relating to child protection. Without press coverage it would not have been possible to raise the issues of child sexual abuse to a level which enables more children to come forward and find ways out of terrible pain. However, this should be balanced with a protection of privacy. The press has not generally set itself a sufficiently rigorous code of professional practice and I believe there is now a need for legislation in this area. Freedom is not license but occasionally license has led to the kind of dishonest journalism which has damaged people's lives.

However, there are more sensitive people in the media who do understand that social work issues are more complex than was previously portrayed and it is now the responsibility of all of us to take the opportunity to get the message across. This is particularly true of social services departments who are engaged in a crucial task on behalf of society but whose staff do not always believe they too should actively promote an understanding of their work.

Social work has a lot to shout about. It is essential that the state takes care of those who no other agency will help. Those who, if left to the economic forces of demand, will simply not receive help and care and that is clearly irresponsible. But there are not many discussions of such matters in the media. I think that local government generally, but social services in particular, hasn't thought through how to put its case. The alternative to not having state intervention, just as the alternatives to not really having a national health service, are definable and demonstrable if you take the trouble to generate the appropriate news stories. You can personalize them very easily. That's how the health service issue got onto media agendas. Children were dying because they couldn't get the operation they required. The difficulty of course is that when a child dies in care, the press present it as somebody's fault, but when a child dies in an operating theatre it's the system. We must get our act together to get our message across. But somehow social services don't do it and I think it's partly because social services and local government are so pressurized that they're forced into reacting rather than thinking proactively.

Have your experiences at ChildLine helped you move into a more proactive view of your relationships with the media?

Yes. I have always felt, from my early Lambeth days, that one had a responsibility to try and get the message through about what one was doing. I still believe that is true but my conviction has grown a million times stronger since I've been here at ChildLine. And I know that if you work *with* the media they will listen too.

8 Hidden agendas and moral messages: social workers and the press

Louis Blom-Cooper

The Times, in its issue of 2 July 1986, published an item reporting the final stages of the trial of Mrs Mirella Beechook, a Mauritian immigrant charged with the murder of her daughter and her daughter's friend. The report, which was unsigned and therefore assumed to be an agency report, began by saying that 'a mother who believed in witchcraft and voodoo was given two life sentences at the Central Criminal Court yesterday for the "hideous" murders of her daughter and a neighbour's child'. After stating the bald description of Mrs Beechook and the children and reporting the judgement on sentence by the Recorder of London, the paper reported the following which is verbatim:

> Earlier, social workers told the court how Beechook had tried to poison her younger baby, Sabrina, with sleeping tablets six years before she strangled her daughter Tina, and the child's friend, Stacey Kavanagh.
>
> Although Sabrina, then aged only twenty-two days, was taken from her after the poisioning in 1979 and later adopted, social workers in the London Borough of Southwark allowed Beechook to keep Tina because they believed the child, then 15 months old, would help to stabilise her parents' marriage.
>
> Tina was placed on the 'at risk' register of the social services department and a close watch kept on the family. But in 1982 she was removed from the register.
>
> The last few weeks of her life were spent shoplifting and begging for money on the Swan Road Estate in Rotherhithe, South London, where she and her mother lived.
>
> Mr Ravi Beechook, Tina's father, who left the family home two years ago, blamed social workers for her death.
>
> Mr Beechook, aged 30, an insurance salesman now living in

Stratford, East London, said: 'If they had kept a tighter grip on the case she might not have died. They knew she needed medical help.'

But the social services department said there was no reason to believe that Mrs Beechook would harm the other child at the time of the incident with Sabrina.

Caring agencies who continued to visit the Beechook flat reported no sign of ill-treatment of Tina. And her school, Albion Primary, reported no problems.[1]

(*The Times*, 2 July 1986)

There then followed a brief account of Mrs Beechook's version of Tina's death, and a fuller account of the incident with Sabrina which concluded:

Beechook claimed that she had been told in a dream to harm the child, and alleged that Mr Beechook's old girlfriend was putting the 'evil eye' on her and placing ideas in her mind.

Beechook came to Britain in 1974 from Mauritius, an island in the Indian Ocean, where voodoo remains a powerful force.

(ibid.)

Journalistically speaking, the report was, on the face of it, a fair and balanced account of a criminal trial. The facts stated were accurate and there was no statement in the report that could be said deliberately to mislead the reader. Yet, on a careful study of the report, facts were so juxtaposed as to convey a moral message. The reader was implicitly pointed towards connections and moral lessons, leaving him or her to draw conclusions that were antipathetic to social workers. To substantiate these assertions it is necessary to consider certain features of the reporter's account.

The overall effect on the reader is that this is a cool, factual, unsensational account of a criminal trial that befits a broadsheet newspaper of high reputation. It displays its claim to objective reporting on the sleeve of its style of reporting. One can imagine, without having to cite, how a representative of the tabloid newspapers would have treated the case. Yet lurking behind that aura of neutrality there lies the reporter's account which seeks to persuade the reader of some social and moral lessons.

First, *The Times* did not say, 'social workers might and ought to have prevented this child's death'. To have written that, other than in an editorial, would have breached a basic canon of journalistic ethics to keep separate fact from comment. Nevertheless, the report devoted undue prominence to Mr Beechook's view, at the climax of the narrative, constructed in a way that implies that the real subject of the report is the inexplicable blindness of social workers on the case. Indeed, the lead paragraph focuses on social workers describing an earlier homicide attempt on a baby sibling of the strangled daughter.

The item presents a cumulative picture of Mrs Mirella Beechook as manifestly unfit to be a parent. Woven into the dossier of her parental unfitness are the accounts of the failure of the Social Services Department of Southwark Borough Council to exhibit alarm about Tina. It would be an abnormally sceptical reader who did not throw up his or her mental arms in disbelief and incredulity that social workers had palpably failed to read the signs of maternal unsuitability in Mrs Beechook. Moreover, the chronology of the story told by the reporter serves only to confuse the reader. One has to do some sums to work out that Mr Beechook left the family only *after* Tina had been removed from the 'at risk' register. There are also some conflicting messages about marriage, family and parental responsibility.

Given that this item in *The Times* came six months after the report of the Panel of Inquiry into the circumstances surrounding the death of Jasmine Beckford, *A Child in Trust*, the reader could have been expected to pick up the hint that here was yet another case of shocking child abuse in which social workers had naively put the interests of parents before that of their child: the second paragraph of the item mentioned social workers in Southwark in 1979 as believing 'the child, then 15 months old, would help to stabilise her parents "marriage" '. *A Child in Trust* (the report of the Beckford case) had pointed up the defect in social work training which regarded the parents of a child at risk as the clients of social workers. The fact is that the Beechook's marriage did not 'stabilize', and there is nothing in *The Times*'s account to suggest that the prime onus of responsibility for Tina and her mother might be seen as resting with Mr Beechook. He is recorded as having 'left the family home two years ago', a strictly accurate fact, but juxtaposed with him 'blaming social workers' for Tina's death. The tacit assumption is that the Social Services Department may be the interestingly guilty party in the whole affair. And even when the reader is distracted from the implicit assumptions of social work failure there is introduced Mrs Beechook's fanciful dreams and an unattributed statement that 'voodoo remains a powerful force' in Mauritius.

This news item reflects how easy it is, unless great care is taken by reporter and sub-editor, to construct moral messages within the narrative account. And because the message is a moral one, it pans out into social and political messages. This particular moral message owed much to the press campaign against social workers that culminated in the Jasmine Beckford report and has continued unabated through a series of child abuse inquiries in the late 1980s, in particular the Butler-Sloss inquiry in 1987–8 into the Cleveland child sexual abuse cases.

The public reaction to the case of Jasmine Beckford, a 4½-year-old child in the care of the London Borough of Brent who died on 5 July 1984, was aroused initially only at the time of the trial of the child's mother and father in April 1985. The trial judge excited press interest by prematurely and unjustly reproving social workers from Brent Borough Council while at the same time exonerating members from the Education Department of the same local authority.

The fact that almost none of the agencies involved in the management of the child protection system is entirely blameless for the death of a child at the hands of abusing parents, seems not to deflect the media from focusing on social workers as primarily, if not exclusively, to blame for the failure to protect. It is not always easy to separate the attitudes of the public and the attitudes that are expressed in the media.

Society, not unnaturally, revolts at the repugnance of parents who torment and kill their children. It expresses alarm that such behaviour can happen when there is close monitoring and surveillance of the family with a child at risk by officialdom in the shape of social services. It is aroused to anger whenever it perceives incompetence or negligence on the part of those responsible for ensuring the protection of the vulnerable young. And that anger is directed specifically at social workers, to the apparent exclusion of any other persons engaged in the field of child care and child health, if only because of the pre-existing set of public attitudes to the nature of social work and the character, often stereotyped, of social workers. If that is a correct analysis of public attitudes, it is hardly surprising that it finds a ready echo in the media. Given the media reflection of public attitudes, the excessive concentration on social workers by the media is hard to bear. Social workers have become the butt of every unthinking journalist whenever a scapegoat is sought to explain a fatality or serious injury to a child either in the care of a local authority, or whose vulnerability to parental abuse is known to social services.

Does the press subject social workers to some kind of public trial, and if so, why? To answer the first question, I take two instances: one, the disciplinary action against the social workers in the Beckford case; and second, the press reaction to the recommendation for the future employment of the main social worker in the Kimberley Carlile case.

THE BECKFORD DISMISSALS

The day after publication of *A Child in Trust*, Brent Borough Council dismissed Miss Gunn Wahlstrom, the key social worker to the Beckford family, her immediate supervisor, Mrs Diane Dietmann, and Mr William Thompson, the principal court officer in the Social Services Department whose misconduct of the case before the juvenile court was a crucial factor in the child being fatally returned to her parents' home. While the report of the Panel of Inquiry had been critical of all three workers – and indeed others as well – it refrained from making any recommendations about the future employment of all three. If the Panel had been consulted by the employing local authority, it would have singled out only Mrs Dietmann for possible action, either to terminate her contract or involve disciplinary action. Miss Wahlstrom's employment should continue, but in residential care work. Mr Thompson should have been offered early retirement, with no adverse financial consequences.

Not a single newspaper expressed the slightest doubt that all three dismissals were right, fair and proper. Quite the contrary, there was an immediate sense that nothing less than dismissal sufficed as the appropriate response of a public authority. Only the *Guardian*, in an editorial, observed that no other professional – particularly so a member of the medical profession – would be treated so punitively, even in cases of proven negligence. The broadsheet press – *The Times*, the *Guardian*, and the *Daily Telegraph* – gave full and accurate summaries of the findings and recommendations in their news columns, but were highly selective in editorial comment. The *Daily Mail* and the *Daily Express* did not restrict their selectivity to editorial comment. They concentrated in their news columns and editorials almost exclusively on the named social workers. The *Daily Mail* excelled itself with the headline on the front page: 'Jasmine: Everyone was guilty . . . but WILL NO ONE

TAKE THE BLAME?' There followed photographs of Miss Wahlstrom, Mrs Dietmann and the Director of Social Services, Miss Valerie Howarth, who was not blamed for any action or omission prior to Jasmine Beckford's death.

The *Daily Mail* could not resist including a large picture of Jasmine's grave with its wooden cross and anonymous number to ensure that no one should forget the pathetic victim. The text continued: 'Beckford [Maurice Beckford, the step-father who was convicted of the child's manslaughter and was sentenced to 10 year's imprisonment] is where he ought to be', but went on to ask, what of 'inexperienced' social worker Gunn Wahlstrom and 'ineffective' health visitor, Yeng Leory [who was criticized in the report but not disciplined by her employing health authority]: 'If they are not to be sacked, Diane Dietmann should be.' Interestingly enough, the lay magistrates, who remained anonymous and did not give evidence to the inquiry, under directions from the Lord Chancellor, (although they indicated willingness to appear and did provide written answers to a questionnaire) were mentioned by the *Daily Mail*: 'Magistrates should be named and chastised by the Lord Chancellor.'

In short, the popular press and, in a more restrained fashion, the quality newspapers, spread the blame widely, quoting the report on the shortcomings of magistrates, health care workers, schoolteachers as well as social workers. But on the day after publication of the report, most newspapers responded in ways that added weight to the case of sacking, or at the very least, severely disciplining *someone* in Brent. The *Daily Mail* and the *Sun* were quite open in their demand that heads should roll. All the popular papers used the technique of printing graphic details of the child's suffering alongside accounts of the failures of the named workers, mostly with photographs of those whom the *Sun* labelled 'Guilty Ones Who Let Jasmine Die'.

Such juxtaposing of photographs of the main actors in the tragedy of a child abuse death reached its nadir when the report of the trial of the parents of Kimberley Carlile appeared in March 1987. The popular newspaper showed the photograph of the main social worker between those of the two convicted parents under the banner headline 'Murderers'.

THE CARLILE CASE

The December 1987 report of the Commission of Inquiry into the circumstances surrounding the death of Kimberley Carlile followed the pattern of the earlier Beckford report in that it analysed the events, pointed up the deficiencies in the management of the child protection system, as well as indicating fault on the part of child care and health care workers.

The main social worker, Mr Martin Ruddock, was a team leader but, due to staff shortages, was acting down as the field-worker with the Carlile family.

In the course of the inquiry Mr Ruddock submitted a report which was a commendable reappraisal of his own competence to deal with a child abuse inquiry. He acknowledged his blame for the failure of intervention to protect the child. At the time of the inquiry Mr Ruddock had already given notice to his employer, the London Borough of Greenwich, and was expecting to take up a post with the Family Service Unit at Woolwich. The Family Service Unit delayed making the appointment until it had read the report of the inquiry. In the circumstances the Commission of Inquiry, desirous of ensuring that no obstacle should be put in the way of the Family Service Unit appointment by reason of the criticism of Mr Ruddock's work in the Carlile case, made an exception to the principle that a child abuse inquiry should not involve itself in any consequential disciplinary action. The inquiry report included among its listed recommendations – and in this respect the authors perhaps unwisely gave undue prominence to the recommendation – that Mr Ruddock should not exercise any *statutory* functions in relation to child care.

Although this recommendation was incidental to the main thrust of the report, which was to highlight once again the failure of the child protection system and the deficiencies in giving effect to the multi-disciplinary approach to problems of child abuse, it was seized upon by the media as the single, most important recommendation. By such selectivity, a well-intentioned communication to an intending employer of a social worker distracted much attention from the report and excited, not unnaturally, hostility among social workers towards a report that was supportive of much social work and sought to strengthen the specialized training of social workers and the development of their professionalism.

WHY SOCIAL WORKERS?

The exigencies of topicality and newsworthiness dictate the vision of the journalist. The complex, subtle and often conflicting demands of casework will frequently obscure rather than enlighten the good story. Journalism is largely about rendering the vicissitudes of life simpler and starker. Social workers present to the journalist a prime target for the good story. They operate in a field of competing social motives; they are insufficiently rigorous in their practices; they appear to be sympathetic to wrongdoers; they are politically biased, perceived as predominantly left-wing to a press that is heavily tilted in the opposite direction; and they are gullible to every sob story.

There is perhaps not much that social workers can do effectively to counter the most entrenched antipathies. But there are some things that would go some way to correcting some of the falsities perpetrated by the press. Public (or press) attitudes to social workers are often caricatures. Social work is regarded not as a profession, in the way that law or medicine are. However, professional social workers may be in their principles or practice, they cannot escape the fact that they lack universal recognition as professional. There is a dire need for social work to be a licensed profession, subject to the ordinary disciplinary processes of the established professions. Without the backing of a professional association, the social worker is occupationally at the mercy of the politicians of the employing local authorities. Given equality of professional status and a professional body that could speak authoritatively to press and public, the discrimination (used in its, now almost uniformly, pejorative sense) against social workers, would diminish.

Flowing from this would be a constant stream of uniform publicity about the nature of the tasks which social workers undertake in the public's name. One understandable reason for the prominence of social workers in child care cases is the fact that Parliament has made them legally responsible for the child protection system. A greater awareness that the statutory responsibility is in practice a responsibility shared with their agencies, and supervised by an enhanced judicial role for the courts, would do much to diffuse any blame for failure rather than to focus it on the one legally dominant agency.

The training of social workers needs more recognition by governments in order that trainees acquire an academic and practical status commensurate with similar occupations in the legal and medical fields; it fails, moreover, to acknowledge the importance of the task which society places on social workers.

Above all, there should be a conscious attempt on behalf of social work to demonstrate the moral options which reflect current social work orthodoxy as opposed to the primitive and vindictive attitudes that characterize much of the popular press and some of the more serious press. As this chapter seeks to establish, the press attitude to social workers, whether it be *The Times* or the *Sun*, is the same. The only difference concerns presentation and the style of communicating to the different audiences and readerships.

NOTE

1 I am indebted to Mrs Bernia Martin for the reference 'Moral messages and the press: newspapers response to *A Child in Trust*', in *After Beckford? Essays on Thoughts Related to Child Abuse* (Martin 1987).

9 Press reporting of Kincora

Marie Smyth

INTRODUCTION

Kincora has been associated with a variety of different concerns related to social work accountability, sexuality and power, political intrigue and the particular sectarian situation in Northern Ireland. This chapter offers an insight into the affair but will serve, in part, as a case study to assess how far the media, and investigative journalism in particular, can play a positive role in reporting the unseemly and unpalatable aspects of social work.

Social work's view of the media is typically negative, but media can on occasion fulfil an important task in calling social work to account on behalf of both its often powerless clients and the community more generally. To address such questions is difficult since many consider the full story of Kincora has yet to be told; a point underscored by the uncertainties surrounding ex-civil servant Colin Wallace's claims of a government campaign of 'misinformation' in Northern Ireland. In taking on such a task, moreover, media become active participants constructing the issue under investigation. It is necessary, therefore, to assess the way Kincora was presented in the media, but also to note any variations in media coverage and also to assess possible implications. The chapter also provides a comparison with media coverage of other child abuse cases where social work is presented in very negative terms which, interestingly, was not the case with Kincora.

The analysis is based on data derived from press coverage of the initial story during January/February 1980 in Northern Ireland papers and from subsequent coverage in local papers across a two-year period. Coverage of Kincora thereafter is surveyed and sampled by detailed examination of one Irish tabloid and one broadsheet newspaper. Analysis of newspaper content has been supplemented by interviews with journalists and social workers involved in the case.

THE KINCORA SCANDAL: THE 'STORY'

Kincora was the name of a hostel for adolescent boys in East Belfast, run by the local authority, Belfast Corporation and, since 1972, by the Eastern Health and Social Services Board. It opened in 1959 and provided accommodation for adolescent boys between the ages of 15 and 19. All residents were placed there under the Children and Young Persons Act.

The story unfolded as follows:

24 January 1980

The *Irish Independent* front-page headline 'Sex Racket at Children's Home' alleged boys in Kincora were recruited for homosexual prostitution, that there was a cover-up by both the police and the social services department, that a member of staff in Kincora was involved in a loyalist paramilitary group and that he was pimping. Important Northern Ireland businessmen were alleged to have been involved. It was also alleged that one of the children had committed suicide and another had attempted suicide.

May–December 1981

A police investigation led to the conviction of seven men, three of whom worked in Kincora. Former assistant warden in Kincora, Raymond Semple, was convicted on four charges of buggery and gross indecency and sentenced to five years' imprisonment.

Joseph Mains, formerly the warden in charge of Kincora, was charged with a number of offences allegedly committed during 1961–79 involving eight different boys. He was convicted and sentenced to six years' imprisonment.

William McGrath, 64, was charged on eighteen counts but convicted on fifteen of the charges and sentenced to four years.

15 January 1982

James Prior, Secretary of State for Northern Ireland, announced the setting up of an inquiry under Stephen McGonagle, Commissioner for Complaints for Northern Ireland, to investigate allegations that a homosexual vice ring in Kincora had been covered up.

January–February 1982

Press reports alleged the homosexual vice ring had been covered up.

12 February 1982
The McGonagle inquiry stood down after one day following the resignation of three of its members; continuing police investigations was the stated reason.

18 February 1982
Jack Hermon, Chief Constable for Northern Ireland, announced a police inquiry headed by Sir George Terry, Chief Constable of Sussex, to investigate allegations of a homosexual vice ring and the involvement of civil servants.

24–26 February 1982
Miss A. M. Sheridan, Deputy Director for Social Work Services in the Department of Health and Social Services in London, visited Northern Ireland to advise the DHSS in Northern Ireland on the supervision of homes and hostels for children and young people.

June 1982
The Sheridan report recommended increased monitoring of children's homes, more staff training and the introduction of a complaints procedure for residents.

22 March 1983
A debate on Kincora took place in the Northern Ireland Assembly.

29 October 1983
The Terry inquiry found no evidence of the involvement of residents of children's homes in homosexual vice rings or that any vice ring involved police officers, civil servants, military personnel, justices of the peace or the legal profession.

9 November 1983
A further debate on Kincora took place in the Northern Ireland Assembly.

3 November 1983
An *Irish Times* article alleged connections between Kincora, McGrath and military intelligence.

18 January 1984
An inquiry was set up under the chair of Judge William Hughes into whether the abuse of residents could have been prevented by the administration of homes and hostels by the DHSS and social services.

June 1985
Continued press coverage of MI5 interest in Kincora.

December 1985
The Hughes inquiry report was published. It made fifty-six recommendations, including staff vetting, increased staff training, the possible use of psychological tests on prospective staff, increased

DHSS supervision of homes and that the DHSS establish the legality of excluding homosexuals from employment in residential children's care.[1]

THE PRESS AS AGENTS OF DISCLOSURE

The role of the press in revealing the abuse in Kincora began with Peter McKenna's article in the *Irish Independent*, 24 January 1980. The story had been brought to him by two social workers who felt they had exhausted all other avenues. According to the Hughes inquiry report:

> At some time about December 1979, Mrs. Gogarty and Mrs. Kennedy met socially and Kincora was discussed. As a result of their discussion and their shared concern that nothing appeared to have been done to resolve suspicions about the hostel, they decided to approach the press . . . this culminated in the 'Irish Independent' printing its 24 January 1980 article. . . . *The real significance of its publication was that it resulted in the initiation of the RUC's investigation which eventually led to the convictions of Messrs. Mains, Semple and McGrath* (my emphasis).
>
> (DHSS NI 1986: para 4.211)

Perhaps the media's most important function in the Kincora scandal was in bringing it to light in the first place. Repeated attempts by residents and others to expose the abuse in Kincora, using the normal channels, failed to elicit a response from social services, or any police investigation. Eventually the press was used by social work staff to draw public attention to a situation in their own agency.

There is, of course, too frequently resistance within organizations to such information (Ennew 1986:5–6). In 1980, moreover, neither social workers nor the public were as sensitized to sexual abuse as they are today. One male social worker, who had placed a child in Kincora, attended there regularly and knew Joseph Mains stated:

> As far as I am concerned, Kincora was a vital facility which I used as a social worker and which I recommended others to use. . . . Bloody hell fire, we must have been so blind and so naive and so unbelievably ill-equipped in our perception of what was an appalling, grotesque environment for vulnerable young kids in care to spend their teenage years.[2]

Attitudes and values on sexuality, moreover, take a particular form in Ireland, and this militates against an awareness of sexual abuse. The divorce referendum, the abortion referendum and the legislation on homosexuality and contraception in the Republic of Ireland, and in the North the relatively recent decriminalization of male homosexuality coupled with restrictive laws on abortion, signal a society with extremely conservative attitudes. Taboos around sexual issues are strong, making it even more difficult to deal openly with issues such as sexual abuse. Going to the press was a powerful device to overcome the organizational and professional paralysis which previously had not detected the abuse.[3]

THE INITIAL REPORTING OF KINCORA

Coverage of Kincora varied from front-page articles reporting major developments – the various revelations, the allegations of cover-up, the inquiries – to features on particular aspects of the case – the MI5 connections and the alleged involvement of the Revd. Ian Paisley. Editorials and opinion columns also sporadically commented on Kincora (see McGournan 1984 and *Sunday Independent*, 24 January 1980). A number of themes were used to frame the story. These included:

(a)   Political story – political involvement of politicians
(b)   Security, MI5 involvement
(c)   Sexual abuse/abuse of power over children in care
(d)   Personal, sexual, scandal, homosexual story
(e)   Institutional failure, social work negligence and incompetence
(f)   Cover-up and conspiracy story
(g)   Victim story/human suffering
(h)   Northern Ireland story/divided society/paramilitary
(i)   Vice ring, prostitution, 'perversion' story
(j)   The perpetrators

Analysis reveals how these different themes were reported, how they occasionally fused together, but sometimes how they were ignored.

The front-page article in the *Irish Independent* (24 January 1980) which broke the story was headlined 'Sex Racket at Children's Home'. The first paragraph referred to a 'major scandal' erupting 'in the North last night' based on allegations of an official 'cover-up' over the recruiting of boys 'at a Belfast children's home for homosexual prostitution'. A politician, Gerry Fitt, announced his intention to raise the matter at Westminster and was reported to be 'shocked to the core'. 'If these allegations are true', he claimed, 'there has been some kind of Watergate cover-up and those responsible should be brought to book.' The article suggested that 'reports on certain cases were destroyed under orders from a senior member of the social services department'. It also stated that a member of staff was 'alleged to be involved with a loyalist paramilitary group' and that this was known to the social services but that 'he has retained his job – despite being accused of encouraging children to engage in homosexual acts for money and exacting money for pimping'. The article reported other allegations concerning the involvement of businessmen in the affair as well as allegations that one of the children had committed suicide and that another 'now living with an elderly homosexual' had 'attempted suicide'. It mentioned that two police stations held files on the allegations and that an investigation had been undertaken by the police and the file had been sent to the Director of Public Prosecutions. The article ended by quoting 'a reliable source' who claimed that 'the man suspected of having made large amounts of money by 'hiring out' teenage boys still held a senior position in the home.

This single article embraced a number of the diverse story 'elements' identified above: the sex scandal; the cover-up and the conspiracy; the vice ring; the homosexual and prostitution elements; the involvement of a politician. Only the headline 'Sex Racket at Children's Home' gave special weight to two of the concerns over the others, the sexual matters and the children in care aspect. The article reported so many elements that the reader risks overload. This 'overload' occurred with some of the *Irish Times* coverage from 1982 which presented the reader with a tangled web of intrigue, conspiracy, MI5, politicians and a 'mystery' witness called Mr X (who eventually revealed himself to be Roy Garland, a former associate of William McGrath).

The *Belfast Newsletter*, a Belfast-based daily newspaper with Unionist affiliations, also gave the story front-page coverage under the headline 'Cover Up in Sex Scandal Alleged' (*Belfast Newsletter*, 25 January 1980). The article contained allegations about the recruitment of boys for homosexual prostitution, Gerry Fitt's proposed questions at Westminster and the alleged involvement of important businessmen. There was no further coverage in the *Belfast Newsletter* over the next month.

The *Irish News*, a Belfast-based daily with Catholic or Nationalist leanings, carried a small piece on the front page entitled 'Children Used For Sex Probe', announcing the social services inquiry into 'allegations of homosexual recruitment at a boys' home in Belfast'

(*Irish News*, 25 January 1980). The *Belfast Telegraph*, a Belfast-based evening daily gave it no coverage, nor did the *Irish Times*, a Dublin-based daily broadsheet with an editorial office in Belfast.

This modest initial media interest is surprising given the substantial attention devoted to Kincora in 1982. The political potential for anti-Unionists makes the minimal coverage given by the *Irish News*, particularly unexpected. The *Irish Times* reported the connection between McGrath and Ian Paisley and other politicians in later coverage – perhaps prompting Paisley's press conference on 26 February 1982 – but initial coverage was minimal. The *Belfast Newsletter*'s coverage repeated much of the *Irish Independent* article but gave the story more front-page space than the *Irish News*. A journalist suggested 'The *Irish News* didn't play it because it was a squalid, sordid type of thing. . . . It's not the thing in Northern Ireland society that you bring up' (*Irish Times*, 1 February 1982). The lack of initial coverage perhaps reflects journalistic taboos on covering 'sexual' stories in the context of a society and culture which renders coverage of such matters unacceptable for certain newspapers. This taboo seemed initially to override every journalistic desire to exploit such a newsworthy story as Kincora.

KINCORA AND NEWS ANGLES

Increasingly press coverage grew and began to define some concerns as central, interesting and newsworthy while others were relegated to the status of background material. Many journalists identified the security aspect of the story as the central issue: 'whether British security services, either military intelligence or the civilian equivalents, had been aware . . . and had used that information to blackmail people who were in charge of Kincora.[4] But a different journalist described his interest in the story as: 'The persistent ill-treatment of boys which had become institutionalised. I spoke to the victims, it was sad and depressing – a shameful reflection on society.'[5]

This was an exceptional response and the journalist spoke of his own experience of abuse which perhaps influenced his attitude to the story.

The overriding concerns of journalists centred on the alleged political connections of the perpetrators, the security aspects and the cover-ups. A tabloid journalist claimed: 'It wouldn't have been a running story except for the fact that McGrath was a member of the Orange Order and had protestant paramilitary links, and that in the early days Paisley's name was thrown into the hat.'[6]

That political interest was primary for journalists is reflected in the press focus on the 'cover-up', with words like 'Kincoragate' appearing in one article.[7] The appearance of a mystery witness at one stage (Pollak 1982) gave the coverage an element of conspiracy and intrigue.

The reason underlying the press emphasis on the security rather than the sexual aspect is quite simple. The editor of a Sunday tabloid explained that 'the reason would be a purely commercial or professional one. Somebody else had broken that story – the shock, horror, young boys being abused in a boys' home. We were looking more underneath it at the political thing.'[8]

Sexual matters do not, in themselves, constitute a major story. The crucial factor is who is involved. A tabloid journalist explained. 'In our case we were interested in the British intelligence, the spy connection . . . the murky world of the secret service; did they allow this to continue for anything up to eight years? Was this allowed to go on simply so that they could get information? I think that caught the imagination as well.'[9]

A number of quite divergent news angles began to emerge. Kincora became a story involving 'important people', especially political people; a story of intrigue concerning spies and the British secret service and a story which revealed something that has been covered up. The focus on the cover-up quickly became a more prominent news angle than the events which had allegedly been covered up.

When the media constructed the Kincora story as a sexual matter, it typically ignored issues concerning the abuse of power over children or sexual abuse. The reporting of Kincora touched on an existing raw nerve – the issue of homosexuality. Northern Ireland had witnessed the 'Save Ulster From Sodomy' campaign involving a number of prominent Loyalist politicians. This campaign was aimed at preventing the decriminalization of homosexuality by amending the Offences Against the Persons Act. 'Homosexual' was the word used in press coverage when the nature of the sexual relationship between the staff and residents in Kincora was described. The terms in contemporary use, 'child sexual abuse' or the more technical terms 'pederasty' or 'paedophilia' do not appear. A journalist acknowledged with hindsight: 'We weren't talking about homosexuality necessarily, although that's the way it was presented – we were talking about pederasty, talking about physical and sexual abuse on minors.'[10] It is difficult to assess the extent to which the media mirrored the existing homophobia in Northern Ireland and the degree to which they fuelled it. But by failing to draw a distinction between homosexuality and pederasty, the public remained unclear about the difference between sexual preference and sexual abuse. Media coverage confirmed the erroneous view that homosexuals are necessarily sexually interested in young boys and that they are more likely to be abusive.

Journalists' attitudes varied markedly about covering the story from the victims' standpoint. A broadsheet journalist claimed:

> I just didn't have any stomach for delving into that sort of side. . . . To a certain extent we followed up the victims but . . . it would have struck me as a wee bit salacious to overconcentrate on what happened to these people. . . . The story for us was not so much the nitty gritty details of what happened to these boys . . . but why the authorities had done fuck all about it.[11]

The journalist's clearly stated interest here is in institutional failure. But some tabloids printed features on the victims of sexual abuse (see *Sunday World*, 20 December 1981). The story filled two pages and was headed 'My Story By Kincora House Victim'. A sub-title 'The Sex Scandal That Shocked Belfast – Now One of the Youths Speaks Out' described the 'sordid revelations in a Belfast court-room' and announced 'one of the witnesses gives evidence . . . tells how he was used as a sexual plaything by men who were supposed to be looking after him'.

This victim's account, unlike some others, contains little about physical violence but focuses on pornographic photography, car rides and sexual approaches made to him by Semple, Mains and McGrath. The explicit accounts of the brutality of attacks on the boys which one of the journalists 'had no stomach for' are not referred to, nor do they appear in the press coverage, although the paper did not shy away from other forms of brutality and printed a very clear photograph of a headless corpse in Latin America.

Overall, the coverage of Kincora was primarily focused on the security angle, and gave only a small indication of the suffering of the victims, with tabloid coverage giving the most detail and explaining their enthusiasm in market terms. When asked if child sexual abuse constituted a 'good story' in tabloid newspaper terms, a journalist said: 'We probably show more interest in these stories than some of our rival newspapers. It's a lurid subject but ours is a commercial newspaper. I don't necessarily like everything we do, but it sells newspapers and that's my job'.[12]

Interestingly, the Kincora story was covered by most journalists who worked on that paper, with the possible exception of the sports journalist. The story was not seen as any particular journalist's 'property', nor was any specialist knowledge judged to be necessary to write about it. In the larger Dublin-based newspapers, the coverage was provided by the journalists in their Northern office who also covered any other aspects of Northern Ireland affairs. In the British newspapers, again for the most part, it was their Northern Ireland correspondent who provided the coverage. Given that the average 'Northern Ireland story' is about Northern Ireland politics, security, paramilitaries, this may predispose journalists to look for these elements in any story they are researching. Furthermore, journalists covering the story would have no particular expertise in social services, children or sexual abuse, which again would affect the coverage.

A number of other technical and commercial factors seemed to influence the type of coverage which the story received. First competitiveness between journalists to get a new 'angle', an exclusive or a scoop which might become that journalist's or newspaper's property, was one such factor. On a story with the longevity of Kincora a division of labour seemed to develop with different papers covering different facets of the story which then became their fields of expertise. The editor of a Sunday tabloid newspaper, for example, explained, 'The story had been broken and we had to find a new angle on it . . . one which clicked with me immediately.'[13]

Second, the type of newspaper affected coverage, with the tabloids tending to cover the 'human interest' angles whilst the broadsheet newspapers covered the political and other 'hard' or 'serious' angles. Moreover, since it was more likely that social workers would read broadsheets while their clients read tabloids, the selection of information and the 'story angle' each read would tend to be different. Broadsheets gave detailed information on the cover-up, the military and political connections, almost to the point of overload, but the tabloids contained less information and were more likely to focus on other aspects of the story, especially the human interest aspects.

Third, the frequency of publication of a newspaper, whether weekly or daily, influenced the type of coverage. A journalist working on a daily paper at the time he wrote about Kincora commented, 'There was more room and more days to cram the stuff in. It would have been very difficult to cram all that stuff in on a Sunday newspaper.'[14]

Finally, media silence at certain points in the coverage was also very significant. One journalist explained why the *Belfast Telegraph* gave no initial coverage to the story in January/February 1980. He recounts how a letter written by, or on behalf of, a social worker alleging sexual abuse in a children's home arrived in the *Belfast Telegraph* office. According to him it 'disappeared' into the editor's office and wasn't heard of again. Two months later the Kincora scandal broke in the *Irish Independent*. Some time later, a victim of sexual abuse telephoned the *Telegraph*, angry at the light sentences passed on the perpetrators and anxious for his side of the story to be known. The editors in the *Belfast Telegraph* were not interested in printing it. The journalist wrote the story and sold it to another newspaper for £50 which he gave to the victim. The journalist said he sold the material because there was no other outlet for it. The *Belfast Telegraph* considered itself

> a family newspaper and it was not a family story. It was a dirty, nasty story involving homosexuality, buggery. . . . If you paid a lot of money for an advertisement in the paper and it appeared opposite a story like that, it would be very upsetting for advertisers. . . .[15]

The same journalist was reprimanded by the *Belfast Telegraph* for writing a story which was printed when editorial control was slack over a weekend. The story was an account of a young woman who died as a result of a backstreet abortion. His conclusion was that his newspaper considers such issues best left unreported.

The journalist who ran the story as a security/conspiracy/political story stated that editorially he experienced no censorship. When journalists were asked about censorship, with the exception of the last journalist cited, the factor they mentioned most was legal constraints in the form of libel laws. This accounts for the lack of coverage during the period immediately after the story broke in January 1980. During this time a police investigation was on-going and the three Kincora staff were charged and awaiting trial, so the matter was *sub judice*. Two of the three, Mains and Semple, pleaded guilty; McGrath refused to plead guilty and it appeared that all the evidence against him would have to be heard in court. McGrath pleaded guilty at the last minute. Press coverage began again after the trial was over, but since the full evidence against McGrath was not heard in court due to his last-minute change in plea, the trial itself did not receive coverage. In the process of researching and writing stories, legal restrictions clearly shaped the coverage. A journalist on a Dublin-based paper said, 'The major constraints were legal constraints. They are always scared about libel. The whole Paisley involvement. . . . We had written it up. . . . The *Irish Times* took one look at it and shit a brick.'[16]

It is noteworthy that the *Irish Independent* and the *Irish Times* are both based outside Northern Ireland, in Dublin. In the words of one of their journalists, 'I doubt very much if it (the newspaper) would have been so enthusiastic to cover this story (Kincora) if it involved Fine Fail politicians covering up, or allegations of them covering up a scandal in Dublin.'[17] Journalists expressed doubt that the story ever would have emerged had it not been for Dublin-based newspaper coverage.

HOW THE SOCIAL WORKERS SAW KINCORA

Predictably social workers saw the Kincora affair rather differently. One social worker claimed that 'the most profound tragedy of the whole thing was the exploitation of the kids in care. . . . I don't think the media were as interested in that as they were in intrigue and political cover-ups.'[18]

This judgement was confirmed by a second social worker who saw Kincora,

> strictly in terms of child abuse . . . and it was more horrific that the boys who were placed in care because their home circumstances were not suitable . . . were subsequently abused in care and abused so horrifically as well. It was such an abuse of power. I know there's some kind of political element . . . but the details I don't know.[19]

Such assessment stood in sharp contrast to media concerns. The primary focus for social workers was on the child care and child abuse aspects of the case, rather than on political matters. One social worker expressed concern about

> the length of time it took to come to light, that it could have gone on for as long as it did, that the supervision of the home and the people who ran the home was so poor, and that the hold they had over the boys was so great.[20]

When asked about other aspects of the case, for example the allegations of cover-up, a social worker claimed,

> That's a different agenda entirely which I know nothing about. I'm speaking very much from a social work point of view. I

would say as a citizen that if there were all sorts of shady connections . . . I would have a reaction . . . how any reasonably decent citizen would react, but that's way out of the context of social work.[21]

Social workers seemed to separate social work concerns from those of the wider society. To detach the child care issues of Kincora from the rest of the material allows Kincora to be seen purely in 'safer' social work terms. One social worker seemed to acknowledge as much:

I have no direct experience for this but in knowing the society we live in and the sinister influences which can be brought to bear on people, it wouldn't surprise me at all . . . if those who were called to give evidence to the Kincora inquiry, not just the social workers, but the managers from the personal social services, had a wee visit and were told 'you speak up and you take the consequences'.[22]

There is an awareness of the wider sinister and dangerous world, and as in other fields in Northern Ireland, social workers may have their suspicions, may be aware of the sinister aspects, but narrow their focus to exclude those dangerous and frightening aspects, in the interests of survival. There is little or no open discussion within social work of such matters, and to open such discussions is seen to be problematic. The method of coping is to restrict social work interests to a narrow band of social work concerns leaving the 'political' side to others.

PRESS COVERAGE OF SOCIAL WORKERS

The initial press coverage of Kincora barely mentions social workers and when it does it is in terms of the Belfast welfare authority and its failure to respond to complaints of abuse. There is little evidence in press coverage of an anti-social work bias, any naming of social workers, or the allocation of blame to individual social workers. That the information for the original story came from two social workers (DHSS (NI) 1986) may have coloured the perceptions of the press. One journalist said:

I don't think that social workers were hard done by the press. I think it was the very fact that the story was exposed that caused problems, not just for social workers but for some politicians and for some people in the health authority who must have known what was going on. But at a much more senior level.[23]

The revelations of abuse and the allegations of cover-ups discomforted the social work world, but the unease was felt more acutely at management rather than the field social work level. It was only during the coverage of the Hughes inquiry that the performance of social workers was scrutinized directly by the press. The reaction in the Northern Ireland social work world was tense and anxious but overall social workers felt that

the inquiry was justified. I would be up-tight about inquiries if I felt they were looking for scapegoats but the inquiry was necessary and right to be called. . . . It is inexcusable that it (the sexual abuse) went on under the Eastern board and before that under the Belfast welfare authority and didn't come to light. . . . I found the inquiry embarrassing in that I'd buy the *Belfast Telegraph* and every night I'd think, 'Oh god, who said what today?' But I felt it was right to hold it. I was just sorry that the performance by my colleagues was so abysmal in the main. . . . Some of my colleagues . . . went along to hear it . . . [and we] talked about [it] in terms of 'if you should ever find yourself in this position appearing before an inquiry justifying what you've done or not done'. So that it was frightening to think that your work could be under that kind of scrutiny.[24]

Unlike press coverage of scandals involving social workers in Britain, the press coverage of the Hughes inquiry was restrained and stuck mainly to factual reporting. There was little or no scapegoating by the press, perhaps because in the years leading up to 1985 the press had clearly established Willie McGrath as the scapegoat. It is interesting to note that few of the commercial newspapers made the connection between social work and the perpetrators or referred to McGrath, Semple or Mains as social workers, residential social workers or house fathers. The latter terms were used in inverted commas in a number of newspaper articles, with an implication of sarcasm. The photograph of McGrath, which is repeatedly used in all the papers, portrays him, head erect, wearing an orange sash, suggesting again that his political identity is a more important factor in Kincora than his abuse of a caring role. The primary focus on the political aspects of the story by the media may have acted to displace coverage of the social services and social work aspects of the story, which were seen as less important, less newsworthy.

Northern Ireland and indeed the Republic of Ireland, moreover, are societies in which welfare ideology is not long-standing and its welfare benefits, state housing and other welfare reforms were introduced by a reluctant Stormont Unionist government. The expectation that the prevention of child abuse is the total responsibility of social workers is perhaps not as prevalent as in Britain. This may explain why when child sexual abuse has occurred, as in Kincora, it has not led to the same scapegoating of social workers evident in the British press.

IMPACT AND AFTERMATH

The power of the media is illustrated in a variety of ways. Press reporting and television coverage was a factor in the McGonagle inquiry which had to stand down after only one day because of on-going police investigations into 'press reports . . . that a homosexual vice ring . . . involving Northern Ireland Office officials, policemen, legal figures, businessmen and boys in care at Kincora had been "covered up" by the authorities in Northern Ireland' (DHSS (NI) 1986, para 1.4). Perhaps the most potent illustration of the power of the media was the role of the press in the disclosure of the abuse in the first instance.

In the aftermath of Kincora there was a discernible growth in homophobia which must in part reflect media unwillingness to distinguish between child sexual abuse and homosexuality. According to the Northern Ireland Gay Rights Association, at least one homosexual lost employment during the early period of disclosure.[25] A social worker described the atmosphere at that period in social services:

> It was quite unbelievable. People working in residential care were scared to touch a child. They were scared to give a child a cuddle. When they went into children's bedrooms they were frozen. All sorts of completely over-the-top rules and regulations were made by agencies to protect themselves and apparently to protect the staff and the children.[26]

Another social worker stated:

> There was a kind of backlash reaction to Kincora in terms of 'we have to weed out these perverts', and it was as blatant as that . . . anyone who deviated from the sexual norm of heterosexuality was suspect and was weeded out. . . . I think there

would be grave suspicions around homosexuals looking after children.[27]

The extent to which this bigotry can be attributed to the lack of clarity in the press coverage about the differences between pederasty and homosexuality is unclear, but it must surely have been a contributory factor.

SUMMARY

The relationship between the press and social work in Northern Ireland as illustrated by Kincora is complex. The concerns which journalists and social workers bring to the Kincora affair are different. This is at least in part because social workers tend to narrow their range of concerns to filter out the 'dangerous' political aspects of the case. It is also because of the similar limitation on the interests of journalists obsessed with 'Northern Ireland' stories and their perceptions of the newsworthiness of the sexual abuse aspects of the case, which in turn partly reflect the moral postures of the newspapers on which they work. Editorial policy is clearly also important with certain newspapers being unwilling to print stories, either for commercial reasons or because of their judgement about what is 'decent' or in 'good taste' or 'suitable for families'.

The media enjoyed a virtual monopoly of information about Kincora. Since social work agencies appear not to have briefed their staff about Kincora, most social workers received their information from the media. Consequently the media not only shaped and informed public opinion but also formed social work opinion about Kincora. Social workers used media to break the story but subsequently the media reported Kincora in ways which extended beyond the remit of concerns which social workers in Northern Ireland identified as relevant. The coverage of social workers in Kincora was moderate by comparison to reporting of social work involvement in cases elsewhere; interestingly, social work managers were judged more responsible than social work staff. The question which remains, however, is whether this milder treatment of social workers was due to the press perception that social workers' involvement in Kincora was peripheral or simply not as interesting as the 'political' concern which, according to several journalists, was the key ingredient in making Kincora 'a good story'.

NOTES

1 For a more descriptive account of the Kincora affair see Smyth 1988.
2 Interview with social worker 2, Belfast, September 1989.
3 Mason 1989, points out that under the new Official Secrets Act the Kincora scandal may never have come to light.
4 Journalist 1, interview September 1989.
5 Journalist 2, interview September 1989.
6 Journalist 3, interview September 1989.
7 See, for example, *Sunday World* and *Daily Telegraph* 28 January 1982, the *Guardian* 17 December 1981, 27 January 1982.
8 Journalist 1, interview September 1989.
9 Journalist 1, ibid.
10 Journalist 2, interview September 1989.
11 Journalist 2, ibid.
12 Journalist 1, interview September 1989.
13 Journalist 1, ibid.
14 Journalist 2, interview September 1989.
15 Journalist 3, interview September 1989.
16 Journalist 2, interview September 1989.
17 Journalist 2, ibid.
18 Social Worker 2, interview September 1989.
19 Social Worker 1, interview September 1989.
20 Social Worker 1, ibid.
21 Social Worker 2, ibid.
22 Social Worker 2, ibid.
23 Social Worker 1, interview September 1989.
24 Social Worker 1, ibid.
25 Interview with Geoff Dudgeon, Northern Ireland Gay Rights Association, 1988.
26 Interview with Social Worker 2.
27 Social Worker 1, ibid.

Part IV

Remedies and strategies: improving the public image

10 Promoting positive images of people with learning difficulties: problems and strategies

Steve Dowson

A recent public information leaflet announcing a health authority's plans for community care offered the following description of people with learning difficulties:

> They are mostly simple and gentle people, like children in many ways even when they are adults.
>
> (Warrington Health Authority 1987)

A leaflet which ostensibly aims to inform thus turns out to be peddling stereotypical images. The author of the leaflet, if not revealing mere thoughtlessness or ignorance, must have judged that the path to community acceptance lay in persuading readers to trade in their old, unsettling prejudices for these more comfy new ones. Instead of being introduced to some of the variety and complexity which would challenge casual stereotyping, we are offered the image of a race of people who might well be inhabitants of Middle Earth or Wimbledon Common.

This trade in stereotypes, which characterizes so much public debate about the place of people with learning difficulties in our (and their) society, has a large stock to draw upon. For as long as they have been identified as a group, people with learning difficulties have been invested with characteristics justified by a variety of once-fashionable religious and scientific theories. The theories have been largely forgotten,[1] but the fears and fantasies which they expressed still live on in an assortment of stereotypes. The high degree of contradiction between these stereotypes itself attests that they have little basis in fact.

At one end of the spectrum, the 'eternal child' image of the health authority leaflet is elevated to the stereotype of the 'holy innocent' or 'little angel without wings' – a gift from God. Less positively – though hardly more a burden on those who have to act the part – is the image of poor unfortunates, victims of their handicaps, incapable of achieving anything or of speaking for themselves, and reliant on others for charity. By elaboration, they can then be regarded as *sick* and in need of care by nurses in hospitals.

Moving further into negative imagery, we pass from pity into guilt. Humanity has never been satisfied with sheer bad luck as an explanation for the unequal distribution of events which are categorized as misfortune. The traditional Christian explanation for a disabled child has been that it is a punishment for the sins of the parents. Even in our more secular society, parental wrongdoing survives in the folklore of causation, though now the emphasis may be shifting to bad parenting before or after birth: the mother smoked during pregnancy, the father dropped the baby on its head. Further advances in medicine are unlikely to remove this tendency to pass blame: not so far into the future, a disabled child will be taken as proof of a mother's failure to submit to pre-natal screening, or of her obstinate refusal to have an abortion.

In stark contrast to the image of the 'holy innocent', people with learning difficulties are sometimes supposed to have abnormal sexual appetites and reduced moral awareness. Prior to the introduction of the 1959 Mental Health Act, the categories into which 'the mentally defective' were legally divided included 'moral defectives' alongside 'the feebleminded' and 'imbeciles'. There was a fear, dressed up as a theory by the eugenics movement in the early part of this century, that such people would breed faster and so pollute the 'good blood' of the population as a whole. It was this fear that formed part of the explicit justification for institutional confinement. Though involuntary sterilization has never been approved by English statute, it received much official support and many such operations were carried out (Ryan and Thomas 1980:109). Even now, some elderly women living in mental handicap hospitals will tell how they were admitted years ago because they had an illegitimate child. Though the law is no longer so explicitly oppressive, society's attitude towards the sexuality of people with learning difficulties, and its willingness to allow them the opportunity of parenthood, still reflect these prejudices. Much more immediate fears are evident in the views commonly expressed by the public contemplating the opening of a community home for people with learning difficulties, who are seen as amoral animals. Suddenly the women and children are in danger of sexual molestation, properties at risk of theft and housebreaking. Sadly, supposedly informed authorities sometimes support these views. In 1983 a letter from a community representative to local people, seeking support for opposition to a proposed community home in the north of England, quoted the 1978 edition of *Forensic Medicine for Lawyers*, by J. K. Mason, which included the following statements:

> even those [the mentally subnormal] who can read – and many cannot do these basic essentials – have a very limited comprehension of what society expects of them, of fundamental concepts of right and wrong. . . . Baulked of normal sexual outlet they [male defectives] turn to children. If the children resent or resist their advances they panic and kill them. In any circumstances a defective may kill because of frustration or a lack of appreciation of what he is doing, particularly when alcohol, to which he is unduly susceptible, is involved.

It is important to recognize that the strength and variety of these stereotypes do not merely indicate confusion in the public mind. They are the products of a process by which a social group is defined and given meaning. Like other groups which are perceived to be different in some way, people with learning difficulties become a screen onto which public fears and uncertainties – the shadows of the collective unconscious – are projected. Once perceived as a group, rather than as individuals, the process is self-sustaining. Behaviour by members of the group is emphasized if it fits the prejudice, explained away if it does not. The mental age of the offender is only likely to be mentioned when it is below normal, so leaving the impression that there is a correlation between intelligence and crime. As the self-advocacy movement has developed over the last decade, challenging the stereotype that people with learning difficulties cannot speak for themselves, conference audiences have had the novel experience of hearing speeches, often cogent as well as forceful, from people with learning difficulties. A frequent reaction on such occasions has been to insist that the speaker 'wasn't really handicapped'.

In three ways, people with learning difficulties have been especially at the mercy of this process. First, the system of health, education and social services has contrived to ensure that the population has little direct contact with people with learning difficulties. The great majority of children with special needs (an educational term which includes other disabilities) still go to segregated schools. Most people with severe learning disabilities move straight from school into segregated day centres, and are likely to find their leisure-time social activities in segregated clubs. About 20 per cent of this group, approximately 30,000 people in England (DHSS 1989), are still living in mental handicap hospitals, mostly in remote rural locations. Consequently, popular prejudice is rarely challenged by direct experience. But at the same time, and this leads to my second point, this system also functions to reinforce prejudice. Common sense would suggest that these people must surely be poor unfortunates if they need to be protected in this way. Or perhaps, if they have to be kept in closed institutions, they do indeed pose some sort of threat.

Third, the perpetuation of stereotypes is also in the interests of the service industry. Progressive services based on the principle of normalization (O'Brien and Tyne 1981) aim to enable disadvantaged people to achieve socially valued lifestyles, rather than surrounding them with devaluing images which create additional handicaps. However, the supposed need of people with learning difficulties for specialized services has provided the *raison d'être* for several professional groups. It is easier for staff to wield power if they can believe that people they 'serve' cannot make choices for themselves. There is also a special kind of satisfaction in being perceived as a dedicated worker caring for poor unfortunates. Madden and Maund (1987) nicely illustrate this last point with an account of a worker who took a group of people with learning difficulties to a village bonfire. While with the group, the worker was able to exude caring feelings because he was obviously 'doing a good job'. However, he was left for a while looking after only one woman, and someone asked whether she was his daughter:

> He vociferously denied this in a way that was out of all proportion to the question and showed up just how hypocritical his position really was – that he did not really value either the woman or any of the others he was responsible for with any real dignity.
>
> (Madden and Maund 1987:18–19)

In this way, the images which professional groups and service agencies wish to cultivate for themselves feed parasitically from the negative images attached to the people they support. As discussed below, this frequently shows in media representations which depend on professionals for the supply of information.

The route to community acceptance must lead through to the stage where there is sufficient everyday, individual contact between people with learning difficulties and 'ordinary' people in the community; at school, at work, down the road, and in the pub. Then

- and probably not before - stereotypes will simply be unsustainable. Each person will be recognized as an individual; as someone with feelings, preferences (even if not expressed in words), and rights. It will be discovered that each person has likeable and irritating qualities, in varying degrees and in unique ways, just like everyone else. At least some social contact will be taking place just because both sides like it, partly replacing both paid services and the artifice of the visiting volunteer. By this stage, the average community resident would be hard-pressed to give any working definition of mental handicap: 'People who need some extra help', perhaps, but even that would include many others in the average neighbourhood.

This vision may sound like an integrationist's nirvana, but it can and does happen. Robert Perske is one American author whose true stories of acceptance and friendships inspire more hope for the capacities of the community than any amount of statistics. He tells, for example (Perske and Perske 1988:45–7), of 14-year-old Katherine, who had been diagnosed as having a profound retardation and lived in a world of her own, twiddling objects in front of her eyes, until she enrolled in mainstream school. At first she was supported by the school's integration facilitator, but gradually other students took over without being asked. As well as sharing their activities and teenage dress styles with Katherine, the students carry out a schedule of support and guidance throughout the day. Her mother reported:

> For the first time we and Katherine have a sense of belonging. She has a real school to belong to. She even went to a regular dance without her parents. She's not a *case* any more. Now she's a person who is a student, who has friends, and she goes to different classes like a real teenager.
>
> (Perske and Perske 1988:45–7)

The tale illustrates that the first stage to community acceptance is to enable people with learning difficulties to be physically present in the community, in contact with other people. They have a right to be there, and do not need to be invited. Community acceptance must never be regarded as the precondition for community presence. However, there is a stage between the transition to community-based services and the formation of everyday individualized social contact. Until recently, service providers largely ignored this middle stage, preferring to regard community education only as important when public hostility threatened a proposed community project.

Even when the community home has been opened, and hostility has faded into silence, the new residents may still find themselves ignored by the neighbours and taunted by the local children. It is here that use of the media can promote a social climate in which positive, individual social contact can flourish.

TOWARDS A COMMUNITY EDUCATION STRATEGY

The typical social services department or health authority would probably say that it was not undertaking a programme of educational activities to promote public acceptance of people with learning difficulties. In reality, statutory agencies are almost inevitably drawn into a miscellany of activities with the potential to have a significant effect on community attitudes. The failure to recognize the connections between these activities, and to bring them together within an overall strategy, is as much a problem as the overall level of investment in public education.

In the absence of a strategy, the activities are likely to have been initiated externally as responses to friendly interest or sudden hostility. Many authorities have produced information leaflets aimed at parents, workers, the neighbours or – vaguely and confusingly – at all three simultaneously. A few have produced videos. Managers give talks to the Round Table or Women's Institute, social workers get called in to give talks at local schools. Some Community Mental Handicap Teams produce a newsletter, and staff working in community residential services are often left to work out how to make contact with the neighbours. Newspapers run cheerful stories about charity fundraising and Christmas outings, as well as providing a vehicle for prejudice when there is an outcry against the opening of some new community service.

The changing of attitudes, at least in a free society, can never be a science, and the evaluation of the effectiveness of any method is bound to be problematic. In the commercial sector, a marketing strategy can at least be judged by the subsequent trend in sales. There is no equivalent measure for public education about disability. Attitudes can be tested before and after exposure to an educational experience, and again after a period of months. Even by that time, other influences may have been at work for better or worse, and there is no reliable way of knowing whether improved attitudes will be maintained against the infamous nimby ('Not In My Back Yard') factor. Consequently, the research[2] – much of it carried out in the United States – remains equivocal, and is more helpful in indicating the factors which should be incorporated in any educational approach, rather than clearly favouring any educational model. It is clear that any strategy will be more effective when it is planned with care and implemented with skill and consistency. No competent commercial manager would give backing to a marketing exercise which had not identified the target audience or the central message to be conveyed, and which instead left an untrained sales force to say and print whatever they felt appropriate at the time. Yet this is the state of play in most statutory services for people with learning difficulties. If private and voluntary service agencies are more organized, it is generally only because they have a keen financial interest in maintaining their own image and this, as noted earlier, may not serve the interests of the people they are in business to support.

Even though it is not possible to offer a method of public education which is bound to be a success, agencies can be encouraged to think more clearly about the task, and to select the options which seem appropriate to the particular circumstances. First, they should consider the *time-range* they are aiming for. Are they investing 'for the next generation', or because they know that the planned closure of the mental handicap hospital will, in two years' time, create an influx of people with learning difficulties? Or are they simply trying to get the home opened next week in spite of the petition now circulating round the neighbours?

The second consideration is the choice of *target audience*, which will in turn affect the *message* and the *medium*. For example, staff in a mental handicap hospital which is to be closed will need to have information about the new services, including not only an assurance that they will continue to be employed, but also that their work in the hospital has been valued. However, a public information leaflet explaining the same closure will be confusing if it praises the hospital system while also announcing its termination. Furthermore, leaflets and the mass media are obviously not ways to convey a message specifically and solely to one narrow target group; better, perhaps, to arrange personal contact with the group or its representatives.

Finally, there are choices in the *style* in which the message is delivered. It may be coolly informative or passionately evangelistic; arouse concern or celebrate the positives. If the medium allows, the audience may be invited to be actively involved. Or the message may be subtly incorporated in other activities so that the audience is not even aware it is being educated.

When these sets of choices are brought together they offer a multidimensional matrix of options. Certainly, not every cell in the matrix is a practical option: interactive leaflets, for instance, strain the imagination! Nevertheless there are a great many choices, and the service agency which contemplated them systematically would probably move beyond the ubiquitous twice-folded A4 leaflet. Nor is it suggested that every feasible option is equally effective or indeed ethical. But if those who designed educational initiatives knew precisely whom they were trying to reach, and what they wanted to say to them, they would be far less likely to make the blunders which are now so commonplace.

One common mistake is to include some feature in the design of the educational event or materials which implicitly contradicts the intended message. There are newsletters which try hard to present people with learning difficulties as adults, but have excess pages filled with childish drawings. Similarly, in a desperate attempt to make pamphlets look attractive, some (usually amateur) graphic artists resort to comic book animal cartoons. The same error can be observed in the workshop where it is asserted that people with learning difficulties have opinions and can speak for themselves, but the organizers have failed to invite anyone with learning difficulties to attend and contribute those opinions.

At a time when local authorities are being urged, indeed coerced, into being enablers rather than providers of services, they might do well to commission independent groups to undertake community education projects. This will reduce the likelihood that the projects will serve the local authority rather than people with learning difficulties. More importantly, it is also more likely to allow disabled people to have some ownership of a task which is ultimately their own struggle. On the other hand, it needs to be recognized that disabled people do not have any inherent expertise in community education, any more than graphic designers or public relations officers necessarily have enlightened views about disability.

Direct contact with people with disabilities can be a powerful educational experience, but it is not necessarily so. Research indicates (Donaldson 1980:504–14) that it is important for the meeting to take place on the basis of equal status. Institutional open days certainly do not provide this condition. Meet a person for the first time in the thirty-bed villa where they live, and one's perception of the individual will almost certainly be shaped by their abnormal and deprived circumstances. Get to know that person first, however, as an individual, identify with them as a human being, and then see where they live: the impact may be devastating. Open days and guided tours confuse pride in the service with the promotion of positive images of people with learning difficulties. Agency pride can also surface in the announcement of bold, innovative new community services. The implicit message is that the agency is undertaking an experiment in social engineering – a message which is unlikely to go down well with either the community or the families of the people being resettled.

One further error is inappropriate diffidence. There are occasions when it is both right and suitably diplomatic to invite a debate on the merits of integrated education, employment, or community living. But asking for the opportunity to make the case in favour implies that there is also a legitimate counter-argument. Sometimes service providers would do better to undercut the intellectual arguments and instead appeal to the emotions (surely the successful marketing strategy of the 1980s), or otherwise engage in whatever machiavellian tactics might be required in order to uphold the rights of people with learning difficulties.

THE ROLE OF THE PRESS

The matrix outlined above makes it clear that the mass media, and the press in particular, represent only part of the range of options which may be used to promote positive images of people with learning difficulties. Nevertheless, they are important because they are ready-made channels which, with or without the intervention of the service agencies, are constantly influencing public attitudes. Their obvious disadvantage, from the point of view of the community educator, is that they may not share the same concern to offer images which challenge negative stereotypes.

In 1987, CMH – the national campaign for people with learning difficulties, now re-named as Values Into Action (VIA) – commissioned a press-cuttings service to collect, over a six-week period, every item in national, regional and local newspapers (including freesheets) which included the words 'mental handicap' or 'mentally handicapped'. By sheer chance two major news stories about people with learning difficulties arose during this period; the court case to determine whether the woman 'Jeanette' should be sterilized without her consent; and the cousins of the Queen who were living in a mental handicap hospital. As shown in Table 10.1, a total of 1,489 cuttings were collected. Of these, 513 concerned the sterilization issue, and 160 the Royal Family story, leaving 816 which might be regarded as the usual 'background level' of newspaper references to people with learning difficulties. The categories into which the cuttings fell are shown in Table 10.2.

Table 10.1 Types of press cutting during six-week survey period, 1987

	General		Royal Family		Sterilization	
		%		%		%
News stories	708	(86.8)	130	(81.1)	381	(74.3)
Features	33	(4.0)	9	(5.7)	14	(2.7)
Comment columns	8	(1.0)	6	(3.8)	35	(6.8)
Letters	63	(7.7)	12	(7.5)	65	(12.7)
Leaders	4	(0.5)	3	(1.9)	18	(3.5)
Totals	816	(100)	160	(100)	513	(100)

Source: Wertheimer 1988

Table 10.2 Topics covered in news stories (excluding sterilization and Royal Family stories)

		%
Services to people with learning difficulties	296	(37.6)
Fundraising	232	(29.4)
Individual people with learning difficulties	91	(11.5)
Other charitable activities	81	(10.3)
Care in the community (general)	36	(4.6)
Local groups/clubs for people with learning difficulties	15	(1.9)
Parliamentary/legislative issues	7	(0.9)
Personal benefits/income	5	(0.6)
Miscellaneous	25	(3.1)

Source: Wertheimer 1988

Note: The total exceeds the number of new story cuttings as some items covered more than one topic.

Analysis of the content of the cuttings (Wertheimer 1988) confirmed that, in spite of some positive images, the overall representation of people with learning difficulties served to support the familiar negative stereotypes. Fundraising and other aspects of charitable work provide good material for local newspapers, often with the opportunity for a photograph of a famous politician or 'star'; but these stories do not help people with learning difficulties. Like stories about services, they reinforce images of dependency and passivity.

Two-thirds of all news stories (excluding the sterilization and Royal Family stories) fell into these categories. Such strong images could not be compensated for by the relatively small number of stories about individuals, even if they had all been positive. In fact, of the ninety-one stories concerning individuals, only twenty-four described achievements. The most striking finding of the survey must be that nowhere amongst the 1,489 cuttings was there a single instance of a direct report of an opinion expressed by a person with learning difficulties.

Community care also fared badly in the cuttings. Of the news stories which covered the topic of community care, only 22 per cent were wholeheartedly in support, while half painted a wholly negative picture, dwelling entirely on 'failure stories'. Two lead articles discussed community care, but they confined themselves to setting out the arguments, and neither of them expressed any great support for people's right to live in the community. About 14 per cent of the news stories about services concerned neighbourhood protests against proposed service provision. Furthermore, the letters columns provided people hostile to proposed community services with an excellent opportunity to display their prejudices. If the writers of these letters are to be believed (which they should not be), people with learning difficulties are noisy, dangerous to children, create parking problems and run into the middle of the road; and, of course, lower property prices.

The broad statistical findings of the survey are exemplified by the kind of language which was used repeatedly. People were described as 'poor souls', 'the more unfortunate of God's creatures', and 'a race apart'. As suggested earlier, service workers tend to get a better press, at the expense of the people for whom they care. A manager of an Adult Training Centre – the predominant model of day service for people with learning difficulties – who was also a bowls champion was described as 'the winner who looks after life's losers'. The sterilization story invoked other, yet more negative stereotypes of people with excessive urges and inadequate morals; images which rested uneasily alongside the stereotype of the eternal child. Jeanette was portrayed simultaneously as a sexually aware, fertile woman and yet also as a 'girl who will always remain a child', in need of protection from the sexual advances of the rest of the world. One newspaper tried to make sense of it all by suggesting that 'mentally deficient children are affectionate and outgoing, with the kind of warm instinctive sexual responses of puppies'.

Newspapers reflect other people's prejudices by making use of quotations and letters to the editor. Therefore the press cannot be blamed entirely for the negative imagery revealed by the CMH survey. In any case it would be foolish to suppose that journalists – who also suffer from some negative stereotyping – are somehow free of the prejudice and ignorance which effects most of the population. The constructive conclusion is that those who undertake community education should add journalists to their list of key target groups.

In fact, the National Union of Journalists has a voluntary Code of Conduct which deals with the reporting of people with disabilities. It states that a journalist shall not originate or process material which encourages discrimination on grounds of race, colour, creed, illegitimacy, disability, marital status (or lack of it), gender or sexual orientation. In the light of the practices of some sections of the press, such highflown principles do seem incongruous. But those of us who work with and for people with learning difficulties should contain our hollow laughter. The NUJ code recognizes that disability should stand alongside other targets of discrimination, and in doing so offers us a challenge. If the kinds of depths of prejudice discussed in this chapter were being openly applied, not to people with learning difficulties but to members of an ethnic group, most of us would be outraged. Do we – genuinely – feel the same outrage when it is 'only' people with learning difficulties who suffer? If we do not, then before we set about the education of the community we might do well to attend to our own attitudes.

NOTES

1 For a full account of the historical development of stereotypes, see Ryan and Thomas, 1980, ch. 5.
2 See, for example, Donaldson, 1980, pp. 504–14; Sandler and Robinson, 1981, pp. 97–103; Snart and Maguire, 1987; and for a general review of the research, McConkey and McCormack, 1983, ch. 3.

11 Growing old in the eyes of the media

Tim Dant and Malcolm Johnson

INTRODUCTION

In the Sixties there was a theory which suggested that as people got older they 'disengaged' from society. The evidence was slim but comforting because it suggested that it began 'during the sixth decade with a shift in self-perception which may reflect both a withdrawal of object cathexis and a beginning of anticipatory socialization to the aged state' (Cumming *et al*. 1960). In other words it was natural and therefore society could not be blamed. The theory was based on data from a study of 211 people in Kansas which seemed to show that people's perception of constriction in their 'life space' of interactions with others preceded their experience of such constriction. Of course this theory is not yet dead even though it has grown older. The belief that it is 'natural' for people to 'disengage' as they get older can excuse the way we think of older people and reject them as equal and active members of our society.

This belief often seems to underlie much of the media's treatment of ageing; old people are seen as a special category with certain features (poor, poor health, handicapped, dependent, helpless). Because people are old, as evidenced by these features, they should withdraw gracefully from activities thought of as the prerogative of the young:

> Old enough to be her father at 52 (indeed his 28-year-old son Stephen was best man) Bill had made a special effort for his wedding, with freshly hennaed hair and blue suede shoes. . . .
> Bill had obliged the world's media with privileged invitations. Watching on television the procession of ageing rock stars strutting up to pat him on the back, I turned to my companions with

a derisive comment on the horrific appearance of all these haggard old men, grinning away for the cameras like gargoyles . . .

This is not from an article in a teenager's magazine or even a snide account of the media occasion of Rolling Stone Bill Wyman's marriage but a feature article in the *Guardian* (8 June 1989), one of the heavy, thoughtful newspapers. The article appeared under a small headline 'Knowing When to Call it a Day' with the banner headline of AGE OLD PROBLEM. The writer of the article, Jane Ellison, has a very young view of old age: 'To the post Sixties people they are merely a collection of raddled old men, prancing about in pathetic imitations of their former selves.' Her notion of growing old is clearly that people should 'disengage'; if not from life, then from ideals and fantasies, from activities that are clearly the prerogative of youth:

> few of the Sixties people actually felt like calling it a day when they reached that fateful fourth decade. Unfairly, life did not arrange for them to vanish softly and suddenly away. . . . The sight of the Stones refusing to go out quietly, is their inspiration.
>
> *Guardian*, 8 June 1989

Such an image of growing older as being an unhappy alternative to 'vanishing softly and fading away' is a vision of the young who do not look forward to the prospect. Those of us who have progressed further through the process may wish to think of it more optimistically and tend to feel some sympathy for the rock stars who 'refuse to go out quietly' at the relatively early age of 50.

Ageism in the media is seldom so stark and is not usually directed at such a young age group. More common are stereotypical views of what being old means. We do not wish to argue that newspapers, the television or other forms of mass media determine how we think about old people (or any other group). But the media do provide a stock of images that we all utilize in our everyday perceptions, even if we do not believe they are 'true'. Social workers (along with doctors, nurses, housing officials, social security staff and many others) act as agents for our society, dealing with old people amongst others who have problems. How they perceive and relate to old people is important not only in terms of their professional conduct but also in representing how we as a society see older people. Inevitably, social workers deal with a particular group of old people – those who need some form of help or support – and they are not typical of older people in general. They are, however, often the group of elderly people who are treated by the media as standing for old age. The older clients on the social workers' caseload might well seem to confirm the stereotypical view of old age.

In this chapter we will look at some of the images of ageing to be found in the media and discuss them in the context of some academic research on attitudes and communications. In drawing attention to the undoubted ageism in media representations of people in later life, we have overstated the position to create impact – as the media do themselves. In fact there are positive images, reports and representations to be found in broadcasts and the printed word, but they are overwhelmed by the negative. Unfortunately there is an almost complete absence of reliable empirical research on this subject in Britain, so what follows is more impressionistic and less rigorous than we would wish it to be. Our claims, therefore should be treated as challenges to more systematic enquiry, where generalizations are being made. Our aim is to encourage a critical perspective toward images of ageing, including those presented in the media; we feel that growing old in the eyes of the media is different from the actual experience of growing older.

GETTING INTO THE NEWS

People's age, like their sex and occupation, is a feature that locates their identity quickly and simply as a distinct individual. It often features in the reporting of stories of individuals in newspapers and the style not only identifies individuals but also categorizes them:

GIRL OF 13 LEADS GANG IN RAID ON PENSIONER

Three schoolchildren led by a 13-year-old girl robbed a half-blind pensioner in his home.

The 'angel-faced' blonde youngster shoved retired council worker E____ C____, 78, aside when he opened his front door.
Daily Express, 16 August 1989

The contrast of youth and age is heavily stressed in this item: youth is strong enough to shove aside the pensioner; youth is angel-faced and blonde, age is half-blind; youth acts as a group in a 'gang' while age is apparently alone (a 'widower' we are told later in the piece). The image is of power in the hands of youth (in this case schoolchildren, under the age of consent or legal responsibility) and vulnerability and dependence in the old (retired from work, apparently dependent on a pension). This was one of three items in that particular edition of the *Daily Express* which featured people over 65. One of the other two was a comment on the retirement of P. W. Botha as President of South Africa ('Old Croc That Finally Snapped'). The third, a tailpiece to the gang raid story, was of another old victim ('A teenage thug beat a frail 95-year-old woman to the ground in the street . . .').

A glance at any newspaper or television news report shows that older people seldom appear as individuals in stories and when they do it is in a particular way. It is not unusual for there to be no older characters at all in a newspaper – the concentration of stories around sport, television personalities and politics seems to ensure that the 15 per cent of the population over 65 are under-represented. When older people do appear it is not only as victims of violence but age seems to coincide with some sort of victimization. It may be to do with their poverty, or their vulnerability:

ELDERLY URGED TO KEEP WARM
The charity Age Concern today repeated its plea for elderly people to keep warm during the severe cold weather.
Gloucester Citizen, 13 January 1987

OAPS' MEALS UNDER THREAT
Cut-price meals for the elderly and disabled could be axed unless Gloucester city councillors agree to back a Matson lunch club.
Gloucester Citizen, 13 March 1989

'PENSIONS ARE CHEATING AGED'
Britain's 'forgotten' senior citizens are being cheated out of £7,000 million by the Government each year claims a Gloucestershire union chief.
Gloucester Citizen, 22 August 1989

People who have reached a certain age, usually retirement and the onset of pensioner status, are lumped together and treated as an homogeneous group as 'the elderly', 'OAPs', 'pensioners', 'the aged'. It is implied that they share a similar need to be told to keep warm, receive state pensions and even cut-price meals.

The tabloid newspapers also feature the older person as a hero:

GEORGE DIED WITH THE COURAGE OF A LION
George Adamson, the lion man, died fighting like a lion, it was revealed yesterday.
Daily Mail, 22 August 1989

This story reported Adamson's death during a heroic struggle with game poachers while he was trying to rescue his young driver and a young woman. Adamson's age is not mentioned for a number of column inches when it is revealed as 83; his heroism is neither attributed to his age nor emphasized by it. Another story that allows the person's actions to be reported without reference to their age as significant is rather different:

MAN FINED FOR WATERING HIS TREE

Norm defies hose ban

Gardener Norman R____ was fined £200 yesterday for watering a dying tree – then he said he would do it again.

Norman, 70, became the first person to be prosecuted in the parched South-West of England for defying a hose-pipe ban.

Sun, 23 August 1989

These old people who have been reported in news items do not sound like people who are 'disengaging' in preparation for the final stages of life. While 'Norm's' act of heroism is not so dramatic or normally associated with youth, he is represented as a man of the people (Norm) who went up against a state bureaucracy and stood his ground – he even says he would do it again.

Until recently the most frequently featured old people in the news were 'world leaders'. President Reagan was depicted as the stereotype of a forgetful, reactionary, simple-minded old person who was really past it while maintaining his extraordinarily powerful position. Until the arrival of President Gorbachov, Russian leaders had also been traditionally 'old' and it was easy for the western media to cast doubt on their ability to govern competently. The death of President Hirohito in Japan removed another world leader who was apparently out of his time. It seems as if the Chinese alone persist in having a leader of great age and indeed Deng Xia Ping displays some stereotypical aspects of old age: ill-health and intolerance.

There are older personalities (Alistair Cooke, Ludovic Kennedy, Bob Hope) who still command attention in the media not for their age or even their power but for what they do. It is, however, notable that there are fewer older women in such positions, although this probably reflects the shorter time that women have taken central roles as presenters and personalities. In 'selling' things to the consumer, be it news or deodorant, women are regarded as having to add a desirable image and this continues to be associated with youth. Older men may not add desirability to a product but they can add authority and continuity.

AGEING AS A PROBLEM

So far we have looked at images of individual older people and of how they are represented in the media. But the media also deal with ageing itself in a different way, as a social issue and often as a problem. The *Guardian*, for example, reported in 1987 on its Society Tomorrow feature page, 'A Change in the Older Order', quoting figures from Professor Alan Pifer from New York who was in England to talk on the ageing of society. The article includes some horror talk about the changing age structure of US society:

> The early years of the next century, he says, could be a nightmare, as this relatively small group of workers bears not just the usual brunt of securing the national living and security and caring for the young, but the support of the unprecedentedly large numbers of old people as well.

But also includes a view of the ageing society that is not simply gloomy:

> Thirty years from now, not far short of a third of Americans will be in that third quarter of their lives – and they are the most educated and assertive generation in their country's history. Opportunities for them to continue to be productive must be found – as both full time and part time workers as well as volunteers.
>
> *Guardian*, 4 February 1987

There are a number of ageing-as-a-problem issues that recur. One is to do with poverty:

> TRAPPED IN THE UNDERCLASS BY A PENSION THAT DENIES DIGNITY
> *Independent*, 20 September 1989

Another is how the government is treating elderly people:

> At Reading, Mrs Currie said: 'The message to the nation's grannies and grandads is: please look after yourselves.' Even she did not add, 'you are on your own', but she might just as well have done.
>
> Malcolm Wicks, *Guardian*, 21 November 1988

A favourite topic is the type of care that is provided in old people's homes:

'TOO RIGID' REGIME IN OLD FOLKS HOME
A 'far too rigid and institutional approach' has led to problems at a County Council-run old folks' home at Stroud, social service chiefs heard this afternoon.

Gloucester Citizen, 20 October 1987

While the issues of health, warmth, pensions and institutional care are all unquestionably important and worthy of public debate, the image of the ageing population presented in these serious political commentaries is in danger of coinciding with the stereotypes of old people. The tendency is to always present older people as those in need of warmth, care, pensions and health services which lumps all old people together and assumes their needs are the same. This perspective implies that all of us will experience old age and the problems associated with it in much the same way.

FICTIONAL IMAGES

The most influential images of growing old in our times are provided on television. The sixties spawned characters like the middle-aged 'young' Steptoe, who was contrasted with the 'dirty old man' portrayed so powerfully by Wilfred Bramble, and the clutch of old ladies led by Ena Sharples gossiping in the Rovers Return in *Coronation Street*. While these characters are gone now and the actors who created them are sadly dead, in the newer soaps like *Prisoner Cell Block H* and *EastEnders* there are still eccentric old characters, past it but tolerated by the younger ones. In *Neighbours* there is the difficult older woman in Mrs Mangel, who is self-willed, inflexible and unable to understand the lives of young people. But here there is also another older woman, Helen Daniels, who is apparently grandmother to a man in his twenties yet is a fit and active person who paints, who recently set up an art show and who is treated as counsellor and social worker for all the other 'neighbours'.

The current trend of 'human relationship comedy' from the United States has exported the *Golden Girls* and *Empty Nest* to the United Kingdom. These take an ironic look at features of ageing to do with lost partners and lost families. The characters are all fit, physically and mentally, but they show an eccentric quality which makes them 'interesting' in the absence of being 'attractive'. Their sexual activity (or lack of it) is not presented as erotic or exciting but as humorous and occasionally romantic.

The play-off of young against old is also a traditional topic for drama and fictional stories (Heidi and her grandfather, *Great Expectations* and so on). In a television play like *Past Caring*, written by Tom Clarke and directed by Richard Eyre, the play of young against old takes some risks. The central character, Victor, is a resident in an old people's home who has an affair with the much younger 'matron', Linda. While Victor is clearly out of place in the home because he is so fit and independent, the setting accentuates the contrast between young and old and enables the introduction of a third character, Edward, who does need care and support and is clearly near the end of his life. He asks:

> can anyone really care about us, decrepit hulks whose self hate and fear of death would render us uncontrollable were it not for the drugs that stupefy us into imbecility . . .

Whereas Edward bemoans the passage of time, Victor lives in the moment with apparently little concern for the past or future: 'One's age. It's not something of any real importance.'

The more subtle view, possible in literature, that puts elderly people and the business of growing older at the centre of things, produces not just stereotypes but also questions presumptions that the viewer/reader holds. The contrast of young and old characters becomes an especially powerful device when each of the characters grows older and the tension between ages at different stages in life can be explored. This is more possible in the form of a novel and in *Duet for Three*, Joan Barfoot explores the present and past relationships between three generations of women. Aggie is eighty and near the end of her life, reflecting on the difference between her origins (a large family working on the land), her daughter June's and those of her granddaughter Frances. The commitment of the three women to men and marriage is contrasted partly as a consequence of their different personalities and partly as a consequence of the times in which they lived.

The determination of Aggie to remain independent of a nursing home as long as possible, even now she is becoming incontinent, is a theme that runs through the novel while its contradiction with her dependence on June is not shirked. It is Frances of whom Aggie is most fond and feels most at home with, but it is June who feels responsible for providing a home for Aggie. June was invited into Aggie's house when her marriage ended but it is the home of both women now, both old, although of different generations. Aggie is willing to claim it as her own and stay put whatever the risk:

> 'Look June, it's my risk after all. It's my death you seem to be worrying about. And as I said before, it's my house. You may stay or go as you please, but I stay.'
>
> But this house is in June's blood. This is the one place in the world she belongs.

(Barfoot, 1986: 44–5)

This sort of novel cannot be accused of creating stereotypes or of fudging issues of growing older. Just as gerontologists, after a period of infatuation with disengagement theory, began to point out the logical absurdity of any statement of generalized withdrawal from life (Hendricks and Hendricks 1986), so too novelists and other writers have struggled to provide glimpses of a greater variety of responses. Both Paul Bailey (1967) in his novel about an old peoples' home and Ellen Newton (1980) in her first-hand account of life in an Australian nursing home, provide graphic evidence of refusal to disengage. Bailey's Mrs Gadney exhibits resourcefulness and social skill as she enters the residential home her niece and nephew have contrived to place her in. In *This Bed My Centre*, Ellen Newton's diary reporting shares with the reader a deeply disturbing view of the world of a helpless old woman, neglected and underfed but still wonderfully lucid and capable of acute social observation.

The life course, the personal biographies, the cohort effect, all need to be taken into account to understand the experience of growing older. A fuller view reveals that growing older does not lead to the absence of desire, or absence of the need for independence, self-determination, affection and companionship. At the same time neither does it obscure the difficulties in meeting these needs because of declining mobility, poorer health, declining income and loss of partners, family and friends.

ATTITUDES AND AGEISM

Robert Butler coined the term 'ageism' in 1968 and has sustained an attack on the use of stereotypes of old age:

> Those who think of old people as boobies, crones, witches, old biddies, old fogies, pains-in-the-neck, out-to-pasture, boring,

garrulous, unproductive and worthless, have accepted the stereotypes of ageing, including the extreme mistake of believing that
substantial numbers of old people are in or belong in institutions.

(Butler 1974:529)

It is these stereotypical images of ageing that the media are in
danger of fostering. In their review of attitudes, stereotypes and
prejudice about ageing Slater and Gearing quote evidence from a
Harris Poll in the United States that shows that the public's view
of the problems faced by the elderly is much more extreme than
the experience of elderly people themselves (Slater and Gearing
1988). The study suggested that older people themselves had been
influenced by stereotypes of ageing and for many, life had turned
out better than they had expected. Slater and Gearing point out:

> Such expectations often find expression in a well-meaning but
> ultimately harmful presentation of old age as necessarily a prob-
> lem state. Problems which affect some older people – often a
> small minority – are present in an 'overdrawn' picture of inevi-
> table decline seen in the necessary accompaniment of old age
> which affects all old people.

(Slater and Gearing 1988:31)

While they are keen to point out that it is not just social workers
who tend to operate with stereotypical images of ageing, they refer
to a series of studies of social work with older people that suggest
that it is low status, attracts low priority and apparently involves
only straightforward practical tasks rather than trying to achieve
environmental and personal change (Slater and Gearing 1988:32).
There seems to be a congruence between the practice of social
work and the limited, stereotypical view of growing older that is
frequently portrayed in the media.

There has been a tradition of research in the United States
looking at the generation of attitudes to ageing. Kosberg and Harris
reviewed the research on social work attitudes towards elderly clients and found the problems in the professional orientation of social
workers rather than in the working out of generally held attitudes:

> social workers are dedicated to and have been trained to effect
> the improvement or restoration of their client's ability to func-
> tion, but they may view the elderly individual as being incapable
> of responding to treatment.

(Kosberg and Harris 1978:77)

Not surprisingly perhaps these authors recommend changes in the formal education and in-service training of social workers to make them more aware of what is known about later life. They also suggest that social work has a responsibility to engage in advocacy to challenge ageist values and to work to bring about change in the lives of older people rather than just to help them adjust to their stage in life. It is, however, notoriously difficult to measure attitudes and even more difficult to measure changes in attitudes or to find causes (such as the media) for particular attitudes (for a review of the methodological problems see Kogan 1979).

What is known about the process of ageism and attitudes towards ageing may be equivocal and beset by methodological dilemmas but, as one recent researcher has pointed out, there is basic evidence that is sufficient to go on:

> the elderly are still the most heterogeneous stratum in the age spectrum . . . however . . . older people continue to be lumped together and negatively evaluated, even on characteristics for which there is no evidence, or poor evidence, for decline.
>
> (Levin 1988:146)

One of the theories that has been explored is that stereotyped images of older people form a 'basic category', that is, a category that is used in perceptual processes spontaneously. Alternative versions of what it means to be older can co-exist but they do so in relation to the basic category and need longer to process and recall (Brewer *et al.* 1981). There is, however, a danger in assuming that stereotypes are necessarily negative, or applied universally to all old people (Branco and Williamson 1982:380); some are clearly positive in their view of old people (Braithwaite 1986). Moreover, stereotypes can serve a purpose for society as a whole and are not simply mistakes:

> even if disengagement theory is guilty of what some people consider the worst sin of social science – simply rephrasing the 'common sense' view in scientific terms – it can be useful for understanding why these negative stereotypes persist. The negative stereotypes do not just occur; they are functional for maintaining the status quo of age relations in modern society – a status quo that continuously sees younger people being phased into important social roles, and older people as being phased out.
>
> (Branco and Williamson 1982:389–90)

This view may seem to attribute to stereotypes a function that might lead us to tolerate them – but then the stereotypes are only functional to a society that also tolerates the disadvantaging of elderly people merely on the grounds of their age. It has also been argued that the very practice of pointing out stereotypes in attitudes is suspect. Schonfield suggests that a 'mixture of altruism and egoism' has caused anti-ageist spokespersons to 'misread the evidence' (Schonfield 1982:272). He questions the evidence of ageism in people's attitudes which depends on the method of asking people to respond 'true' or 'false' to attitude questions. He shows that even when people do say that they think a statement like 'Old people tend to be inflexible' is true, they also recognize that there are a large number of exceptions.

> It is therefore dangerous to predict not only behaviour from an answer to a question but even existing beliefs and opinions.
>
> (Schonfield 1982:269)

Whatever their precise impact on attitudes, it is clearly a political issue whether stereotypical images should be tolerated or challenged and it is one that has been taken up by women studying sexism in the media. Catherine Itzin reviews the literature on images of ageing and women and comments on the strength of her own study of women's experience:

> Because of the extent to which we have internalised age-sex stereotypes we lead double lives. We live both our 'reality' and the 'reality' of the oppression. . . . We submit to the stereotypes and resist them simultaneously.
>
> (Itzin 1984: 176)

To resist stereotypical images of growing older seems a task we all need to undertake but perhaps those working directly with older people need to more vigorously than others.

THE PROCESS OF IDEOLOGY

The recognition of ageism and the pointing out of stereotypical images of old age is a first step that gerontologists have made in understanding the importance of media images of ageing in contemporary society. There is a need to counter negative images and challenge stereotypes especially when, as Alison Norman puts it, 'the poor image of old age inevitably rubs off on those who are working in this field' (Norman 1987:9). There is, however, a second step that needs to be made that goes beyond challenging stereotypical images with 'true' images derived from gerontological study. This second step involves locating media images in a social context – Fennell and his colleagues argue that rival images of old age, both negative and positive contribute to a 'social construction of old age' (Fennell *et al.* 1988:9).

This sociological perspective implies a much more complex situation than one in which stereotypes are seen as 'misrepresenting' reality. In our earlier examples it became clear that there are considerable variations around the stereotypes of old age and while the research literature supports the existence of stereotypes it suggests that there are both positive and negative images and their effect on 'attitudes' is far from clear.

It is not surprising that the images of older people in the media are distorted in a systematic way (Habermas 1970), given the context of production of media images, it is difficult to see how they could be otherwise. This context is one of an imbalance of power; it is not old people who produce media images for themselves. Older people are keener watchers of television, for example, than younger people (22 per cent of those over 75 watch at least once in twenty-four hours, compared to 12 per cent of those between 25 and 44 – Wober, forthcoming). However, the media are, by and large, produced by a group of young to middle-aged people who are locked into a process of reproducing a set of cultural values. This ideological process of reproducing and reinforcing a certain set of cultural values has been recognized as a feature of the media for some time in sociology and media studies (e.g. Hall 1977). The way that the process works has been subjected to some detailed analysis (e.g. Kress and Hodge 1979, Fowler *et al.* 1979) that has focused on the way that language and other sign systems (such as two-dimensional images) have an ideological effect. This approach has been applied in the fields of sexism (e.g. Coward 1984; Billig *et al.* 1988; Hodge and Kress 1988) and racism (e.g. Potter and Wetherell 1988; Billig *et al.* 1988) but there has not, as yet, been an analysis of ageism that confronts the ideological effects of discourse. There are the beginnings of interest in the sociolinguistic effects of communicative interactions between older and younger people (Boden and Bielby 1983 and 1986; Coupland *et al.* 1988; Grainger, Atkinson and Coupland, forthcoming; Dant 1988) but there has, as yet, been no attempt to broaden the attention to mass communications and older people.

CONCLUSIONS

Social workers cannot hold their breath waiting for gerontologists to undertake analysis of ageist discourse in the media but the outcome for practitioners can be anticipated from other analyses. There will, for example, be no unearthing of an ageist conspiracy perpetrated by a power élite of young people hoping that they will not grow any older. What will become apparent is that ageism is a process of producing and reproducing an imbalance of power between people of different age groups. The process is not discrete or distinct from other ideological effects such as those deriving from racism or sexism (producing what Itzin calls a 'double jeopardy' for older women). Neither is the process peculiar to the mass media. The same process that occurs in the media also occurs in relatively formal interactions (e.g. between professionals and clients) and in informal relationships. Structural features of these different contexts legitimate the use of images and categories that effectively diminish the power and autonomy of those who are old. So, in the media old people are often stylized as vulnerable, dependent and a social problem for the sake of brevity, in professional relationships their problems are attributed to their age (rather than poverty, ill-health or handicap), and in less formal relationships presumptions are made about the extent or significance of disabilities which lead to 'caring for' people rather than helping them care for themselves.

The second step, seeing media images of growing older as part of a process of social construction, changes our response to those images. We need to be critically aware of the disadvantaging effect of ideological processes on older people (including our ageing selves). This means going beyond rejecting stereotypes (which often involves putting a 'better' stereotype in its place) to recognizing the continuity between mass media, professional and personal practice. What the media present and what we articulate are interconnected in a more subtle and pervasive way than mechanically adopting or rejecting attitudes. There can be an illusory satisfaction derived from pointing to the excesses of some media images; critical awareness should involve reviewing our own presuppositions and the concepts adopted in professional practice, as well as the range of images in the media.

12 Running a campaign: appropriate strategies for changing times

Tom White

INTRODUCTION

Since the Second World War 'campaign' techniques have improved enormously in the United Kingdom, often incorporating and elaborating ideas first developed in the United States. Political parties' election campaigning and the media strategies and lobbying of commercial organizations are obvious examples.

Social work and social policy interests have not been immune to these broader tendencies and have developed their own techniques of campaigning for social policy changes. Organizations like CPAG (Child Poverty Action Group) and Shelter were specifically established as pressure groups, but professional associations of social workers like BASW (British Association of Social Workers), ADSS (Association of Directors of Social Service) and SCA (Social Care Association), as well as service-providing voluntary organizations like NCH (National Children's Home) consider campaigning to be an important component of their work.

Descriptions of two very different campaigns organized twenty years apart will help illustrate the way in which two voluntary organizations sought to influence events: (1) SIAG (Seebohm Implementation Action Group), a time-limited, for-one-specific-purpose organization, established on the initiative of a social work professional association, ACCO (Association of Child Care Officers) and (2) the other very different kind of campaign, organized by a long-established child care charity, NCH.

Comparison of the two campaigns illustrate the important changes in the socio-political context in which social work operated in the two periods and how the role, impact and use of the media was quite different.

SEEBOHM IMPLEMENTATION ACTION GROUP (SIAG): BACKGROUND

In the mid 1960s considerable concern was being expressed about the effectiveness of the organization of social welfare services for families in England and Wales. A particular focus for concern was the separate organization of children's welfare, health, education and probation services, with their overlapping responsibilities in aspects of provision for families, which prompted Sir Keith Joseph to describe personal social services at that time as 'islands of welfare in a sea of confusion' (Younghusband 1978:232).

The Seebohm Committee (the Committee on the Local Authority and Allied Personal Social Services) was set up in 1965 'to review the organisation and responsibilities of the local authority personal social services in England and Wales, and to consider what changes were desirable to secure an effective family service'.

The Committee's report was published in 1968 and received a mixed reception from the various relevant professional groups. A history of social work claims that 'When the report appeared, it was naturally hailed with enthusiasm by social workers and their supporters. Indeed, "Seebohm" became as much a rallying cry in some quarters as "Beveridge" had been over 25 years earlier. Predictably, many doctors were far from enthusiastic about proposals to tear apart, what to them, were essential elements in the Health Service. Some politicians were also against the proposals' (Younghusband 1978:239).

There was quite an influential group of civil servants and politicians who wanted to delay any decision relating to change in the Local Authority Social Services until after the reorganization of Local Government and the Health Services scheduled for the mid 1970s, and they persuaded the powerful Local Authority Associations to agree to their stance. Some individual local authorities (particularly in London) jumped the gun by bringing their Health, Welfare and Children services together under the Medical Officer of Health. Social workers were very worried by this development, and Social Work Associations contested fiercely a form of integration which would have resulted in medical rather than social work direction of these services.

ACCO (the Association of Child Care Officers) was the most politically sophisticated of the eight professional associations who then formed the Standing Conference of Social Workers (which eventually developed into BASW). The Standing Conference did not feel able to campaign for Seebohm implementation, but gave its blessing to ACCO taking a lead in such a campaign.

As a past president of ACCO and Chair of its Parliamentary Committee, the author organized the early meetings of this group and later chaired SIAG. SIAG soon had seventeen member organizations and was committed to campaign for the implementation of the major recommendations of the Seebohm Committee Report.

SUPPORT FOR SIAG

The seventeen organizations represented the eight professional associations of social workers (covering child care, medical, psychiatric and family social work, as well as probation officers); chief officers associations representing children's and welfare officers; other social welfare organizations (e.g., Institute of Social Welfare) and a number of 'consumer' bodies e.g., CPAG, DIG (Disabled Income Group), Patients Association, Council on Children's Welfare and National Corporation for the Care of Old People (later to become Age Concern). Keith Bilton, employed as ACCO's General Secretary, acted as Secretary to the Committee.

SIAG deliberately sought wide membership support – particularly from the consumer groups – to broaden the base of its appeal. Many of the organizations were very much 'sleeping' partners, happy to let the enthusiastic social workers get on with the actual campaigning – but the wide spectrum of apparent support was influential in a significant way for many people anxious about the proposed reforms.

PLANNING THE CAMPAIGN

Enthusiastic preparation took place for what was to prove the most sophisticated and successful of social welfare and social policy campaigns of the time. The central aim was to convince Government of the need for urgent legislation (in advance of local government re-organization) to implement the Seebohm proposals. Determined efforts were made to influence official, parliamentary, ministerial and public opinion. Member organizations donated funds which were supplemented by a grant from one of the Rowntree trusts for the Group's educational work.

A great deal of effort was put into preparing briefing materials. Extensive 'speakers notes' in a book-size loose leaf folder were soon produced and gave confidence to SIAG representatives in their contacts with the media, officials, MPs and Ministers.

An orchestrated campaign of letters and articles to the press and weekly journals was successfully organized. An initial letter from Lord Donaldson published in *The Times* caused the paper subsequently to be inundated with letters (many published) from the well-organized social work lobby and its friends.

PARLIAMENTARY CAMPAIGN

Many SIAG member organizations prompted their individual members to write to their MP, with briefing notes being provided to assist in the preparation of the letter (which emphasized the need for 'individualized' correspondence).

Visits to MPs in constituency 'surgeries' were carefully orchestrated. It was not simply a matter of urging supporters to contact MPs for individual meetings, but of co-ordinating joint visits when more than one person in a constituency was prepared to act on SIAG's behalf. The degree of support offered by SIAG was very important in encouraging larger numbers of people to confront MPs in their constituencies than is normally the case in campaigning of this kind.

Separate group meetings were held at the House of Commons with back-bench MPs of the Labour, Conservative and Liberal Parties and a good deal of correspondence took place between the officers of SIAG and individual MPs.

Sympathetic MPs and peers were prepared to 'plant' questions for Question Time in the Commons and the Lords. A Lords debate was stimulated and a number of peers were given individualized briefs by SIAG officers and member organizations (I do not know whether this was the first occasion Lucy Faithfull[1] wrote a speech for the House of Lords, but certainly as the Association of Children's Officers representative on SIAG she prepared material for a number of peers' speeches on that day).

A lobby of the House of Commons, the first ever by social workers, added to the effectiveness of the parliamentary campaign.

There can be little doubt that the campaign's ability to generate cross-party support influenced ministers and helped ensure a speedy passage for the subsequent Bill before the 1970 general election.

INFLUENCE IN WHITEHALL

Considerable effort was expended to influence officials in the Home Office and Health Departments with meetings in offices and over lunch and dinner. Ministers at Cabinet and junior level were also button-holed at informal meetings, and formal meetings were sought. Delegates from SIAG met Richard Crossman, the Secretary of State for Social Services and James Callaghan, the Home Secretary, individually and again later at a joint meeting. The Prime Minister was written to on more than one occasion and statements of support for the implementation of the main Seebohm recommendations from 131 university and college teachers, including five professors (there were not so many social work professors at that time!) were sent to the Prime Minister.

EXTRA-PARLIAMENTARY CAMPAIGNING AND THE ROLE OF THE MEDIA

Local SIAG groups sprang up to bring influence to bear on leaders in Local Government who were judged to be potentially influential. A residential conference with distinguished participants was arranged through INLOGOV (Institute of Local Government Studies at Birmingham University). PEP (Political and Economic Planning) organized a day conference, and the National Institute of Social Work organized a series of 'consultations'.

Unusually, members of the Seebohm Committee themselves were active behind the scenes – and sometimes on the platform – very much encouraged by Robin Huws Jones (Principal of the National Institute of Social Work) who was himself a member of the Seebohm Committee.

While the media was not neglected they were probably less central to the campaign than they would be in any such campaign organized twenty years later. This reflected the wisdom prevalent at the time concerning how to conduct a campaign. S. E. Finer's book *Anonymous Empire* (1958) enumerated the belief that only pressure groups without influence in Westminster and Whitehall resorted to media campaigns in order to influence public opinions. The general rule of thumb that the higher a group's public profile the less its real 'clout' was accepted as axiomatic. Nevertheless, articles appeared in the professional and intellectual weeklies. Robin Guthrie, now Chief Charity Commissioner, who then worked at Peterborough Development Corporation, wrote a weekly column for the 'new' *New Society*, in which he gave sympathetic support to SIAG efforts. There was coverage in the 'heavies' and some of the popular press for the regular press releases issued by SIAG. For a child of its generation SIAG was untypically media conscious. Limited, but telling use was made of radio and television.

One significant fact which influenced parliamentary and public response at that time was that social work and social workers were well respected. They were very much the 'goodies' rather than the 'baddies' in any public media coverage of the debate relating to Seebohm. They were seen to be representing the interests of their clients who were unable to speak for themselves. The contrast with today (and the media hostility to social work) could not be more marked.

I am still surprised, more than twenty years later, that the Labour Government decided, with all-party support, to implement the Seebohm Committee recommendations, despite the opposition of the well-established and powerful medical and local government lobbies (see Hall 1976, Cooper 1983). SIAG played an important part in that decision and the success of that voluntary organization's campaign was due, particularly, to three factors:

1 Meticulous attention to detailed organization – with checks and 'backup' systems for all the major components of the campaign.
2 Infectious enthusiasm, which ensured widespread support of individuals in a variety of organizations spread widely throughout the country.
3 A social climate which was sympathetic to social work and in which public and media attitudes were supportive.

NCH'S CHILDREN IN DANGER CAMPAIGN: BACKGROUND

National Children's Home was established in 1869, and has for many decades maintained a position as one of the major child care voluntary organizations in the United Kingdom. With over 200 projects, 2,000 staff and a £37m budget in 1989/90, it works in a variety of ways with children and families in need.

NCH runs Family Centres, provides a wide range of residential homes and schools, undertakes community-based work with families, organizes more 'replacement to custody' schemes for young offenders than any other organization, and is developing work with young offenders in the age group 17 to 21. It organizes family placement services, telephone counselling services, specialist child abuse services, and is involved in a range of other social work activity. Most of its work is undertaken in partnership with statutory agencies – social services, health and probation – and it is committed to working in partnership with the users of its projects.

A CAMPAIGNING ROLE

The founding fathers of the large child care charities in the nineteenth century were concerned not only with providing services for deprived children but also with campaigning to change the atrocious conditions in which children were growing up. The Revd Thomas Bowman Stephenson, the founder of NCH, was clear from the very beginning that NCH was not solely a residential institution for orphans, but had a wider 'advocacy' role for children. Dr Barnardo took a similar stance.

Some would argue that over the last fifty years, the child care voluntary organizations have played down or even ignored the 'campaigning' role that their founders prescribed. They have concentrated on the service provision aspect of the work and perhaps, as a consequence, seen other voluntary organizations develop specifically with a pressure group role, e.g., Child Poverty Action Group. One possible explanation for the reluctance to campaign vigorously on behalf of children might be the concern that this would adversely affect fundraising.

It is interesting, therefore, to note that a number of the major child care voluntaries have made 'social policy adviser' type appointments over the last few years, with the specific intention of ensuring that those appointed are well briefed and can seek to influence the wider social policy issues that affect children. It will be interesting to see how radical and effective this 'campaigning' voice proves to be.

One of the ways in which NCH flexed its campaigning muscle was by launching its 'Children in Danger' campaign in the autumn of 1985. This section deals with some of the dilemmas and opportunities which that campaign highlighted.

THE CAMPAIGN OBJECTIVES

Considering its size, NCH as an organization was little known amongst the general public in 1985. For some time, concern had been expressed, within the organization, about this lack of public awareness. Social work staff had asked, 'Why do other child care voluntaries get more publicity than NCH?' Grass-root fund-raisers had also called for action.

At national level a reorganized senior staff realized the advantages, in social policy and fund-raising terms, which a higher profile would bring. An intention of the campaign was to promote interest in NCH's work and to highlight to the public that there are ways of confronting some of the dangers to which children are exposed. The campaign was planned to stimulate a greater national debate about issues of concern which affect children and families. It was also hoped that greater awareness of NCH would lead to NCH receiving more money from the general public with which to respond to the pressing needs of children and families.

'CHILDREN IN DANGER' SLOGAN

In any campaign which aims to capture the public's attention a 'slogan' which is memorable and dramatic will help. It can also produce one of the important dilemmas of a high-profile campaign within a service-providing organization. Clearly there are dangers in the slogan eventually chosen. 'Children in Danger' could be seen to imply that all children who come into contact with NCH, in whatever way, are potentially 'in danger'. This is clearly not the case. There has been an explosion of public awareness and concern about some dangers in the last few years – sexual abuse, serious neglect, cruelty, etc. – but there is another interpretation of 'children in danger'. This concerns much more prevalent, but less sensational dangers – the effects of poverty, adult and youth unemployment, family breakdown, poor education facilities, etc. One of the aims of NCH's 'Children in Danger' campaign is to suggest that there are links between the gross dangers to children and the secondary dangers. Unless something is done about these secondary dangers, the first set of gross dangers increases.

In the event, the launch of the 'Children in Danger' campaign in September 1985 was dramatically affected by a number of factors outside the campaign itself. The launch coincided with a number of highly sensational child murders and child abuse cases coming to Court. September 1985 saw the beginning of a radically heightened media awareness of children's issues which has continued through the Jasmine Beckford inquiry and Cleveland.

As a consequence, the campaign, which had been planned to cover a very broad range of dangers affecting children, became focused on the specific issues of child abuse. Such a focus provided a rapid escalation of contacts with the media and, consequently, opportunities to talk about a wide range of NCH work. There was much debate within NCH at the time about the appropriateness of the media 'hijacking' the campaign and focusing exclusively on child abuse, but a significant part of NCH work was extensively involved with abused children and we had much to say about their needs and the importance of legal reform and change in public attitudes. On balance we were, therefore, pleased to have the media opportunities. Nevertheless, they left the unfortunate impression that the campaign was largely concerned about child abuse and the consequences for NCH operational work were not always easy.

CAMPAIGN PLANNING

A campaign of this kind involves much planning and preparation. Discussion between various parts of a large voluntary organization: social work staff, fund-raising staff, public relations staff, the organization's external advertising agencies, etc. The preparation can be expensive, not only in the cost of advertising in newspapers and on hoardings and the paying of PR agency fees, but also in the cost of staff time diverted from other urgent tasks. Whenever NCH launches a campaign, all our Regional Directors of Social Work have to be at their desks for time-consuming media attention, and invariably spend many hours in radio and television studios, a process which itself involves expense on media training. (This was first provided for most NCH senior staff in preparation for the Children in Danger launch and has since become a regular feature of NCH senior staff training.)

Media interest in social work projects is not always welcomed by either the users of social work projects or by the staff working with them, and careful preparation is necessary if the organization's credibility is not to be dented in seeking media attention and then being unable to respond to meet media interest. Clearly, some clients do not want their cases highlighted for neighbours, friends and relations to be made aware of their circumstances – particularly where their contact with NCH is related to child abuse, or their poverty or some other unsatisfactory circumstance.

Not all our media contacts have been of the quality we would have hoped, and some clients who agreed to be filmed felt let down when editing of an item created a distorted view of their circumstances. The reporting of such incidents and exaggeration on the internal 'grape vine', make other projects wary of co-operation with the media.

There remains a dilemma which, unchecked, can form a vicious circle. The poor image that social work and social workers have acquired in recent years in the statutory sector, if not in the voluntary sector, requires us to take a proactive stance. The public need to understand better the complexity, difficulties and realities of the work undertaken in residential, day and community work projects. To have such an understanding, the media need to be encouraged to be involved in visiting and probing the effectiveness of this work. An over-defensive attitude on the part of staff is in the long run going to defer the public understanding that we crave.

I believe voluntary organizations have a very much better image with the public and the media than do their statutory counterparts because they are more willing to encourage media attention to their work. Their motive may not be to improve social work's image, but often, simply, the need to raise funds for the organization to continue its work. But the effect is to improve the image of the organization and of social work generally, and Directors of Social Services and their staff could benefit the profession and their own departments by following the example of the voluntary organizations.

The NCH 'Children in Danger' campaign continued into its second year with attempts to highlight a number of particular issues which again provide useful case studies concerning social policy campaigning.

While much had been written about youth unemployment and long-term unemployment within the adult population, relatively little attention had been focused on the effects of long-term unemployment on families as a whole, and children in particular. The campaign tried to focus on this aspect, and one of the benefits was a considerable amount of media coverage of the adverse effect of unemployment on the 1¼ million children who are involved.

Another, and more controversial, aspect of the campaign concerned the effect of family breakdown on children. A nationwide poster campaign was launched with the slogan: 'Since you passed this poster yesterday, another 436 children got divorced. 436 more reasons why NCH works with children in danger.'

Trying to get a message over via a poster campaign in an area as delicate as divorce is extremely difficult and perhaps even foolhardy! Any poster must be concise and contain a dramatic and simple message if it is to be effective, but how is it possible to do this without oversimplifying what is, undoubtedly, a complex topic?

NCH did certainly run into the criticism that this poster implied that all children involved in their parents' divorce are damaged in the process. There was particular criticism from some sections in the Methodist Church of which NCH is a part. In fact, however, NCH was able to use some of the controversy which surrounded this poster to call for much greater provision of conciliation services and for the speedy introduction of Family Courts. This illustrates how unpredictable opportunities can emerge during campaigns which can be eagerly seized to aid the underlying message and secure many more column inches than would otherwise have been the case. This flexibility of response is one distinguishing feature of social policy as opposed to commercial 'selling a product' campaigning.

The launching of a poster of this kind raises a number of general questions. How far is it permissible to 'simplify' a complex debate in order to stimulate wider public discussion of the issue? Is it wiser to avoid the tabloid press altogether with its sensationalism, or given their massive circulation, should efforts be made to present issues to the popular media in such a way that serious points can be made?

I do not think the issues should be shirked. Policy-makers are influenced by the masses as well as by the 'opinion formers', and social policy campaigning must be directed at both ends of the spectrum.

EFFECT ON USERS

Whenever the media is involved there is a danger of things being 'blown out of all proportion'. You can have no real control over what is written in an article or what appears on the screen. Reporters have a way of chasing what they see as 'a good story' rather than helping you get across the point you want.

In the current state of relationships between the media and social work, it is not surprising that both social work staff and the users of our services are hesitant about putting themselves in the 'front line' with the media (although social workers' assumptions about client attitudes to the media are often wrong, particularly if it offers the opportunity to appear on television – see Chapter 4 by David Perrin).

NCH would maintain that attempts must be made to generate

public discussion about the difficulties encountered by families with little or no influence over events which affect them. Sometimes this attempt is successful, sometimes it is not. Articles were written in the popular press about the role of NCH Family Centres in supporting families living in desperate conditions. Articles were written about NCH's work with young offenders which helped to dispel some of the many myths in this area of work. Sympathetic radio interviews were secured with users of NCH projects and these enabled those individuals to speak out about how bad housing, poverty and lack of employment all put tremendous strains on their family life.

It is considerably more difficult to encourage the media to focus on what can be achieved – on a successful family centre, or 'replacement to custody' schemes, etc. – rather than focusing on the dangers and crisis points themselves. It has always been more difficult to gain resources for, or interest in, preventive work rather than in crisis work, but it is perhaps only by learning painful lessons and developing a greater expertise that the very wide range of media outlets can be utilized to greater effect.

MULTIPLE AUDIENCE

Voluntary organizations engaged in campaigning activities must be aware that one of the difficulties of running any campaign on a broad topic such as 'Children in Danger' is that the material will inevitably reach a number of different audiences, all of whom have different perspectives and different relationships with the organization. Those who give funds to a voluntary organization are likely to see a campaign differently from the clients of that organization. Individual donors and the corporate donors of the industrial and commercial world do not have the same motives and will be influenced by different factors. Statutory authorities, who provide financial help for voluntary organizations, might again take a different view. Presentations which are directed mainly toward the general public are inevitably over-simplistic, sometimes seen as offensive by fellow professionals in the field.

In planning such a campaign, slogans and text must be carefully examined to avoid any danger of inadvertent offence, but if the sensitivity is taken too far the message becomes so bland as to be ineffective.

EVALUATING SUCCESS

When all the campaigning money is spent, articles filed in scrap books, television reports recorded on video cassettes on the shelf, how do you measure whether the campaign has been successful?

NCH is unaware of any effective evaluative techniques for this function. There are public awareness surveys, which charities diligently scrutinize to determine the level of 'unprompted' awareness with the general public, and debate whether 'unprompted' awareness or 'prompted' awareness (where someone is given the name of the charity and asked if they know of its work) is the more relevant criteria.

The aim of a voluntary organization like NCH, which has a variety of objectives (greater public awareness, better public appreciation of its work, influencing public opinion about the needs of children), makes it very difficult to be certain about any judgement of 'success'. In this particular campaign, where NCH secured significant television exposure and many column inches of print, NCH staff felt the campaign *was* successful. Fund-raising performance has improved significantly over previous years, and shows healthy annual increases in income – from the general public, from commerce and industry and from legacies. Clearly, that part of the campaign was successful, despite the fact that we lost a few supporters who felt that the campaign was too radical, too anti-government and too anti-establishment for them to continue to support our organization. In the main, our social work staff have been delighted to see the organization taking a lead in pressing for social policy improvements, although there continues to be a debate about whether the money spent on newspaper or hoarding advertising would be better spent directly on services to children in need.

These dilemmas will continue, but voluntary organizations and, perhaps in the future, the more courageous of the statutory social services could get together and use media campaigning to improve public attitudes to the care of children and take the opportunities such campaigns provide to open up to the wider world the hidden work of social services departments and social work voluntary organizations.[2]

CONCLUSION

These two campaigns were clearly very different both in setting and in primary objectives, yet both were concerned, in part, with influencing public opinion on social policy/social work issues.

The first campaign by SIAG was based in a coalition of organizations and had a specific 'one-off' objective. The media was seen as having a useful but peripheral role and the major effort was concentrated on the direct influence of parliamentary and governmental opinion.

The twenty-year gap before the very different NCH 'Children in Danger' campaign had been a period of growing influence for television and a greater recognition of the power of the media, generally, in influencing both public attitudes and government decision-making. A SIAG-type campaign today would clearly have to give much greater attention to the media if it was to be successful.

The combined tools of both campaigns:

(a) Published material.

(b) Media contact – press conferences, press releases, interviews with television, radio and press, photo opportunities.

(c) Availability of spokesperson for briefing of parliamentarians; meetings with political parties, senior civil servants and ministers.

(d) Cultivation of 'friends' in high places.

These remain the essential features of a successful campaign.

NOTES

1 Lucy Faithfull, then Children's Officer, Oxford City, became Baroness Faithfull of Wolvercote, Oxfordshire, in 1975.

2 The author first wrote about the 'Children in Danger' campaign in the National Children's Bureau journal *Children and Society*, vol. 1, no. 4 (Winter 1987/88).

13 Speaking up: community action and the media

John Callaghan

'Be a pal to handicapped'

VOLUNTEERS are needed to befriend mentally handicapped people in Bradford.

The appeal has gone out from Sue Haigh, a senior social worker responsible for mentally handicapped people living in the community. Many have been placed in group homes after release from hospital. They are supervised by qualified staff who attend regularly to keep an eye on their progress. They all either work or attend social education centres during the day.

Sue said: 'We would like to recruit people who could take part in social activities with them in an evening or at weekend. It might be just going to the pictures with them, or to the pub.

'It might be going to their home for a meal or inviting them round to your own house for a cup of tea and a chat.'

The scheme is being set up all over the Bradford area, which already has 12 group homes and more planned for the future.

Anyone who would like to volunteer or receive more information can contact Sue at the Alternative Care Section, Springfield, Squire Lane, Bradford 9, telephone Bradford 490944.

The special way of life for a mum

IN some parts of the country, Special Constables are called upon to police mainly garden parties ... and are rather looked down upon by the "regulars".

BY JOHN HEWITT

But it is not like that in West Yorkshire.

Here they are given the same status as the professional bobbies. They have a real job to do and women get every chance for promotion.

Which is why Mrs. Anne Jones, a 47-year-old mother of three, of Queens Road, Ilkley, loves the work.

She's Divisional Staff Officer, the equivalent of Chief Inspector, in the Bradford North Division and has been a Special for 18 years.

'There is a lot of work to do, but then, I get carried away with it. I enjoy it so much,' she said.

'I can think of what I am going to say at the next crime prevention meeting while I'm washing the pots. And I have a very understanding husband. He backs me all the way.'

Which is not really surprising as she and her husband, David, used to live in the West Country and joined the Devon and Cornwall Specials together.

'The last bus used to leave at 9.20 p.m. so we couldn't go out to the films and I was looking for something useful to do,' she says. 'We would take it in turns to go to the evening lectures while the other one acted as babysitter.'

Though her husband had to quit the specials when they moved to Ilkley – as a representative he has to travel a lot – she continued and found that the specials certainly occupied her time. Her recruiting and training work includes arranging a mock court in a real courtroom to give specials a taste of what it is like to give evidence.

She has organised the Balldon Armistice Parade for the last three years.

Figures 13.1 and 13.2 Newspaper articles from the Bradford *Telegraph & Argus*, 17 February 1986.

One of the most common purposes community and voluntary organizations have in using the media is to recruit volunteers. The above two stories appeared on the same page of the Bradford *Telegraph & Argus* on 17 February 1986. Anyone reading that paper and interested in doing something more fulfilling with their time would be offered information on two opportunities. But which sounds the more attractive?

'The Special Way of Life For a Mum' is a story that, in spite of the mum-washing-the-pots references, does on the whole give readers a strong and positive image of a woman doing a valuable job which she greatly enjoys, and where her achievements are recognized. We also learn that being a Special is not incompatible with family life, and that recruits receive training. Though it contains no overt appeal to join up, it seems likely that the story was set up by the West Yorkshire Police Press Office, as part of a Special Constable Recruitment Campaign. And if it wasn't, it should have been.

By contrast, the story 'Be a Pal to Handicapped' has plainly not excited anyone on the newspaper and is unlikely to inspire any readers. The story-line that has been selected is 'social worker makes appeal'. This is probably not the most interesting story that could be told about what volunteers and people in group homes do. It certainly does very little for the public image of mentally handicapped people, who figure as 'they' and 'them' throughout, usually as the passive objects of impersonal verbs. If you want total strangers to make friends then it's probably not helpful to start off by talking about 'release from hospital' and regular supervision by 'qualified staff who attend regularly to keep an eye on their progress'. That language smells of the official report. For 'mentally handicapped people' you can substitute any one of half a dozen 'problem' categories and the piece still makes perfect sense. However, the article does warm up with the quote, giving examples of what volunteers might be doing and it gets full marks for telling people how they can get involved.

WYRA (West Yorkshire Radio Action) is a project that helps community and voluntary organizations and other public services to avoid the 'Be a Pal to Handicapped' treatment and, more positively, to use the approach and the techniques behind 'The Special Way of Life For a Mum' to further their aims.

ABOUT WYRA

Since 1981 WYRA has helped hundreds of local organizations make more effective use of the press, radio and TV in order to contact thousands of West Yorkshire people – getting them involved, giving them information, taking up their offers of help, and bringing hundreds of thousands of pounds of otherwise unclaimed benefit into the local economy. In 1988, for example, a total of 150 voluntary and statutory organizations from West Yorkshire used our services.

Over the last nine years WYRA has acted as the umbrella for a wide range of initiatives with community and voluntary organizations and other public services involving young people, users of unemployment centres, women, Black and Asian communities, community health and self-help groups. Our most consistent work has been in providing two services to the voluntary/public sector. First the supply of information, advice and training in using the media, and second, regular action-line slots on local radio through our Pennine Action project. More recently we have launched a vocational training course (Positive Action Radio Training or PART) which aims to get more members of ethnic minorities, women and disabled people into the broadcasting industry.

WYRA is part of the Media Programme of Community Service Volunteers (CSV), a registered charity. CSV's main aim is to create opportunities for people to play an active part in their community. The Media Programme works with television and radio stations throughout the United Kingdom, promoting what in the trade is known as 'social action broadcasting' through a network of about forty media projects. These are mounted in partnerships with the BBC, independent television and radio companies and a wide range of national and local agencies as well as some commercial sponsors.

WYRA is also mounting an IBA-funded project to improve the services that ethnic minorities receive from the social action broadcasting provided by CSV media projects across the country. It is one of CSV's older and better established media projects, set up in 1981 with the very open brief of developing community uses of local radio. All the projects vary, of course, but WYRA's development and priorities have been different from most in that we are tied to no single radio station or media company. Though we do work closely with our partners in the media, we have preserved financial independence and autonomy in our programme of work.

Maintaining funding for a project like WYRA is an uncertain business but it is a task that has been eased by core funding from the West Yorkshire Metropolitan County Council, and from its successor, West Yorkshire Grants (the Joint Committee for Grants to Voluntary Bodies). WYRA also currently receives funding from Yorkshire Arts, the European Social Fund, the Opportunities for Volunteering Fund and the Sir George Martin Trust.

TRAINING IN USING THE MEDIA

WYRA has been running 'Using the Media' training courses and advising organizations since its inception. We are presently training about ninety people a year on courses and advising about sixty organizations. A precondition for successful work with media is a fully worked through media strategy. We have come to view the skills and techniques of public relations work (press release writing, handling a radio interview), and a background knowledge of the media industry (newspaper deadlines, journalists' methods of work, conventions on radio programming) as being of little help unless a group has first clearly defined its publicity goals and has the confidence to manage their public relations in pursuit of them.

The local media generally offer very few opportunities to present detailed discussion on questions of social policy. WYRA takes the view that it has been more valuable for community and voluntary organizations to use the media to make contact with people, rather than to persuade them or inform them of something. The power to reach out to total strangers – to individuals outside the existing networks of contacts that all organizations possess – is perhaps the greatest strength of the local media and of local radio in particular. Once you have people on the end of the phone, or have got them along to a meeting or an open day, or simply have their name and address, you can make a much better job of persuading them to join, or in giving them useful advice, or getting money out of them.

To argue a complex case through the local media is often impossible because it would take too long, or would be seen by broadcasters to be 'boring to most of our listeners'. Often the attempt to do so entails the risk of dangerously misleading simplifications and generalizations.

It is helpful for organizations to formulate clear, concise and comprehensible statements about their aims and objectives, about their programmes of work and about the issues that currently affect people they are working to help. But this does not necessarily mean that they need to simplify their thinking about complex issues. They should, however, be able to summarize the relevant key points for a given audience.

Preparation for effective use of the media can be a powerful acid test of an organization's clarity of purpose and relationships with the rest of the world. The community or voluntary organization that has a poor understanding of how others view it must necessarily be less effective – not just in its public relations but also in the whole range of its activities whether care work, service provision or fund-raising.

Any group seeking publicity must ask itself two questions. First, 'Why are we doing this?' Publicity should not be judged as an end in itself. Successful publicity, moreover, usually creates extra work, even though it may also attract more people to help complete it. The trick, of course, is not simply to get coverage. Groups should know in advance who they most want to talk to (audience), what they most want to say to them (message) and, since they are probably trying to promote some kind of social action, what they most want their audience to do (objective). 'Most' is a key word, since a clear understanding of priorities is crucial to organizations with limited resources of people and money.

The second question must be, 'Why bother with the mass media?' Face-to-face communication is more persuasive and gives complete control over the message. Consequently, producing leaflets, newsletters, posters, or videos may prove a more effective strategy. The problem with media which are readily controlled is one of limited distribution. Mass media are vital to get messages to a large number of people, or put pressure on remote decision-makers.

Contact with the press, radio and television, however, can put tremendous strains on a group and WYRA always advises groups to discuss issues and make sure there is agreement within the group concerning publicity aims. It is not possible to deal with media by committee and clear procedures must be established in matters such as authorizing statements, etc.

WYRA's basic training message is twofold. First, expressed briefly, 'Know your enemy.' Groups should get to know the various reporting styles of different local media. What types of stories and messages do they like to print or broadcast? What subject areas do they typically ignore? Groups should make contact, ask questions, pool information. Second, try to make it as easy as possible for local media to do and say what you want them to. This usually means doing as much of their job for them as you tactfully and discreetly can. Invite them to meetings, offer information and issue press releases. These procedures offer no guarantees against inaccurate, misleading or downright malicious reporting, but like any preventative measure they do reduce the risks.

The most important element in all this is that groups should learn how to spot a good story which conveys their message. The aim is to find an angle which is so attractive to the journalist or broadcaster that they do not trouble to look further for other, potentially

damaging, angles of their own invention. Finding that story calls
for creativity and open-mindedness. WYRA offers three broad rules
of thumb.

First, organizations must be wary of taking the public's interest
in their cause for granted. In using the mass media they are addressing a large and general audience, and not preaching to the con-
verted. Using mysterious jargon and abbreviations, assuming that
what is obvious to people in the group is equally obvious to outsiders are things which can be very off-putting and should be
avoided. This is no easy task and requires groups to step outside
of their activities and beyond what happened at the last committee
meeting to get a sense of how others perceive them. The history
of the group from the year dot may be fascinating to members but
can be very boring to those not yet involved. In brief, groups must
start from the audience's point of view – their interests, desires,
problems or needs – and then proceed to show the ways in which
the group can help.

Second, presenting a case effectively needs advance preparation.
There will always be limited amounts of time or space in which to
argue a case. WYRA's advice is to emulate market traders and put
the good stuff at the front: get straight to the point that most
concerns the target audience. It's best not to try to tell everything
to everyone all at once. Instead, hammer home one point at a time.
Groups that have several points to make will get more coverage
if they find different angles for each that can be timed and co-
ordinated into a campaign. Similarly, planning publicity up to, say,
a year ahead allows groups to anticipate opportunities to give their
campaign a boost.

Third, groups trying to persuade individuals to do something are
advised to make their target's role in the story an obvious, valuable
and positive one. Language needs to be used sensitively, employing
words that people would choose to describe themselves and avoiding those which would not be used face-to-face. Has anyone, for
example, ever described themselves as 'jobless'? The key technique
is to present arguments in terms of what people are doing, or what
is happening to them, and to let vivid example and anecdote make
the point stick in the audience's mind.

Any organization making sustained use of the media will suffer
disappointments and, occasionally, disasters. But the more publicity
work they do, the more practised, confident, and hence more effective, they become.

PENNINE ACTION

Pennine Action is WYRA's community information and advice service to Bradford, Calderdale and Kirklees. It uses scripted announcements, interviews, and phone-ins on Pennine FM (formerly Pennine Radio). These are always prepared in conjunction with partner organizations – community and voluntary organizations, statutory services, and sometimes a combination of all three. Listeners are encouraged to ring the Pennine Action line for further information, advice or counselling by trained workers or volunteers. The Pennine Action spots are broadcast throughout the day, and are also rewritten or translated for specialist programmes like 'Eastern Ear' aimed at the Asian community.

At the time of writing we are in the process of re-organizing the Pennine Action format to accommodate both the changes in broadcasting style of the radio station, and to create new links with other radio stations in the area, so that we can offer our partners in the community a more comprehensive service. New staff will also be bringing fresh experiences and contacts to the service.

However, we want to maintain our commitment to mounting features and campaigns only in conjunction with community and voluntary organizations, or other local public services, so that responding listeners can be properly catered for. We also want to continue to give space and time to smaller organizations and sections of the community who are not well represented in the media more generally. We don't want to become the 'good works' department of the radio station, and their only point of contact with groups in the community, or the sole vehicle for them on the air. So the following snapshot of Pennine Action's work is relevant, even if details may date.[1]

Between January and October 1988, Pennine Action received 1,481 calls in response to features ranging from voluntary conservation work, statutory wage increases for low-paid workers and changes to the social security system (not including calls direct to some organizations). The consultation, research, preparation of on-air and back-up material, telephone answering and referrals of calls relating to those features involved the collaboration of sixty-seven local and national organizations. Other Pennine Action features gave general publicity to events with no specific off-air follow-up. We will never know, for example, how many of the 140 people who came to a home-workers conference held in June that year came because they heard it on a Pennine Action spot.

Pennine Action has been a resource for community and voluntary groups serving the West Yorkshire area. A growing number of 'regulars' like Age Concern find our service a useful and efficient way of contacting potential volunteers. Similarly, Bradford's Community Dietitians, have supplied popular interviews, phone-ins and information sheets on all aspects of healthy eating.

Welfare rights take-up work has been a major part of the Pennine Action's work for some years. The 1988 Social Security Act introduced major changes to the benefit system. Pennine Action provided regular information and advice before the changes were implemented to ensure that as many people as possible knew how they would be affected and what they could do to protect their income. Once the changes had taken place, Pennine Action also ran a campaign on the very complex transitional protection arrangements. These campaigns resulted in the payment of £139,000 (Bradford Benefits Campaign estimate) in otherwise unclaimed benefits to several hundred of the poorest people in the three metropolitan districts served by Pennine Radio.

There were a large number of calls to Pennine Action from people who, whilst confused and distressed by the new regulations, also experience great difficulty in finding accessible information about their rights. We know from our callers that there is a substantial audience of people who are effectively isolated by disability, the care of children or relatives, unemployment or simple poverty, for whom Pennine Action features are an important source of information and help. The lack of alternative sources of information is underlined by the word-of-mouth ripple effect producing calls on features like our low pay series for up to six months after broadcasts.

Pennine Action has only been able to cover such a wide range of issues and offer useful back-up for listeners because of the collaboration with voluntary and statutory organizations across the three districts of Bradford, Calderdale and Kirklees. And Pennine Action's work would be impossible without the particular support and co-operation of advice agencies.

CHANGING TIMES

There has never been any statutory responsibility laid on radio stations to give coverage to voluntary and community organizations, except in the very broadest terms of 'serving the community'. Some individual broadcasters and station managers have made conscious efforts to interpret this in a positive manner, taking the initiative to talk and listen to community and voluntary groups. For others the phrase simply means a couple of days 'snowline' a year and a bit of fundraising for handicapped kiddies. Even then the professionalism and marketing magic that goes into promoting the station itself is not always apparent in the promotion of the worthy cause.

Stations may not even be obliged to pay that kind of lip service if the large-scale deregulation of broadcasting envisaged in the new Broadcasting Bill goes through. CSV, together with many other voluntary organizations has been campaigning for a statutory requirement on broadcasters to undertake Social Action Broadcasting.

But even in advance of new broadcasting legislation, local radio – indeed the entire media industry – has been changing, and in ways that offer new barriers to fair or effective coverage. First, ownership and control is increasingly concentrated into the hands of large conglomerates with extensive holdings in all forms of communications. This must have a profound, if indirect, effect on editorial policy towards the coverage of many issues.

Second, broadcasting is on the brink of an explosion in the number of channels and services, which will divide and segment the audience into more saleable chunks. This replaces the very idea of broadcasting with one of narrowcasting, and threatens to isolate some groups in society still further. Third, production costs are forced down. Daytime and satellite TV schedules, for example, are full of cheap, live, talk shows which, while they are suitable for some kinds of appeals and social action broadcasting, do not have the resources or programming policies to produce in-depth or sustained coverage of an issue, even within the rather special meaning that phrase has in the television industry (i.e. not very deep and not very sustained coverage).

Deregulation and increased competition may however bring some benefits to some community and voluntary organizations. Community radio stations may offer more airtime for issues and campaigns that are presently given little attention on the BBC or independent radio stations. This may be poor trade-off, however, if that simply encourages the latter to drop their coverage entirely. This is a particular danger for minority groups whose voices may simply never be heard by others.

Hitherto, the people who work in the more powerful mainstream media have not formed a representative cross-section of our society. Black and Asian people, people with disabilities, and women are particularly under-represented in all areas of broadcasting. The coverage of community and voluntary organizations representing those groups is generally stereotyped, marginal, or both. WYRA believes that the changes in broadcasting have given rise to new opportunities for employment (and self-employment). Two specific and very different kinds of opportunity are presented by the legalization of community radio and the implementation of Equal Opportunities policies within the BBC.

WYRA's Positive Action Radio Training (PART) courses are aimed at changing that imbalance, and exploiting the rapid and profound change that the British media are currently experiencing. PART gives the women and men on the course a solid basic training in radio production skills as well as relevant training in the areas of electronics and computing, work experience in the radio industry, and practical help and advice from professional broadcasters about how to get started in a radio career, and the wide variety of possibilities open to them.

The PART courses are designed specifically for people who want a career in broadcasting and are determined to get in. It won't guarantee employment in the industry but PART is an invaluable stepping-stone towards traineeships and other junior positions.

By the end of 1989, WYRA will have trained twenty-four students from West Yorkshire, with financial help from a range of sources, mainly our core funders, West Yorkshire Grants, and the European Social Fund. Funding permitting we will be launching a larger, three-year programme of PART training from 1990 onward and intend to develop a similar package of training in electronic newspaper journalism.

The early 1980s, when WYRA was founded, was a time of expansion in both the independent and BBC local radio systems. Many interest groups at the time saw local radio as a useful new channel of communication. There was also widespread agreement that the voluntary sector was generally poorly prepared to exploit the new opportunities presented by the new stations. Since then the voluntary and public service sector has become more aware of, and more skilled in, media manipulation. It has also learnt to be more cautious in dealing with any media initiative that has the label 'community' pinned to it.

The 1990's will bring a new competitiveness and new complexities to the fabric of the media in Britain. Voluntary organizations want to promote issues that are vitally important to millions of media consumers, but unless they push they may find that the media revolution has relegated them to the 'Be a Pal to Handicapped' corner, where hardly anyone can see or hear them.

NOTE

1 There is generally very little in-depth evaluation of the effectiveness of Social Action Broadcasting. A good starting collection would be *On-Air, Off-Air, Case Studies* and other publications of the Media Project at the Volunteer Centre (29 Lower King's Rd, Berkhamsted, Herts, HP4 2AB). These chart the development of Social Action Broadcasting, but are strongly weighted towards the experiences of larger agencies and their collaborators in broadcasting. *Radio City Report* by Greater London Arts, 1989, gives a stimulating discussion of the consequences of changes in radio for public service broadcasting.

14 Public relations and social services: a view from the statutory sector

Lynne Walder

THE WAY IT WAS

As the publicity says, Bradford is a surprising place. After seventeen years as a journalist I came to live in the Bradford area while the Honeyford affair was still raging. The national media had descended on the city and the council was at the centre of a storm over alleged racist comments by a head teacher in one of the city's schools. The local authority was getting a very bad press but Bradford's unpopularity in newspaper reports was not untypical. Local authorities in general have frequently proved ideal targets, sometimes rightly, for media criticism.

Bradford was getting a bad press because of Honeyford, but nationally, the public image of social services seemed to be at an all-time low after media reporting of several child abuse scandals. As always, social workers were being vilified by the popular press out for a story at any price; an uninformed serious press offered only marginally better coverage.

I was appointed, as far as I am aware, as the country's first Social Services Public Relations Officer, in 1987. Surprisingly, I may well still be the only one based within the directorate, rather than the press office, which underscores Tom White and Valerie Howarth's observations concerning the relative reluctance of the statutory sector to 'grasp' the public relations 'nettle'. It was certainly an interesting challenge. It was frightening, but in a certain sense I didn't have much to lose; the situation simply couldn't have been much worse in terms of the local press coverage local authorities were receiving at that time.

When I first arrived, the local press were predictably suspicious. As a former reporter I know that journalists never want to talk to a press officer. They feel there may be a cover-up, that the press officer may not know what they are doing or understand the journalists' needs. Journalists also have a healthy cynicism about local authorities and a fairly unhealthy scepticism about social work. But more worrying were the suspicions of the social service staff. Not surprisingly they were unsure if they could trust someone who came from what they perceived as the dreaded media world. Many felt that I shouldn't be privy to confidential information and that I would not understand the complex issues involved which demanded a professional's expertise. I felt I had to work promptly but carefully to change the attitudes and relationships between journalists and social services staff.

A major factor, indeed a precondition to make any public relations strategy work, is a director who is trusting, supportive, committed to the job and keen to be proactive in creating an improved image for social services. It was also important to get the support of the people in my Policy and Information section who were helpful, enabling and very caring.

With hindsight it was perhaps fortunate that I was 'thrown in at the deep end'. I started in April just before the local elections with fur flying in all directions as politicians looked for publicity either to improve their own chances or to attempt to decimate the competition. The council workers were often caught in the middle. Within this climate I was quickly able to show that I could understand the issues, that I could be trusted and that I could actually take the heat off many of the staff in the social services. For their part, local journalists also learned to trust me fairly quickly. I knew what they wanted, I didn't 'cover up', I didn't tell lies and I was always as pleasant and helpful as I could be. These first hectic few weeks set the agenda for the philosophy and strategy which subsequently we have implemented.

PUBLIC RELATIONS PHILOSOPHY AND STRATEGY

One of the problems of working in local government is knowing that strictly you are not your own boss. You are accountable to at least three groups of people. First, you are ruled by a political group and have to work within the parameters of that group's philosophy and strategy. Second, it is necessary to recognize that other officers and senior managers will expect certain things from a public relations officer. Finally, but equally importantly, is an awareness that you are accountable to the councils, clients and ratepayers in general. This multiple accountability creates some very difficult situations, some very worried and insecure people who are not keen to adopt a high media profile because of the possible consequences. Consequently, establishing a public relations philosophy and strategy was not the simplest of tasks and confronted problems unique to the statutory sector. It was necessary to set down three very basic but important ground rules at the outset. First, media inquiries will be treated very seriously and our reaction will be prompt; second, we will anticipate bad press; third, we will 'open up' to the media. We judged each of these points to be vital elements in a successful public relations strategy. But the crucial element in establishing successful media relations is to take the time and trouble necessary to be briefed fully to deal with any crisis. It's no good giving ill-informed 'off-the-cuff' comments which might rebound the next day. We had to make sure that we always reacted quickly and worked within media deadlines, however unreasonable they may sound on occasion. Whenever there is a crisis, officers brief me as fully as possible before the story hits the media. It's not always possible to anticipate where difficulties and problems arise but we try to be as prepared as possible in advance. If a major situation arises I will have a meeting to discuss the issues with the director and the officers involved. The director will make a decision on the case practice and I will advise on what information the media might want and how the matter should be handled in its presentation to reporters. Occasionally we will take the initiative in contacting the media to tell them about a situation, instead of waiting for it to 'break', so that they are informed about the issues and have our side of the story first. I will decide who is to be interviewed on television, radio and for the newspapers. Another aspect of my job is to make sure the politician or officer is fully briefed. They will not always need an in-depth knowledge to answer all the questions but being well prepared gives people confidence. It also means they are unlikely to be caught out and 'dry up'. Most importantly it means that they are likely to convey the positive elements in a situation from the authority's perspective.

When it is judged necessary to play a low profile on an issue because of the sensitive nature of the problem, or because of the legal position, a statement is prepared in advance so that social services are not caught out by giving 'no comment' or by being 'unavailable for comment'.

But how has this strategy worked in practice? Soon after I started, Bradford became the centre of a child sex scandal. A politician had made comments about the vice ring he claimed was operating in the city. The local news agency leapt on his comments and overnight Bradford became the child vice capital of Europe without any firm evidence whatsoever to support the allegations. The story was front page news in the local press. The popular or 'gutter' press were keen to print and some did so without checking anything out with us. One of the serious nationals and BBC television also pounced.

To get a grip on the story we gathered the available facts and figures together, admitted that there was a problem concerning teenage girls and boys on the streets, but stressed that it was no worse than in other cities. We realized it was a good opportunity to air some of these issues in the community and try to point out the community's responsibility, at least in part, for them. We suggested it would be advisable for the Child Protection Co-ordinator and the Area Officer to offer to be interviewed as part of an in-depth feature. The Director agreed to do a live television interview and pieces for the radio. Then we began negotiating with the media. We persuaded them to forget the 'child vice capital of Europe' angle. This wasn't easy because once the media are committed to a story 'line' they are reluctant to relinquish it. Reporters sometimes convey the impression they don't want the facts to spoil the story.

The tactic I suggested at this time was to offer the media case histories. This was not popular at first, especially among social workers who felt it was a breach of confidentiality. But I felt strongly that they were powerful vehicles through which to illustrate the problem social services were attempting to resolve. We arrived at a compromise by agreeing to present cases with small details changed to protect the identities of the people involved. We have incorporated this strategy into all our publicity work. We have come to understand that adopting press techniques can help to get our case across. By agreeing to play the game according to their rules we can emerge the winners.

We try to turn every potentially 'bad' story to our advantage by using it to convey as much positive information as possible. A crisis can be used to educate the public. Additionally, we have continued our policy of 'openness and honesty'. If we have made a mistake we admit it and apologize. If there has been a serious case of complaint against the department, an inquiry is conducted and we discuss the outcome with the media.

Confidentiality continues to be a problem. I have always taken the view that if you have established successful working relationships with the media it is possible, and often a good idea, to talk 'off the record'. If you make it very clear that the information is not for quoting, the media will mostly respect that judgement. I have also taken the view that if clients have already given details of their case to the media then it is permissible to talk off the record about our side of the story. On record we would probably issue a statement claiming that we could not discuss particular cases but suggesting that typically the following difficulties tend to arise in these kinds of cases. We would also try to reassure the public about how the department was handling the situation. The purpose of speaking off the record is that it might change the slant of the story more to our favour. There seems little point and, indeed, I have always refused to fight with my hands tied behind my back. To put the matter bluntly, if we don't use all the weapons we have, we have only ourselves to blame if the outcome is not to our liking.

When the Cleveland child sex abuse story broke we felt we had to try even harder to make the media understand the role of social services in these matters. There were some local cases of child abuse where individuals had gone to the press. In order to help journalists put the issue in perspective and discredit some of the sensational misinformation coming from some quarters in Cleveland, Bradford social services sponsored a lunchtime seminar. We invited local media to an intensive session to explain some of the central issues involved in child sexual abuse. We asked a local paediatrician to bring slides illustrating examples of abuse. We were well briefed with facts and figures about our case loads, without disclosing any confidential details about particular clients. We had evidence of good multi-agency work in Bradford. We showed the press the disclosure dolls.

The subject of child sexual abuse seemed to fascinate the media because it seemed to involve so much mystery, so much closing of ranks by doctors and social workers. We decided we should try to show it was only one element in a difficult job and try to explain how difficult decision-making can be in this area. Journalists were presented with a contrived case history and asked, 'What would you do?' Eventually, of course, they began to realize that cases of child protection do not lend themselves readily to clear-cut decisions. But in addition to 'enlightening' the press, I had to convince the social services staff that journalists are not two-headed monsters and explain that without our side of the story the press have few options other than to write a negative story. I also needed to show them why the press reacted in certain ways on certain occasions.

Two different media training courses were held for social services staff. The first concerned newspapers, which I tutored, with the second about television, where a professional company was invited to offer the course involving role-play techniques. The newspaper day started with very basic information about the differing professional cultures, structures and work schedules and deadlines in social services and the press. The chief reporter from the Bradford office of the *Yorkshire Post* spoke about his job and gave some hints on how to achieve positive press coverage. The remainder of the course was devoted to looking at past press coverage and how we might have done better. I had to face some degree of hostility from social services staff on those days. A number of issues were argued quite keenly but, in the end, almost everyone who attended reported feeling that in future they would feel more in control, more able to deal with situations, and confident in speaking about their work to the press. We also had lots of fun.

The television course was more frightening. People were put under a lot of pressure and an impression of a real television studio was created when the hot lights blazed down and the video cameras rolled on staff as the interviewer probed all kinds of horror stories supplied especially for the day. The course began with a discussion about what television is looking for in a story and how to handle the medium by learning some basic techniques. Then there were short stand-up interviews along very general lines, followed by the in-depth studio ordeal. The playback and feedback was incredibly difficult to face but entertaining. We laughed a lot, almost cried a lot, but discovered that we were actually quite good. As with the press course, most people emerged feeling confident. A minority vowed never to go near a television camera again in their lives. The course has certainly stood us in good stead on many occasions when we have been asked to take part in television programmes.

Shortly after the course, television became the major vehicle for one of the most successful national initiatives. Bradford's high-profile approach to media brought the use of social work counselling following a disaster to the very forefront of media attention. I'm convinced that our stance in Bradford following the football ground fire has made other social services departments more prepared to be proactive following such tragic disasters. We were not always popular within the directorate, or even the town, for initiating so much coverage from media but we were determined to get a good image for social work – away from the more typical and disparaging child abuse scandals. We instigated publicity and made sure we always responded positively to requests. I knew we had been successful and perhaps had established a precedent in this area when we were headlines on the 9 o'clock news following the Hungerford disaster as an example of good social work practice on such occasions. It is now part of the journalist's brief always to contact social services following disasters. We can claim we have achieved for counselling the recognition it deserved but have also helped to bring the taboo subject of death into the open and have tried to educate people about how to cope with bereavement.

Since I came to Bradford there have been many disasters and at one time we were having problems juggling people to meet requests for interviews from television, radio and the press. One councillor was heard to say she was sick of seeing the director, John Crook, every time she turned on the television. Now we feel able to adopt a lower profile approach and let other areas tackle media work to publicize a very important aspect of social work.

Another national first with television for Bradford social services was our participation in the thames Television *Witness* series. Never before had a social services department opened its doors so wide and laid its activities so open to public scrutiny. But we had nothing to hide and were prepared for the heavy negotiation with television staff who became great friends. Again, there was conflict from within the department. Some people were very keen to show the public what goes on in an area office; others felt it was a gross breach of confidentiality to allow cameras in. We had to work these issues through over a long period of time as David Perrin has noted in Chapter 4.

I felt the end product was a fair reflection of the different kinds of cases we have to help with, of the pressures under which social services departments operate and the inevitable risk-taking, on a daily basis, which the department must undertake in order to protect and support.

The workers who took part were also mostly happy with the outcome. The only problem we had was when one of the tabloid papers chose to sensationalize a child protection case from the programme. The client was very upset and needed a lot of support which left the workers involved feeling very responsible. It was a sad conclusion which again did little to help our relationship with the popular press. We have learned to be very cautious of news agencies and the popular press; it is difficult to envisage any improvement in these matters.

THE 'CHILD SAFE' CAMPAIGN

Since my appointment there have been a number of major social work stories which have hit the national media. There was the death of Kimberley Carlile, the pre-birth wardship of the Rayner baby in Tameside and, of course, Cleveland. On each occasion social workers have been tried, convicted and sentenced by a vitriolic press. Staff in social services departments around the country have responded angrily to press coverage. Part of their anger expressed the fact that mistakes had been made which reflected badly on them, but their anger was mostly a consequence of the treatment the social workers received.

In Bradford we also suffered from the reflected bad public image of our work. We tried on each occasion to do our 'opening up' and invited people to write features on the issues being faced. However, Cleveland was so big, and the public reaction so strong, that we knew we had to do something much more radical to achieve any counterbalance. We provided stories and seminars for the press while the scandal blazed. It felt like an uphill struggle but luckily social workers, doctors and police all over the country were also working hard to try and inform the media about the issues and try and reassure the public (see, for example, Chapter 15 by Sally Arkley and David Jones). We realized that with the publishing of the Butler-Sloss inquiry, social work was going to face its heaviest onslaught to date. Our strategy was to stick our necks out and to go on the attack. We decided to launch a child protection campaign the day after the Cleveland report was published. It was a difficult period because the inquiry took much longer than anticipated and hence the report was published much later than we expected. It was decided to stick with the original decision and to use the time to prepare with even greater thoroughness. We had negotiated an extraordinary deal with the local newspaper, the Bradford *Telegraph & Argus*, to run the campaign jointly. The deal was that although the newspaper would have to publish any story of complaint about us, it would also be counterbalanced by our positive stories which would be published over a period of weeks and which would attempt to explain the major issues involved in child sexual abuse. The main aim of the campaign was to get a multi-disciplinary group of people together to endorse what we were doing and to help us get the message across to the public. We prepared six leaflets: one targeted at the general public, another specifically for parents, and four for different school-age children, starting with tiny tots and going up to teenagers. The *Telegraph & Argus* designed a logo and posters and lots of coloured balloons. The campaign was launched in a blaze of glory with television, radio and press coverage. But undoubtedly the most significant aspect of the campaign was the series of features in the *Telegraph & Argus*. We arranged for people to talk to the press about their experiences; some of these were adults who had been abused as young people. We encouraged doctors, the police, social workers, the NSPCC, voluntary groups and council chiefs to contribute short articles to the press. We gave the public the facts and, more importantly, tried to convey an idea of the kinds of things that some older people can inflict on younger people. On the whole the campaign offered an incredible insight into child abuse.

Inevitably, whenever you attempt to achieve a high media profile on any subject there is a risk of backlash because some aspects of social services work involve making difficult and sometimes unpopular decisions. Someone is always going to be unhappy and complain. However, in the case of the 'Child Safe' campaign, I think we had only two bad press stories as a consequence of our efforts. By any standards that was a resounding success. We also managed to reassure the public that Bradford had a first-class child protection unit, that teachers were trained to recognize child abuse and that the police, doctors and social services worked together to protect children. We also reassured the public that rehabilitation was the main target of our work, not removing children from their parental home.

SUMMARY

Working with the media entails risks. We don't always get it right and sometimes feel very let down. Despite our very good working relationship with the local press there are still quiet news days when they have big spaces to fill, few good stories and so they 'jack up' half a story simply to fill the paper. But we in public relations and social services remain optimistic and always counterbalance any disappointments by looking to our successes. We refuse to be defensive and remain proactive in our attitude. We are committed to the view that for a social services department public relations is essential and that working with the media is the best way to communicate with thousands or even millions of people. While we need to work hard, we often have lots of excitement, fun and enjoyment.

Ultimately our commitment to public relations means that we are able to inform our clients about what we do, what help is available to them and where it is on offer. I am sure that in many cases this means that services are improved because of the authority's high degree of accountability.

15 The social work profession and professional public relations

Sally Arkley and David Jones

Many professional groups approach public relations with suspicion. More established professions may have come to expect automatic recognition by, and even a degree of deference from, the public. 'Stooping' to public relations may therefore appear demeaning and unnecessary. Social work has never been in that situation and indeed, in the current climate of public and political suspicion of 'professional conspiracies', professional organizations have been forced to learn the effective use of public relations. Social work has probably been less successful than, say, nursing or medicine in attracting public support and sympathy. The British Association of Social Workers (BASW)[1] has clear public relations objectives. They are: providing membership and so sustaining the organization; publicizing policy initiatives that the Association wishes to pursue; responding effectively to external initiatives; promoting a positive image of social work in general and BASW in particular, and helping social workers to take pride in their profession. These objectives have to be pursued within the limited resources of the Association. This means, frustratingly, that BASW is generally more successful in responding to situations than in setting the agenda.

A significant constraint on effective media response by the social work profession is the fragmented nature of the personal social services (PSS). There is no recognized national voice for all PSS interests; no agency or local authority will ever yield its final right to pursue its own strategy and the many different organizations in the field are all competing for media attention. The organizations providing services also control access to examples of good practice, to essential or effective campaigning. The major national bodies have recognized the need to work more effectively on co-ordinating public relations, the most conspicuous example being the 'Community Care Now!' campaign which successfully pressed the case to Government for local authorities and social work to be given lead responsibility for community care management. BASW is campaigning for the creation of a national Social Work Council or similar regulatory body to set standards and to develop a national presence, even though this could detract from the Association's own national profile.

BASW – AN EVOLVING PUBLIC RELATIONS STRATEGY

BASW always responded to media enquiries but it was the Maria Colwell case in 1974 (the first of several child abuse tragedies involving social workers) which first brought home the importance of effective media relations. Child abuse cases have been a constant focus of media interest ever since, paradoxically offering BASW many opportunities for developing a public profile, albeit often in a critical climate.

At first the Association responded by developing public relations as one component of the job of a social work staff member. Inevitably, this task often took second or third place to other professional and organizational demands. It proved especially difficult to invest time in developing essential media contacts. In the early 1980s the Association commissioned a survey of social workers from which it became clear that effective public relations and a high parliamentary profile were two activities which members and potential members valued highly. A staff restructuring at the time enabled the creation of a full-time public relations post and a part-time parliamentary post, both of which have significantly changed the emphasis of the Association's campaigning and contributed to a higher profile. Media experience and ability was also a significant factor in the appointment of a new General Secretary in 1985. It was not entirely coincidental that his professional area of specialist expertise had been child abuse, where he had a reputation as a practitioner and writer.

Coming to terms with the demands of the press, radio and television has not been easy for a membership organization with a strong emphasis on formal democratic procedures. The process of approving policy can be time-consuming and a report or statement can emerge several months after public interest has waned.

There can also be the dilemma of identifying the spokesperson. The media is always attracted to personalities and trusted 'performers', yet a membership organization's strength lies in the diverse expertise of its members, some of whom wish to exploit public interest in their specific subject. Balancing these conflicting objectives is a constant challenge.

The Association has consciously given staff and Honorary Officers the authority to make immediate comment on topical issues, subject to their own assessment of current Association thinking. The benefit of a public profile is seen as outweighing the risk involved. The General Secretary and Public Relations Officer usually determine who speaks on a given subject and when; there has been a balance of staff and members. This has not proved controversial and members have welcomed the immediacy of the BASW media presence. In practice, this has meant that on major issues, such as child abuse inquiries or significant government policy changes, a small group of key members and staff have worked closely together to agree the statement and strategy to be promoted.

BASW, however, also exists in its local branches, which have considerable autonomy over local press contacts. Some have developed very effective links with local papers and radio, others find it impossible to use the media at all. Branch spokespersons are always more vulnerable to attack by local agencies and politicians, especially when the public comment is usually about the organization that employs them or funds their work. It is not unknown for threats of legal action against individuals to follow a local branch media statement. For this reason, the Association approved guidance for branches on public relations and media initiatives in 1988.[2]

There exists a clear gap between the role BASW has defined for itself in its relations with the media and how the media itself wishes to utilize the Association.

THE MEDIA AND BASW

BASW closely monitors media coverage of the social work profession and social issues. As well as releasing statements and detailed briefings on professional matters the Association believes it has a responsibility to raise public awareness about a number of issues, particularly the effects of social legislation. To this end BASW frequently distributes press releases and employs its media contacts. The response is patchy and a source of some frustration to the organization. A survey of a typical six-month period in BASW's Public Relations Office illustrates the point.

In the first half of 1989 the Association issued press releases about Association issues, wrote to letters pages in newspapers, and

complained (verbally and in writing) to the media about its treatment of social workers. In addition BASW issued statements on
the following: Community Care and the Griffiths' report,[3] the Children Bill, juvenile offenders, the Hillsborough disaster, the tagging
of offenders and the Local Government and Housing Bill. Media
response was, on the whole, poor. Community Care and the Association's response to Sir Roy Griffiths' report being the only issues
to attract real interest.

When unsolicited media approaches to BASW are analysed, however, a different picture emerges. In the first half of 1989 BASW
received slightly under 200 enquiries from the non-trade press.[4]
Most requests were for background information on a particular
issue. A few led to television or radio appearances by BASW staff
or members and the occasional direct quote was printed. Nearly
half the enquiries received were related to child sexual abuse. These
were especially prevalent when the report of the Doreen Pearson
inquiry was published in July 1989. The next biggest area of enquiry
was about the Association's views on the Government's response
to Sir Roy Griffiths' report. This was mostly in response to BASW's
intensive publicity on the matter and so cannot be regarded as
'unsolicited'. Table 15.1 (p. 222) shows the range of subjects about
which the media approached BASW from February to August in
1989.

From this it would appear that the media recognizes and exploits
BASW's specialist knowledge about diverse social issues. It prefers,
however, to use this knowledge to discover and validate information
for stories of its own choosing, rarely acknowledging BASW as
the source, rather than pursuing BASW initiatives. The media is,
seemingly, particularly reluctant to investigate and publicize stories
about professional issues or to present the social worker's point of
view. An exception to this is the fairly consistent interest, especially
from the London press, in the 'social worker under stress' story.
The angle pursued here is the adverse effect overworked social
workers have on their clients, particularly children, and the abuse
or deaths of clients that can be attributed to this overwork. In the
period under analysis BASW's Public Relations Officer can only
trace one question about the effects of stress on the social worker.

It is fairly rare for a tabloid newspaper to cover BASW.[5] When
this happens it is usually because the paper hopes to receive a
quote or to discover a BASW policy which will confirm a negative
attitude towards the profession. Recently a tabloid paper asked for
BASW policy on bullying in school. The General Secretary's fairly

Table 15.1 Subjects on which BASW was consulted by the media, February–August 1989

Abandoned babies	Mentally ill parents
Adoption	National Health Service review
Adult survivors of child sexual abuse	Private hostels for young offenders
	Private social work
Black magic	Qualifications for social work
Bereaved parents	Residential care
Bullying	Sexuality in later life
Child abuse	Sexual relations with minors
The Children Bill	Single parents
Cleveland inquiry	Social work and the media
Community care	Statutory powers of social workers
Data Protection Act	Stress suffered by social workers
Day in the life of a social worker	Student social workers
Doreen Pearson inquiry	Tagging
European social workers	The theory of social work
Fostering	Trans-racial adoption
Hillsborough disaster	Violence against social workers
Local Government Act	Women in social work
Local government corruption	Young offenders

pacific response was translated to ' "Spank 'em", says Social Work Chief', when read back to Association staff. To general relief the story never appeared.

CASE EXAMPLES: BECKFORD AND CLEVELAND

Child abuse inquiries have necessarily dominated BASW's relationship with the media in recent years. It is in this area, the meetingplace between the Association's expertise and the media's interest, that BASW's public relations strategy has been at its most effective.

In the Jasmine Beckford case, a BASW working party was already reviewing the Association's policy on child abuse prior to the announcement of the inquiry. The Association was asked to provide legal advice and representation for a senior manager and a student member, both involved in the case. It was therefore essential to reach a speedy conclusion about the Association's response to the case. This was done by a small group including members of the working party, key staff and the Association's solicitor.

The Chair of the working group was called to give expert oral evidence to support the written submission of the Association. The written and oral expert evidence together with the constant presence of a lawyer representing some of the parties (who could repeatedly make public reference to the Association's policy) ensured a number of favourable references to the Association's position in the report itself. Association representatives were then able to draw on these 'marks of approval', from the independent panel, in media interviews after publication.

The report of the working group was accelerated so that it was ready to be launched at a press conference one week before the Beckford report was published. This strategy enabled the professional voice of social work to set some of the terms of the debate for the following week and to argue throughout that social workers had a clear view about the management of child abuse, regardless of the circumstances of that one case. It was not possible for the media to sustain a portrayal of social work as confused and ineffective.

The press conference was well attended and there was published coverage in the press as well as radio and TV interviews. Media interest was then followed up when the report was published, giving the Association over two weeks of constant exposure. At the same time, the Parliamentary Officer was briefing MPs about the wider issues and the many uncertainties in child abuse work. A notable feature of child abuse cases has been that, with only a few exceptions, the Houses of Parliament have recognized the difficulties faced by social workers and MPs have not indulged in the extremes of criticism seen in some popular papers. BASW considers that this is, in part, a result of its effective briefing of MPs.

In the Cleveland case the Association made a significant contribution to the inquiry and was widely quoted in the final report. Involvement began as the public concern escalated. BASW was approached for comment during the early stages when press reports were commenting on the large number of children being admitted to hospital. BASW head office was in contact with the local branch and attempts were made to get briefings from the local departments and other sources. There was a BASW working party on child sexual abuse already in existence and this was consulted about the issues as they emerged.

BASW Chair and General Secretary both gave oral evidence which was covered by the professional press. The General Secretary made personal contacts with the journalists covering the inquiry which were especially helpful when the report was published. As the inquiry progressed it became clear that journalists, who had started out viewing the issue as a 'simple' matter of parents and children 'abused' by authority, were becoming confused and seeking guidance. This BASW was able to supply on a neutral basis. The General Secretary travelled to Middlesbrough for the publication of the inquiry report and was able to react swiftly to events. Staff and members around the country were available to give interviews, the operation being co-ordinated at BASW headquarters.

BASW hosted major conferences on child abuse inquiries and child sexual abuse (in London, Leeds and Belfast) in subsequent weeks which again attracted media interest and enabled the Association to promote good practice. The degree of media interest was intense and highly intrusive, requiring determined handling. For example, a TV crew walked into the conference room without permission as a session was about to begin, seeking to film one of the participants. A press conference prior to the Belfast conference proved a more successful way to meet the needs of the media and, once again, there was coverage on both major TV channels, on radio and in the press. The General Secretary was invited to speak at the major DHSS-sponsored conference at Church House in London, which again lead to radio and TV interviews.

Throughout this period there was a detectable shift in the attitude of the more responsible journalists. After the publication of the Kimberley Carlile inquiry report, just weeks before the Cleveland inquiry was set up and when the cases were already attracting attention, a *Times* 'leader' criticized social workers for being too weak and indecisive and urged that they throw aside their 'theological' belief in maintaining families and do more to protect children by taking them away from their parents. The Cleveland cases, in contrast, involved many children removed from home and a later *Times* leader called for patience and caution and criticized the social workers for impetuosity. Journalists increasingly recognize the inherent dilemma exposed by such hasty moralizing on their part. The Association believes that its strategy over several years of never condoning bad practice and always talking objectively about the realities and limitations of child abuse work have influenced the public climate on an issue where it is all too easy to react with violent emotion. BASW has always kept two simple public relations aims in mind when talking about child abuse. First, to stress that social workers know what they are doing and second, to convey the fact that thousands of children *are* being protected from abuse by social workers.

BASW – PROMOTING POSITIVE IMAGES OF SOCIAL WORK

BASW has ensured that, during a decade of criticism of social work, especially in the popular media, there has been a consistent and confident voice representing social work and challenging the more extreme press ravings. The Association's monitoring of its relations with the media has been valuable in helping to plan future strategy. It is clear that the Association must come to terms with the gap that exists between the subjects it wishes the media to pursue and those in which the media itself is interested. A public relations strategy is evolving which takes account of this. Lack of interest by the media in the professional lives of social workers does not mean that BASW is ceasing to issue statements on their role but rather that the Association is concentrating on communicating how interesting, relevant and indeed vital that role can be. There are some pleasing developments. Television and radio journalists seem more receptive to the positive presentation and serious discussion of social work. Twice in the last year BASW has been closely consulted on major television documentaries about the profession. BASW staff continue to build valuable contacts in the broadcasting media. The Association is now developing a highly assertive strategy, in a time of significant change in social legislation, of 'educating' the media by presenting social workers as 'in touch', realistic and, above all, professional. There are, for example, articles scheduled to appear in women's and career guidance magazines presenting social work as an attractive profession, filled with opportunity and touched with the 'glamour' of caring, the 'nineties reaction to the excesses of the last decade. BASW is not confining itself to the media in its efforts to improve the public perception of social work. The Association, as the social worker's leading voice, is addressing its ways of presentation, designing a range of new literature and launching a campaign to make social workers feel good about themselves.

Social work is, in all honesty, a minor activity, employing a small and poorly paid workforce in a wide diversity of settings. The Association itself has limited resources; the British Medical Association's poster campaign on the restructuring of the National Health Service almost certainly cost more than BASW's entire annual budget. Yet social work issues are of major public interest demanding a highly effective public relations response. BASW has reallocated resources to meet this challenge. While there has been success in reacting to news stories, introducing new topics and setting the agenda is more difficult, especially in a political climate hostile to the interests of many 'consumers' of social work. There is also a need to speak more clearly to social workers themselves.

BASW has a clear analysis of the public relations needs of social work. This recognizes the high value placed by the general public on social work in charitable agencies – no different in content from much local authority work – and the opinion polls which suggest that there is considerable public support for social work. It remains to be seen whether more effective targeting of very limited resources will further enhance BASW's profile and effectiveness. There can be little doubt that any major impact on public understanding of social work will only be achieved by a co-ordinated strategy involving the major national organizations of the personal social services.

NOTES

1 The professional Association for social workers throughout the United Kingdom. It has close to 11,000 members and was formed in 1970 by the merger of a number of older and specialist social work professional associations. BASW represents about one third of qualified social workers and includes some unqualified workers as full members.
2 Media Guidelines, available from BASW, 16 Kent Street, Birmingham, B5 6RD.
3 Sir Roy Griffiths, *Community Care – An Agenda for Action*, London, HMSO, 1988.
4 BASW is in regular contact with all social work's professional journals and enjoys frequent if not always positive, coverage.
5 Other than the regional papers, for example, the Liverpool press did mention BASW after the Hillsborough disaster.

References

ADSS (1986) *Report to Executive Council: ADSS Study Group on Public Relations*, mimeo, London: Association of Directors of Social Services.

Andrews, C. (1974) 'The Maria Colwell inquiry', *Social Work Today* 4, 10 January 1974:637–44.

Association of London Authorities (1987) 'Its the way they tell 'em: distortion, disinformation and downright lies', ALA, April 1987.

Bailey, P. (1967) *At the Jerusalem*, London: Jonathan Cape.

Barfoot, J. (1986) *Duet for Three*, London: The Women's Press.

Barker, P.J. (1975) 'Principal Social Worker', *Social Work Today* 6, 11 December 1975:577–8.

BASW (1981) *Submission to the NISW Working Party on the Role and Tasks of Social Workers*, Birmingham: British Association of Social Workers.

Becker, S. and Macpherson, S. (1986) *Poor Clients: The Extent and Nature of Financial Poverty amongst Consumers of Social Work Services*, University of Nottingham: Benefits Research Unit.

Bell, S. (1988a) *When Salem Came to the Boro*, London: Pan Books.

Bell, S. (1988b) Letter in *New Statesman and Society*, 29 July 1988:24.

Beresford, P. (1988) 'Consumer views: data collection or democracy?', in I. Allen (ed.) *Hearing the Voice of the Consumer*, London: Policy Studies Institute.

Billig, M., Condor, S., Edwards, D., Gane, M., Middleton, D. and Radley, A. (1988) *Ideological Dilemmas: A Social Psychology of Everyday Life*, London: Sage.

Blom-Cooper, L. (1985) *A Child in Trust. The Report of the panel of inquiry into the circumstances surrounding the death of Jasmine Beckford*, London: Kingswood Press.

Blom-Cooper, L. (1987) *A Child in Mind: The Protection of Children in a Responsible Society. The Report of the Commission of Inquiry into the circumstances surrounding the death of Kimberley Carlile*, London: Borough of Greenwich.

Blumler, J.G. and Wolton, D. 'European perspectives on political communication: structures and dynamics', *European Journal of Communication*, 1990.

Boden, D. and Bielby, D. (1983) 'The past as resource: a conversational analysis of elderly conversation', *Human Development* 26:308–19.

Boden, D. and Bielby, D. (1986) 'The way it was: topical organization in elderly conversation', *Language and Communication*, 6, 1/2:73–89.

Booth, J. (1980) *A Different Animal: Local Radio and the Community*, Independent Broadcasting Authority Research Report.

Braithwaite, V. (1986) 'Old age stereotypes: reconciling contradictions', *Journal of Gerontology* 41, 3:353–60.

Branco, K. and Williamson, J. (1982) 'Sterotyping and the life cycle: views of ageing and the aged', in A. Miller (ed.) *In the Eye of the Beholder: Contemporary Issues in Stereotyping*, New York: Praeger.

Brawley, E.A. (1983) *Mass Media and Human Services: Getting the Message Across*, Newbury Park, Ca., USA: Sage.

Brewer, C. and Lait, J. (1980) *Can Social Work Survive?*, London: Temple Smith.

Brewer, M., Dull, V. and Lui, L. (1981) 'Perceptions of the elderly: stereotypes as prototypes', *Journal of Personality and Social Psychology* 41, 4:656–70.

Broadcasting in the 1990s: Competition, Choice and Quality (1988), Home Office, London: HMSO.

Browne, D.R. (1988) *What's Local about Local Radio? A Cross-National Comparative Study*, Paris: International Institute of Communications Study.

Brynin, M. (1988) 'The unchanging British press', *Media Information Australia* 47:23–37.

Butler, R. (1974) 'Successful ageing and the role of the life review', *Journal of the American Geriatrics Society* XXII, 12:529–35.

Butler-Sloss, E. (1988) *Report of the Inquiry into Child Abuse in Cleveland 1987*, Cm. 412, London: HMSO.

Calcott, D. (1990) *Report of the Committee on Privacy and Related Matters*, Cmnd 1102, London: HMSO.

Campbell, B. (1988) 'Champ or chump', *New Statesman and Society*, 15 July 1988:14–16.

Campbell, B. and Sedley, S. (1988) 'A family tragedy: a conversation', *Marxism Today*, July:16–19.

Clare, P. (1988) *Informing the Public: Making Video Material for Use in the Social Services*, Bristol Papers in Applied Social Studies, 6: Bristol University.

Clarke, J. (1988) 'Social work in the welfare state', unit 14, block 3, *Social Problems and Social Welfare* D211, Milton Keynes: Open University.

Cohen, S. (1972) *Folk Devils and Moral Panics: The Creation of the Mods and Rockers*, London: MacGibbon & Kee.

Cooper, J. (1983) *The Creation of the British Personal Social Services, 1962–1974*, London: Heinemann.

Coupland, N., Coupland, J., Giles, H., Henwood, K. and Wieman, J. (1988) 'Elderly self-disclosure: interactional and intergroup issues', *Language and Communication* 8, 2:109–33.

Coveney, P. (1957) *Poor Monkey: The Child in Literature*, London: Rockliff.

Coward, R. (1984) *Female Desire: Women's Sexuality Today*, London: Granada.

CPAG (1988) *Poverty, the Facts*, London: Child Poverty Action Group.

Craig, G. (1981) 'Review of studies of the public and users' attitudes, opinions, and expressed needs with respect to social work and social workers', paper for the NISW working party on the role and tasks of social workers, mimeo, London: National Institute of Social Work.

Creighton, S.J. and Noyes, P. (1989) *Child Abuse Trends in England and Wales 1983–1987*, London: NSPCC.

Cumming, E., Dean, L.R., Newell, D.S. and McCaggrey, I. (1960) 'Disengagement – a tentative theory of ageing', *Sociometry* 23, 1:23–35.

Dant, T. (1988) ' "Now . . . I wobble": relating old age and health', paper presented at Communication, Health and the Elderly: Proceedings of 1988 Fulbright Colloquium, Fulbright Colloquium, University of Wales.

Deutscher, M. (1983) *Subjecting and Objecting*, Oxford: Basil Blackwell.

DHSS (1985) *Review of Child Care Law*, London: HMSO.

DHSS (1986) *Social Work Decisions in Child Care: Recent Research Findings and their Implications*, London: HMSO.

DHSS (NI) (1986) *Report of the Committee of Inquiry into DHSS Children's Homes and Hostels* (chairperson W.H. Hughes), Belfast: HMSO.

DHSS (1989) *Caring for People: Community Care in the Next Decade and Beyond*, Cmd. 849, London: HMSO.

Donaldson, J. (1980) 'Changing attitudes towards handicapped persons: a review and analysis of research', *Exceptional Children* 46:504–14.

Doran, C. and Young, J. (1987) 'Child abuse: the real crisis', *New Society*, 27 November 1987:12–14.

Ennew, J. (1986) *The Sexual Exploitation of Children*, Cambridge: Polity Press.

Fawcett, J. (1987) 'The long road back to normality', *Community Care*, 29 October 1987:16–18.

Fennell, G., Phillipson, C. and Evers, H. (1988) *The Sociology of Old Age*, Milton Keynes: Open University Press.

Ferlie, E. and Judge, K. (1981) 'Retrenchment and rationality in the personal social services', *Policy and Politics* 9, 3.

Finer, S.E. (1958) *Anonymous Empire*, London: Pall Mall Press.

Forsyth, J. and Jones, H.P. (1986) 'Society pays to keep the ugliness hidden', *Listener*, 6 February 1986:10–11.

Fowler, R., Hodge, R., Kress, G. and Trew, T. (1979) *Language and Control*, London: Routledge & Kegan Paul.

Franklin, B. (1986) 'Public relations, the local press and the coverage of local government', *Local Government Studies* 12, 3, July/August:25–34.

Franklin, B. (1988a) *Public Relations Activities in Local Government*, London: Charles Knight Ltd.

Franklin, B. (1988b) 'Civic free newspapers: propaganda on the rates?', *Local Government Studies* 14, 3, May/June:35–57.

Franklin, B. (1989) 'Wimps and bullies: press reporting of child abuse', in P. Carter, T. Jeffs and M. Smith (eds) *Social Work and Social Welfare Yearbook* 1, Milton Keynes: Open University Press.

Franklin, B. and Lavery, G. (1989) 'Legislation by tabloid?', *Community Care* 23, March:26–9.

Fry, A. (1987) *Media Matters: Social Work, the Press and Broadcasting*, Surrey: Reed Business Publishing.

Fuller, R. and Stevenson, O. (1983) *Policies, Programmes and Disadvantage: A Review of the Literature*, London: Heinemann.

Galtung J. and Ruge M. (1981) 'Structuring and selecting news', in S. Cohen and J. Young (eds) *Manufacturing the News*, London: Constable.

Gamble, A. (1988) *The Free Economy and the Strong State: The Politics of Thatcherism*, London: Macmillan.

Gardner, A. (1982) *Public Image of Social Work and Social Workers*, mimeo, Department of Social Administration, University of Birmingham.

Geach, H. (1982) 'Social work and the press', *Community Care* 27, May 1982:14–16.

Glampson, A., Glastonbury, B. and Fruin, D. (1977) 'Knowledge and perceptions of the social services', *Journal of Social Policy* 6:1–16.

Glastonbury, B., Burdett, M. and Austin, R. (1973) 'Community perceptions and the personal social services', *Policy and Politics* 1, 3:191–211.

Goffman, E. (1961) *Asylums*, New York: Doubleday Anchor.

Golding, P. and Elliott, P. (1979) *Making the News*, London: Longman.

Golding, P. and Middleton, S. (1979) 'Making claims: news media and the welfare state', *Media, Culture and Society*, no. 1:5–21.

Golding, P. and Middleton, S. (1982) *Images of Welfare; Press and Public Attitudes to Poverty*, London: Martin Robertson.

Goldsmiths College Media Research Group (1987) *Media Coverage of London Councils: Interim Report*, London: Goldsmiths College.

Grainger, K., Atkinson, K. and Coupland, N. (forthcoming) 'Responding to the elderly: troubles talk in the caring context', in H. Giles, N. Coupland and J. Wiemann (eds) Communication, Health and the Elderly: Proceedings of 1988 Fulbright Colloquium, Manchester: Manchester University Press.

Griffiths, Sir Roy (1988) *Community Care – An Agenda For Action*, London: HMSO.

Guardian, 12 December 1987.

Habermas, J. (1970) 'On systematically distorted communication', *Inquiry* 13:205–18.

Hadley, J. (1987) 'Mum's not the word', *Community Care*, 5 November 1987:24–6.

Hall, P. (1976) *Reforming the Welfare*, London: Heinemann.

Hall, S. (1977) 'Culture, the media and the "ideological effect" ', in J. Curran, M. Gurevitch and J. Woollacott (eds) *Mass Communications and Society*, London: Open University Press.

Hall, S., Critcher, C., Jefferson, T., Clarke, J., Roberts, B. (1978) *Policing the Crisis*, London: Macmillan.

Hartley, P. (1985) 'Child abuse, social work and the press: towards the history of a moral panic', unpublished MA thesis, University of Warwick.

Hendricks, J. and Hendricks, C. (1986) *Ageing in Mass Society*, third Edition, Boston: Little, Brown and Co.

Hetherington, A. (1985) *News, Newspapers and Television*, London: Macmillan.

Hicks, F. (1988) *Survey of Public Awareness of Services Provided by the Social Services Department*, Derbyshire County Council.

Hills, A. (1980) 'How the press sees you', *Social Work Today* 11, 36, 20 May 1980:19–20.

Hodge, R. and Kress, G. (1988) *Social Semiotics*, Cambridge: Polity Press.

Holdsworth, R. (1987) 'Redefining the boundaries of trust', *Community Care*, 12 November 1987:22–3.

Holmes, G. (1987) 'The day Moore meant less', *Community Care*, 12 November 1987:25–7.

Horne, M. (1987) *Values in Social Work*, Aldershot: Wildwood House.

House of Commons (1984) *Second Report from the Social Services Committee: Children in Care*, London: HMSO.

Howe, D. (1986) *Social Workers and their Practice in Welfare Bureaucracies*, Aldershot: Gower.

Hurd, G. (1981) 'The television presentation of the police', in T. Bennett *et al.* (eds) *Popular Television and Film*, London: BFI Publishing.

Itzin, C. (1984) 'The double jeopardy of ageism and sexism: media images of women', in D. Bromley (ed.) *Gerontology: Social and Behavioural Perspectives*, London: Croom Helm.

Jacks, I. (1986) 'Professional journalism', *UK Press Gazette*, 10 February 1986:1.

Johnson, M. (1988) 'Never say die', *Listener*, 23 June 1988:21–2.

Jones, C. (1983) *State Social Work and the Working Class*, London: Macmillan.

Jones, R. (1987) *Like Distant Relatives: Adolescents' Perceptions of Social Work and Social Workers*, London: Gower,

Jordan, B. (1987) 'Counselling, advocacy and negotiation', *British Journal of Social Work* 17, 2:135–46.

Jordan, B. (1989) *The Common Good: Citizenship, Morality and Self-Interest*, Oxford: Basil Blackwell, ch. 2.

Jowell, R. and Airey, C. (eds) (1984) *British Social Attitudes: The 1984 Report*, London: Gower.

Jowell, R. and Witherspoon, S. (eds) (1985) *British Social Attitudes: The 1985 Report*, London: Gower.

Jowell, R., Witherspoon, S. and Brook, L. (eds) (1986) *British Social Attitudes: The 1986 Report*, London: Gower.

Jowell, R., Witherspoon, S. and Brook, L. (eds) (1987) *British Social Attitudes: The 1987 Report*, London: Gower.

Karpf, A. (1988) *Doctoring the Media: The Reporting of Health and Medicine*, London: Routledge.

Kelly, L. (1988a) 'What's in a name? Defining child abuse', *Feminist Review* 28:65–74.

Kelly, L. (1988b) 'Cleveland – feminism and the media war', *Spare Rib* 193:8–12.

King, J. (1989) 'Polish up public image', *Community Care*, 16 March 1989:18–19.

Kitchen, M. (1980) 'What the client thinks of you', *Social Work Today*, June 1980:14–19.

Kitzinger, J. (1988) 'Defending innocence: ideologies of childhood', *Feminist Review* 28:77–88.

Klaidman, S. and Beauchamp, T.L. (1987) *The Virtuous Journalist*, New York and Oxford: Oxford University Press.

Kogan, N. (1979) 'Beliefs, attitudes and stereotypes about old people: a new look at some old issues', *Research on Ageing* 1, 1:11–36.

Kosberg, J. and Harris, A. (1978) 'Attitudes toward elderly clients', *Health and Social Work* 3, 3:67–90.

Kress, G. and Hodge, R. (1979) *Language and Ideology*, London: Routledge & Kegan Paul.

La Fontaine, J. (1988) *Child Sexual Abuse*, ESRC Research Briefing, London: Economic and Social Research Council.

Laking, P. (1987) 'Our own little secret', *Community Care*, 19 November 1987:19–21.

Lees, D. (1979) 'As the hurt fades', *Social Work Today* 10, 19, 9 January 1979:15.

Levin, W. (1988) 'Age stereotyping: college student evaluations', *Research on Ageing* 10, 1:134–48.

Lewis, P.M. and Booth, J. (1989) *The Invisible Medium*, London: Routledge.

McConkey, R. and McCormack, B. (1983) *Breaking Barriers: Educating People about Disability*, London: Souvenir Press.

McCron, R. and Carter, R. (1988) 'Researching socially sensitive subjects: the case of child abuse', in *Annual Review of BBC Broadcasting Research Findings* 13, London: BBC Research Department, 69–77.

McGournan, S. (1984) 'A gay view on Kincora', *Fortnight*, May 1984:12.

McIntosh, M. (1988) 'Introduction to an issue: family secrets as public drama', *Feminist Review* 28:6–16.

Macleod, M. and Saraga, E. (1987) 'Abuse of trust', *Marxism Today*, August 1987:10–13.

Macleod, M. and Saraga, E. (1988a) 'Challenging the orthodoxy: towards a feminist theory and practice', *Feminist Review* 28:16–56.

Macleod, M. and Saraga, E. (1988b) 'Against orthodoxy', *New Statesman and Society*, 1 July 1988:15–19.

Madden, P. and Maund, I. (1987) 'Getting to know you', *Community Care*, 16 April 1987:18–19.

Martin, B. (1987) 'Moral messages and the press: newspaper response to a child in trust' in *After Beckford? Essays on Themes Related to Child Abuse*, Department of Social Policy, Royal Holloway and Bedford New College, Social Policy Papers No. 1.

Mason, J.K. (1978) *Forensic Medicine for Lawyers*, Bristol: John Wright.

Mason, P. (1989) 'The man who won't let go', *Care Weekly*, 31 March 1989.

Mawby, R., Fisher, C. and Hayle, J. (1979) 'The press and Karen Spencer', *Social Work Today* 10, 22, 30 January 1979:13–16.

Mawby, R., Fisher, C. and Parkin, A. (1979) 'Press coverage of social work', *Policy and Politics* 7, 4:357–76.

Millington, B. and Nelson, R. (1986) *Boys from the Blackstuff*, London: Comedia.

Milne, A. (1988) *DG, Memoirs of a British Broadcaster*, London: Hodder & Stoughton.

Moore, J. (1988) 'The question the Carlile report failed to answer', *Community Care*, 14 January 1988:26–7.

Murphy, D. (1974) 'The unfreedom of the local press', *New Society*, 19 December 1974:750–2.

Murphy, D. (1976) *The Silent Watchdog: The Press in Local Politics*, London: Constable.

NALGO (1989) *Social Work in Crisis: A Study of Conditions in Six Local Authorities*, London: National Association of Local Government Officers.

Nava, M. (1988) 'Cleveland and the press: outrage and anxiety in the reporting of child sex abuse', *Feminist Review* 28:103–22.

Nelson, B.C. (1978) 'Setting the public agenda: the case of child abuse', in J.V. May and A.B. Wildawsky (eds) *The Policy Cycle*, New York: Sage.

Nelson, B.J. (1984) *Making an Issue of Child Abuse: Political Agenda for Social Problems*, Chicago: University of Chicago Press.

New Society (1979) 'Findings: what people think of social workers', *New Society* 49, 878, 8 August 1979:248.

Newton, E. (1980) *This Bed My Centre*, London: Virago.

Nicholas, B.B. (1979) 'Image of social workers in fiction', *Social Work* 24, 5:419–20.

NISW (1982) *Social Workers: Their Role and Tasks* (the Barclay report), London: Bedford Square Press for the National Institute of Social Work.

NOP (1989) *Social Workers*, Survey Report 9060, London: National Opinion Polls.

Norman, A. (1987) *Aspects of Ageism: A Discussion Paper*, London: Centre for Policy on Ageing.

NSPCC and Greater Manchester Authority Child Sexual Abuse Unit (1988) *Child Sexual Abuse in Greater Manchester: A Regional Profile 1st March 1987 to 29th February 1988*, Manchester, May 1988.

O'Brien, J. and Tyne, A. (1981) *The Principle of Normalisation: A Foundation for Effective Services*; Campaign for Mental Handicap.

Owen, M. (1989) 'Satisfied customers', *Social Work Today*, 16 November 1989:14–15.

Parton, N. (1977) 'The natural history of non-accidental injury to children', MA thesis, University of Essex.

Parton, N. (1979) 'The natural history of child abuse: a study in social problem definition', *British Journal of Social Work*, 9, 4:427–51.

Parton, N. (1981) 'Child abuse, social anxiety and welfare', *British Journal of Social Work* 11, 4:391–414.

Parton, N. (1985) *The Politics of Child Abuse*, London: Macmillan.

Parton, N. (1989) 'Taking child abuse seriously', in The Violence Against Children Study Group, *Taking Child Abuse Seriously*, London: Unwin Hyman.

Perske, R. and Perske, M. (1988) *Circles of Friends*, Nashville: Abingdon Press, 45–7.

Phillips, M. (1979) 'Social workers and the media: a journalist's view', *Social Work Today* 10, 22, 30 January 1979:123.

Philpot, T. (1982) (ed.) *A New Direction for Social Work?*, Wallington: *Community Care* IPC Business Press.

Philpot, T. (1988) 'What social work must learn from Carlile' (interview with Louis Blom-Cooper), *Community Care*, 7 January 1988:12–15.

Philpot, T. (ed.) (1989) *The Residential Opportunity?*, Wallington: *Community Care* Reed Business Publishing Press.

234 References

Pitt, P.H.B. (1989) 'Social services: the way forward', County Councillor Bob Pitt's address to the Cleveland Social Services Department, 24 March 1989.

Pollak, A. (1982) 'Kincoragate puts Paisley on the spot', *New Statesman*, 12 February 1982.

Potter, J. and Wetherell, M. (1988) 'Accomplishing attitudes: fact and evaluation in racist discourse', *Text* 18:181–202.

Rafferty, E. (1989) 'The social work press', in P. Carter, T. Jeffs and M. Smith (eds) *Social Work and Social Welfare*, Yearbook 1, Milton Keynes: Open University Press.

Raymond, B. (1987) 'A child abuse inquiry – the lawyer's tale', *Social Work Today* 19, 15:16–17.

Reed, D. (1986) 'For social work read scapegoat', *Community Care*, 14 August 1986:17–18.

Rees, S. and Wallace, A. (1982) *Verdicts on Social Work*, London: Edward Arnold.

Reynolds, J. (1981) 'In showing *All Those Hard Luck Stories* did TV intrude?', *Listener* 106, 2736, 19 November 1981:594.

Robards, B. (1985) 'The police show', in B.G. Rose (ed.) *TV Genres: A Handbook and Reference Guide*, London: Greenwood Press.

Robb, B. (ed.) (1967) *Sans Everything: A Case to Answer*, London: Nelson.

Rojek, C., Peacock, G. and Collins, S. (1988) *Social Work and Received Ideas*, London: Routledge.

Rote, G. (1979) 'How to cope with the media', *Social Work Today* 10, 22, 30 January 1979:17.

Royal Commission on the Press (1947–9), Cmd. 6810, London: HMSO.

Ruddock, M. (1987) 'A child abuse inquiry – the social worker's tale', *Social Work Today* 19, 15:14–15.

Ruddock, M. (1988) 'A child in mind: a lost opportunity', *Social Work Today* 19, 20:14–15.

Rustin, M. (1979) 'Social work and the family', in N. Parry, M. Rustin and C. Satyamurti (eds) *Social Work, Welfare and the State*, London: Edward Arnold.

Ryan, J. and Thomas, F. (1980) *The Politics of Mental Handicap*, London: Penguin, ch. 5.

Sandler, A. and Robinson, R. (1981) 'Public attitudes and community acceptance of a mentally retarded person: a review', *Education and Training of the Mentally Retarded* 16:97–103.

Satyamurti, C. (1981) *Occupational Survival: The Case of the Local Authority Social Worker*, Oxford: Basil Blackwell.

Schonfield, D. (1982) 'Who is stereotyping whom and why?', *The Gerontologist* 22, 3:267–72.

Sedley, S. (1987) *Whose Child? The Report of the Public Inquiry into the Death of Tyra Henry*, London: Borough of Lambeth.

Seebohm Report (1968) Report of the Committee on Local Authority and Allied Personal Social Services, London: HMSO, Cmd 3703.

Shearer, A. (1979a) 'Tragedies revisited 1: the legacy of Maria Colwell', *Social Work Today* 10, 19, 9 January 1979:12–19.

Shearer, A. (1979b) 'Tragedies revisited 2: aftermath of the Tragic Deaths of Susan Auckland, Wayne Brewer and Karen Spenser', *Social Work Today* 10, 20, 16 January 1979: 15–19.

Shearer, A. (1979c) 'Tragedies revisited 3: have we learnt the lesson?', *Social Work Today* 10, 21, 23 January 1979:11–16.

Slater, R. and Gearing, B. (1988) 'Attitudes, stereotypes and prejudice about ageing', in B. Gearing, M. Johnson and T. Heller (eds) *Mental Health Problems in Old Age: A Reader*, Chichester: John Wiley & Sons.

Smyth, M. (1988) 'Kincora: towards an analysis', *European Group for the Study of Deviance and Social Control*, Oslo.

Snart, F. and Maguire, T. (1987) 'Effectiveness of the kids on the block puppets: an examination', *British Columbia Journal of Education* II, 1.

Social Worker 2 in the Lucie Gates Case (1983) 'Savaged by the press', *Community Care* 445, 13 January 1983:16–17.

Sparks, C. (1987) 'The readership of the British quality press', *Media, Culture and Society* 9: 427–55.

Stevenson, O. and Parsloe, P. (1978) *Social Service Teams: The Practitioner's View*, London: HMSO.

Sutton, S. (1982) *The Largest Theatre in the World: Thirty Years of Television Drama*, London: BBC Publications.

Taylor-Gooby, P. (1985) *Public Opinion, Ideology and State Welfare*, London: Routledge & Kegan Paul.

Timms, N. (1962) 'The public and the social worker', *Social Work* 19, 1:3–7.

Tindall, R. (1981) 'An exploration of the presentation of social work in the British press', unpublished MA thesis, University of Manchester.

Todd, R. (1987) 'The media and the people', Hetherington Lecture delivered at the London School of Economics, 14 June 1987.

Tonkin, B. (1987) 'A year of living dangerously', *Community Care*, 31 December 1987:15–19.

Townsend, P. (1962) *The Last Refuge*, London: Routledge & Kegan Paul.

Townsend, P. (ed.) (1970) *The Fifth Social Service: A Critical Analysis of the Seebohm Proposals*, London: the Fabian Society.

Treacher, R. (1988) 'The problem with being on the media map', *Local Government Chronicle*, 22 July 1988:15.

Turow, J. (1989) *Playing Doctor*, Oxford: Oxford University Press.

Wagner Report (1988) *Residential Care: A Positive Choice*, National Institute of Social Work, London: HMSO.

Walker, D. (1976) 'Are social workers badly treated by the newspapers?', *Social Work Today* 7, 9, 5 August 1976:292–3.

Warner, M. (1989) *Into the Dangerous World: Some Reflections on Childhood and its Costs*, London: Chatto and Windus.

Warrington Health Authority (1987) *Moving Out*.

Webb, A. and Wistow, G. (1987) *Social Work, Social Care and Social Planning: The Personal Social Services since Seebohm*, London: Longman.

Weir, S. (1981) 'What do people think about social workers?' *New Society* 56, 964, 7 May 1981:216–18.

Wertheimer, A. (1988) *According to the Papers: Press Reporting on People with Learning Difficulties*, London: CMH.

Whitehouse, A. (1982) 'Spreading the word', *Community Care*, 15 April 1982:18–20.

Wilton, G. (1980) 'What they think of you', *Social Work Today*, 11, 36, 20 May 1980:14–18.

Wober, M. (forthcoming) 'Nearer my God, to Thee: how people of increasing age use television, and what they think about an array of programmes, particularly in the realm of religion', paper presented at Communication, Health and the Elderly: Proceedings of 1988 Fulbright Colloquium, Fulbright Colloquium, University of Wales.

Wright, A. (1979) *Local Radio and Local Democracy: A Study in Political Education*, IBA Research Report 1979.

Wroe, A. (1988) *Social Work, Child Abuse and the Press*, Social Work Monographs 66, Norwich: University of East Anglia.

Young, R. (1979) 'Social workers and the media: a social services view', *Social Work Today* 10, 22, 30 January 1979:10–11.

Younghusband, E. (1978) *Social Work in Britain: 1950–1975: A Follow-Up Study*, London: Allen & Unwin, vol. 1.

Index